X

THE YES-I-CAN GUIDE TO MASTERING REAL ESTATE

THE YES-I-CAN GUIDE TO MASTERING REAL ESTATE

HOW TO BUILD YOUR CONFIDENCE AND YOUR WEALTH

Steven Jay Fogel

with Mark Bruce Rosin

𝕿𝖎𝖒𝖊𝖘 BOOKS

All rights reserved under International and
Pan-American Copyright Conventions.
Published in the United States by Times Books, a
division of Random House, Inc.,
New York, and simultaneously in Canada by Random
House of Canada Limited, Toronto.

Library of Congress Cataloging-in-Publication Data
Fogel, Steven Jay, 1942-
    The yes-I-can guide to mastering real estate.
    Includes index.
    1. Real estate investment. I. Rosin, Mark Bruce.
II. Title.
HD1382.5.F64 1987   332.63'24   86-28503
ISBN 0-8129-1637-9

Manufactured in the United States of America
9 8 7 6 5 4 3 2
First Edition

DESIGNED BY BARBARA MARKS

*I wish to dedicate
this book to my wife,
Darlene, to my
partner Howard
Banchik, and to all
the people who sold
me their buildings
and all the people
who have had the
faith and trust to
invest with me. And
of course, Mom.*

—S.J.F.

ACKNOWLEDGMENTS

I would like to thank the people who helped us along the way with our book and became our Free Board of Directors: Sara Blackburn, Robb Creese, Gwen Edelman, Ronald Handelman, Donald Krasne, Gary Krawford, Lola Levoy, Hugh O'Neill, Edwin Reeser III, Howard Stone, Elaine Wane, Bob Weiss, and the Desert Inn.

CONTENTS

Part Three

INTRODUCTION

The intention of this book is to help you to become successful in real estate regardless of whether you currently know anything about real estate, whether you now own or have ever owned real estate, or whether you have the money in the bank to make a down payment on any real estate.

If you think this sounds too good to be true, that's because you believe one or both of the two major myths about buying real estate:

1. It's too complicated for the average person.
2. You can be successful only by playing an angle.

This book is about the *realities* of real estate. By the time you finish reading it, you will see how simple the principles of real estate investment really are and you will have learned my simple, straightforward method for achieving success in real estate. This method is a step-by-step system for teaching yourself to see the actualities of the real estate market in general and learning how to operate effectively in your own real estate marketplace in particular. Once you learn this method, it will help you to build your success in real estate in all types of market conditions. It will help you to deal with such factors as fluctuating interest rates and changing tax laws. In fact, once you know this method for real estate investment, there isn't any factor you won't be able to take into account—and use to your advantage!

The reason this method has the flexibility to provide you with *all* these benefits is that it doesn't depend on somebody else's being a "sucker" or on your finding ways to manipulate a situation that other people have overlooked; it doesn't try to make money on anybody else's misery; it isn't a "hustle"; it doesn't rely on playing any angles at all. *It is a concrete program for developing skills in real estate and learning to apply them in all climates of the real estate market.* These skills help you to know what property you should buy and at what price, and when you should sell and at what price. As part of my method, I will also teach you a step-by-step plan for developing the financial resources you need to build your success—the same way that I built mine.

I discovered the truth about real estate as I pursued my own career in the field. Twenty years ago, I made my first investment, a house I bought with a $5,000 down payment—which I didn't have at the time I made my offer. Today, my company owns over $300 million worth of real estate in seventeen states. And I bought all of it exactly the way I bought that first house, with the same approach I'm going to teach you.

For years after I made that first investment, I felt that I had just used my intuition and common sense in a more or less random fashion while striving to learn the business. But as I began to be a more analytical person, it became a challenge for me to examine the steps I had taken in acquiring over two hundred pieces of real estate, all of them bought quickly and with a substantial profit built in at the time of purchase.

Through this inquiry, I discovered that there was a definite system to how I made these purchases. In fact, there was a clear-cut process I had gone through—and still do go through—on each and every deal. This method is based on a combination of performing certain actions, relying on your intuition, and maintaining a specific mental attitude, and most important, asking naïve (perhaps even stupid) questions in search of answers.

The steps to success with this method truly begin within your own mind. As I saw from examining my own success with real estate investments, if you let the power of your intuition spring forth, it will have a life of its own, guiding you to your goals. The trick is to tune in to the realities of real estate opportunities and then to "reality test" by seeking information as you proceed.

This commonsense method is a point-by-point plan for how you can start from total ignorance about real estate investment and build your career in it the same way I built mine, through a process of self-teaching that connects you with the facts about how real estate works. By the time you finish this book, you will see in detail *exactly* how this process works, and how you can apply it.

The first step in heightening your real estate consciousness is to understand how real estate transactions are made, how the market works, and how people trade in it profitably. I will cover all these areas. I will also provide you with the information I've found helpful in taking the crucial step of improving your self-image so that you are confident in your own ability to trade in real estate profitably. The final step—the most important of all—is entirely up to you: creating movement in your life.

I want to make it very clear to you that the power to do all this is in you right now, just as it was in me when I bought that first house with $5,000 down that I didn't even have. *There are no secrets in real estate.*

If you're saying to yourself, "Oh, no, he's wrong. I don't have that power, I don't have the slightest instinct for real estate," that's because, based on the myth that real estate is too complicated, you believe that you can't penetrate it with your own common sense.

You may not find running your household and earning a living in the field you're now in complicated or intimidating. You may not even be intimidated by investing in the stock or bond markets. But real estate, where you can't just call a broker on the phone to place an order, where there is no buying and selling on whim, where there are calculations, specialized terminology, paperwork, and inspections, where there isn't even a standardization of prices in the same locality—and where you actually have to assume physical responsibility for what you own—seems like an intricate mystery. The truth is that once we know how, we can all penetrate its formidable exterior and get the sweet, rich rewards inside.

My purpose is to penetrate that exterior for you, to demystify real estate so that you feel free and confident in your own ability to achieve success. From reading this book you will learn:

1. how to appraise property (single-family homes, apartment buildings, and commercial, industrial, and office buildings);
2. how to test whether a particular real estate transaction is right for you;
3. how to attract investors if you need more cash to buy than you have;
4. how to structure a deal for maximum satisfaction on all sides;
5. how to negotiate as a buyer or a seller so that it works for both sides;
6. how and when to sell a property;
7. how to plan short-term and long-term goals in real estate investment;
8. how to assess trends and adjust your plans for changes in the real estate market.

We are in a new era in real estate investment. Major tax reform is shifting investment decisions, creating a multitude of activity in the financial sector, particularly in real estate. This activity creates opportunity. Indeed, there has never been a better time to make money in real estate than now, especially for new investors who can learn the new rules unencumbered by knowing the old ones. The principles for doing this are what this book is all about.

Buddha is quoted as saying, "Look within, thou art the Buddha" —meaning that whatever you need for enlightenment is already in you. Whatever you need for success in real estate is also already within you. Yes, there is knowledge you will need to gain for success in real estate, but there are no impenetrable secrets. The techniques I'm about to teach you will help you to bring out the questions you need to ask and the answers you need to find.

—Steven Jay Fogel
Los Angeles, California

Part
One

CHAPTER 1

MY FIRST DEAL IN REAL ESTATE

My real career in real estate began in 1964, the day I quit my second job as a real estate broker—nine months after I started my first job in real estate, all without earning a dime. I was miserable. I had told myself and the world that I was going to be successful in the real estate business. But I had already gone through two jobs and gotten nowhere, and, as far as I could see, no job in real estate fit all my images of where I should be professionally and what I should be doing.

Whenever a character in a movie is depressed, you see him walking the streets or driving around in his car. Since I was very unhappy the day I quit, I took one of my favorite rides near the beach. I was looking for a pretty area, a place where I would be able to indulge my melancholy state of mind. The road to the beach led me to Playa del Rey, an area near Los Angeles International Airport. There I noticed some houses I'd never paid much attention to before and discovered, by using the standards I knew, that they were fairly inexpensive: they cost around $20,000 compared to the houses that cost about $35,000 where I lived.

Just to kill time, I stopped at an "open house" that a broker was trying to sell. Next she took me to four or five other houses, one of which seemed like a real bargain. I went ahead and made an offer on the house even though I didn't have the money to buy it.

Having made the offer, I got so enthusiastic about the house that I told a friend who was also floundering professionally. Before I knew it, he was saying, "Let's do it together. I'll put up half the money." We each had to come up with just over $2,000 for the purchase. Through scrounging around and borrowing from family, we did it. Then we spent $50 on trellises, painted the house white, mowed the lawn, and, lo and behold, the place sold for a profit almost immediately.

My first real estate purchase seemed fortuitous, but I later discovered that luck played only a small role in my success. It took quite a few years' worth of real estate transactions for me to realize a simple fact: *If you have a starting place, common sense, and the willingness to state your plan to the world, to let people know what you're doing and to ask them for advice and support, your real estate transactions will work.* And that's exactly how my first real estate transaction worked.

In broad outline, this is the way it happens: You start to think about making a particular investment (this is your starting place); you make a hypothesis about the investment (why it's a good investment); you start to buy the property; you get excited about buying it; you tell people about it; they start reacting and providing you with information; you investigate to see if the facts you find agree with this information. The net result is that the hypothesis gets tested. If it proves to be right, go ahead with the transaction; if it proves to be wrong, don't.

At each step you take, you ask for directions (whether you need them or not) from any bystander who might have something to contribute. You cannot have too much information or hear too many opinions. The object of doing this is to hear what people say and, even more important, to keep challenging your intuition in light of new information, thus continuously throwing more light on the project's viability.

Let me give you a very simple example of how this works. Let's say you hypothesize that you should buy a particular house for $100,000 because you think it's an attractive house in a good neighborhood and is worth more than $100,000. As you start the process of purchasing the house and you share your excitement with other people, they may tell you, "No, you're wrong—it's overpriced." With this advice, they are attempting to invalidate your hypothesis, in which case you go back, think about it, and ask yourself, "Are they right or wrong?" But you have to do more than just think about it. You have to compare the house to similar houses in the marketplace until you prove whether your assumption is right or wrong.

It is a process of looking at all comparable houses and evaluating whether this particular house is a better value in its physical condition, in its price, in its potential to be improved, and on its financial terms than others for sale in the same market. This process, which will be covered later in detail, becomes a self-correcting mechanism. If the house turns out to be a bad investment at $100,000, you stop and start again with another investment.

Real estate is the perfect field in which to take advantage of this self-correcting technique because, as you will see in later chapters, *it is very easy in real estate to structure a transaction so that it allows for a change of mind.* If your investigation proves that the house is a bargain at $100,000, then, having prepared yourself with the facts explaining why you are correct, you've proven to yourself as well as everyone else that it is as solid an investment as your intuition first told you.

As this example illustrates, debate is an important step toward the goal of buying real estate. The very process of exchanging opinions and the searching for facts either brings you to invalidate your own hypothesis or brings you such enthusiasm for it that you convince other people about the soundness of your investment. As they get convinced, they figure out a way to join in your investment and help you, as my friend did when I told him about the house in Playa del Rey.

Once you've learned how to use this method to evaluate a variety of properties, you'll see that all real estate transactions follow these same basic steps. We will examine the entire process in more detail in the following chapters. For now, the point I want to emphasize is that you don't have to *know* anything to have a starting place. You simply start at one point, and just by sharing your idea and putting it into action, by simply advancing in a direction and by asking naïve questions, you figure the whole thing out.

It all began for me that day I went for my melancholy drive. I suddenly found myself in a place where, without intending to see houses, I saw houses. Then, without intending to see value, I saw value. Then, without intending to buy a house, I bought one. Finally, without intending to take in a partner, I took in a partner.

Of course, on another level, the starting place for me was my desire to own a piece of real estate in order to prove I belonged in the real estate business. This thought was on the periphery of my mind that day, but I had not yet allowed it to become a conscious plan. In making an offer on the house, I was simply acting out my desire to show the world I was a big shot, to stroke my ego.

Now I can see that in that first transaction, several key elements were operating: my intuition told me that the house was a good buy; I was willing to set the ball in motion by making an offer because I felt it was a good buy, and I committed myself to following through on the deal, which meant I was willing to check out my hypothesis that there really was value where I saw value. *The willingness to translate desire into action is essential; it is the difference between daydreaming and doing.* Your dream may be your starting place, but the transaction won't happen unless you actively participate in unfolding your dream. Just plain do it. Remember, with real estate, you can tie up a property before you're obliged to buy it.

Most simply defined, then, my method for investing in real estate allows you to ignore your ignorance.

Later, I'll give examples of how I use my method in various kinds of real estate transactions: private homes, apartment buildings, and office, commercial, and industrial properties. I will show you how to apply my proven techniques to the real estate investment opportunities you are likely to encounter. I will also show you how to apply what you learn to raise the money you may need to purchase investment properties.

But before I do this, I want to address the fundamental principles that make real estate such an outstanding investment opportunity.

CHAPTER 2

IT'S UN-AMERICAN TO LOSE MONEY IN REAL ESTATE

As we proceed with your real estate education, it's important to look head-on at the one basic fear that might stand between you and success in real estate: the fear that somehow or other you'll lose your money. Put in the most basic terms, this fear is: "I want to get rich, but what if I go broke?" A person standing on the street corner of this dilemma won't make a move in any direction. How can you take even one step if your mind is preoccupied by the thought that the whole street could collapse?

The first step in getting over this barrier is to restructure your thinking. Instead of saying to yourself, "I want to get rich, but what if I go broke?" simply state the truth about it: "I want to get rich and I may go broke." That states the risk exactly as it is—a possibility in the realm of all possibilities you face in living, not an insurmountable obstacle that means taking no step at all.

People who dwell on the possibility of catastrophe are also taking a risk—the risk that inactivity will be better than activity. Calculated-risk takers are those who are willing to make choices and act on them, knowing that the only chance they have to achieve their objective is to accept all possible consequences of their action. Inactive people's desire to succeed is not as strong as their fear of the possible consequences of taking risks; they are willing to wait until time tells them if they would have been right or wrong.

While it's true that there are no guarantees, if your goal is to get rich, there's something you should know about American real estate that tends to minimize the potential risks of investing in it. *It's un-American to lose money in real estate.* That's not just a cute chapter title—it's a fact. That's not to say that some people don't lose money in real estate, or that some real estate doesn't drop in value. But over all, real estate generally goes up. Some of the reasons for this have to do with the inherent qualities of real estate; others have to do with the particular social and economic system of our country, a system that supports real estate generally increasing in value.

Let's take a look at the factors that make real estate such a uniquely good investment in our country.

THE ULTIMATE TROPHY

That real estate has inherent value is a long-standing premise in Western civilization. Of course, nobody can really own the earth, but in the Western world we believe that land, as well as the structures on it, can be deeded to individuals, and for centuries real estate has been a symbol of real wealth. If you examine the history of the royal families of Europe, you see that in addition to gold and jewels, they always had land and castles. These were the trophies of the elite. Since the beginning of our history, owning real estate has always been the ultimate trophy of wealth, *the* great status symbol, and perhaps the primary source of our country's great fortunes.

Real estate has a definite aura; people generally associate living "the good life" with owning property. And once they own it, their idea of the good life is for their real estate to maintain its value, which means ensuring that their trophy becomes even *more* valuable. In America, this idea has become so ingrained that by now both property owners and would-be property owners consider owning property a birthright.

Everybody has seen that, in general, real estate just goes up and up and up. Even when prices seem especially high, people are willing to sacrifice luxuries in order to own their own residence. In almost every case, no matter where you are in our country, if you look at any property and ask, "What was it worth fifty years ago?" the answer is astonishing. In many cases, properties have gone up over fifty times in value! The nature of real estate is to keep going up in price, especially over decades, and the consequences of this are very important for the way the real estate market actually works.

THE UNWRITTEN AGREEMENT

Though most people are willing to look foolish losing money in the stock market, they are unwilling to do so by losing money in real estate. When people talk about investments, it's perfectly acceptable to say you lost money in almost anything except real estate. If you start telling people you lost money in real estate, they're going to think, "You're an idiot. You obviously did something wrong. You must have gotten involved with the wrong people!" Why? Because it's *unusual* for anybody to lose money in the buying and selling of real estate. Ordinarily you don't hear about it, because in most cases it doesn't happen.

The reason it doesn't happen is that as a society we have an unwritten agreement that real estate is going to go up. There may be periods in any given area's market history during which properties remain at the same price for a while, or periods during which, due to a very sharp rise in price over a number of years, prices may go down. There certainly are instances of overdevelopment, where the supply of a certain type of real estate temporarily exceeds the demand, and other situations in which an area's image becomes so negative that prices go down sharply. However, if you look at the larger cycles —and the real estate market as a whole—properties in general do go up and the dips are erased as time goes by.

As you learn the guidelines for buying property, you will learn how to evaluate properties and neighborhoods, to take current cycles into account—to figure out ways of using even downward trends to your advantage, for example—and to get an idea of future cycles. Underlying real estate investment is this safety net: the fact that the general trend of real estate is up.

The primary factor reinforcing this upward trend is our commitment to the value of the real estate we own. Let me show you how this commitment is manifested.

LOOKING AT THE WHOLE MARKET—AND SEEING HOW IT WORKS TO PROTECT YOUR INVESTMENT

All real estate is owned by somebody. Elementary as this fact is, it is very significant to real estate's tendency to rise in value, because it means that *every* piece of property is controlled by an individual or group whose expectation is that their piece of property will rise in value.

A property owner's commitment to his property's increasing in value is reinforced by the process everyone must go through to sell a piece of real estate. Property owners can't sell on a moment's notice, so if they hit a cycle in the market during which properties similar to theirs are selling for less than what they feel their property is worth, they tend to say to themselves, "Well, this is just a really bad time to sell; I'll hold on because this is my major asset, and I'll wait till the market improves."

The reason anything goes up or down in value is a function of supply and demand; in real estate value is dependent on the marketplace of buyers and sellers. *The only way the value of real estate goes down is when people start selling it at a loss. When people hold on to real estate, it stays the same and theoretically goes up as the demand increases over time.*

Even if somebody needs money and tries to sell his real estate cheaply, the time it will take and the procedure he has to go through will tend to make him modify his plan. The fact that sellers can't just dump their property quickly and cheaply without having time to reevaluate their decision contributes to real estate's self-preserving quality.

How does this quality of self-preservation affect the real estate market as a whole?

Let's say there is $10 trillion worth of real estate out there, every piece of which has an owner. Since everybody knows there's not much he can do in real estate on the spur of the moment, there will never be a sudden drop in the real estate market as a whole.

Let's compare the real estate market with the stock market. If the stock market were to fall, say, seventy points on an extremely heavy day of trading and 200 million shares changed hands, that would be considered a lot of shares traded. But although 200 million shares is a sizable number, it represents only a small fraction of all the shares that exist. Now think about all the real estate that exists —realizing that you yourself have seen only a tiny fraction of it! Next think about what an infinitesimal fraction of real estate comes onto the market on any given day. It's literally *impossible* for all of it to come on the market at one time!

The potential seller's ideas about the value of real estate are reinforced by personal experience—seeing his grandparents, parents, other relatives, friends, and acquaintances making money in real estate. Time after time we hear of home owners making money on their houses when they sell them. People come to believe that this is how things are, and as a result, most people will do everything they can to not sell in a down cycle.

That's why the time factor involved in real estate transactions is so important. It gives property owners the opportunity to reaffirm their commitment to the value of their property; it also gives them the opportunity to think out strategies to hold on to their property and allow it to appreciate.

With the stock market, we expect shares to be bought and sold and prices to go up and down every day as a result of daily events all over the world. Either interest rates went up or down, the dollar went up or down, or a crisis took place somewhere. The stock market reacts immediately to outside events. But with real estate, with the exception of a Three Mile Island catastrophe, there's no immediate reaction to it; in fact, often you can't tell for a year or two what's happened in real estate as a result of a particular financial or world event. This is why I think of the stock market and real estate as being at opposite ends of the investment spectrum.

THE FUNCTIONAL VALUE OF REAL ESTATE

One of the major factors that make real estate value generally rise over time is also a factor that differentiates it from many other forms of investment: real estate has a *real* value in addition to its perceived value. The real value of real estate consists in its having a function and its being unique: by definition, there can be only one particular piece of real estate on every spot of earth. *Because of its functional value, real estate is a common denominator in everything that goes on in life.* You can't have a business that doesn't have a place to exist; you can't offer goods or services that don't have a base from which to be offered; you can't have a home without a place in which people can live. Real estate is part of everything. The very function of real estate gives a firm foundation to its value—since there is a *real* physical need for it—and contributes to its upward trend in value.

The functional value of real estate also encourages people to hold on to it even in negative cycles. Let's take the example of a house a couple owns and lives in. If the market in their area becomes depressed, most often they just figure, "Well, we'll use the house until we can make money on it, because if we sell it we're only going to have to replace it with something else." If these same people own a portfolio of stocks, however, as soon as they believe that the market is going to go down, they are likely to figure, "What do we need these stocks for? We'll get into gold, or we'll get into real estate . . ."

Even if the owners of a house do decide to sell because they believe that the area they live in is becoming depressed, they still hold out for market value for their house, not a panic price. Since they still need a place to live, they will then either buy again or rent. Either activity continues to support the real estate market's overall rise in value.

If an investment property owner begins to worry about the economy and wonders if he should sell, the first thing he would have to ask himself is "What else can I put the money into if I do sell?" In figuring out what his property will be worth, he has to ask himself, "Compared to what?" If he applies the "what if"s to all forms of investment—the "what if"s being all the awful things he can imagine, from "What if the dollar declines?" and "What if the whole economy goes kaput?" to "What if the entire world falls apart?"—he generally concludes that any economic event that would make his property less valuable would probably make any other form of investment less valuable as well. The basic truth that people *need* real estate to live assures him that if anything will have value, real estate will have value. Thus, in the face of "what if"'s, his best investment is most likely to be the property he already owns —or another piece of real estate.

THE POSITIVE EFFECT OF INFLATION

Another factor that contributes to the general increase in real estate's value is inflation. Though today inflation is not as high as it was a few years ago, it still exists, and most of us expect it to be a permanent factor on the American economic scene. It's crucial to understand that everybody knows innately that even mild inflation drives up the price of real estate. And since everybody knows this, no matter what anybody says about the evils of inflation, every property owner believes he's absolutely entitled to his real estate's going up so that he can make money on it when he sells. Inflation is part of that package: It supports appreciation as the nature of real estate; it supports the self-fulfilling prophecy that real estate value has to rise.

Keeping in mind everything we've learned so far, I now want to turn your attention to the law of supply and demand, which governs the value of real estate as it does the value of every other form of investment. Real estate as a whole will continue to go up because more and more people want it and there is only a fixed supply of it to go around. The supply gets smaller because the population increases. And we are so good as a species at reproducing that even if we don't do anything but blink, there will be more of us—all bidding up the price of the same real estate.

WHAT OUR GOVERNMENT DOES TO SUPPORT OUR COUNTRY'S REAL ESTATE

Our government is very much aware of the value of real estate. Indeed, even with the changes in tax laws, the government encourages us to own real estate by endowing it with unique benefits that add to its attractiveness as an investment. The tax advantages of owning real estate are designed to encourage us to buy property and to hold on to it instead of selling it quickly.

Through such tax benefits as *depreciation* on income-producing properties (being able to deduct from your property's income for a specified number of years an allowance for the theoretical loss of value of the buildings or other improvements on the land due to wear and tear), the federal government is telling you, "If you put your money in real estate, we will make it financially worth your while." It's important to note that as today's tax laws read, current income produced by a property can be converted from taxable income to tax-free income because depreciation acts to shelter that income. Furthermore, depreciation from one piece of real estate can be used to shelter income from other pieces of real estate.

This isn't the only inducement the federal government gives you to invest in real estate. The federal government has even created "tax-free exchanges." Using a tax-free exchange, you can sell your property and use the entire *equity* (the value of the property less what you owe on it) as a down payment on a new property of equal or greater price. The advantage of a tax-free exchange is spelled out in its name: it gives the benefit of using all of your money, including profit, without taxing it now, resulting in a larger down payment, which enables you to buy a more expensive new property instead of paying the IRS now and having no use of the money that would have gone for taxes. There are very strict requirements for doing this, which require the planning and expertise of a knowledgeable attorney.

In overview, the situation looks like this. When you get your paycheck, the federal government says, "Give me your taxes now." But if you own real estate, the federal government says, "You can keep what I would've taken and use it to buy your next real estate investment." If you familiarize yourself with all the provisions, you may never have to pay taxes until you get off the merry-go-round and get out of the real estate business altogether. The federal government has arranged matters so that people keep owning real estate. And all of this supports the value of real estate and its tendency to rise over time.

WHAT ABOUT CHANGES IN TAX LAWS?

In evaluating any future changes in the tax laws governing real estate, the question to ask is, "Taking the modifications into account, will real estate still have the best tax benefits of any other form of investment?" Historically, whatever modifications have been made in the tax benefits of real estate, real estate has always been far superior to most other investments. And this is still true. The point is not to dwell on the benefits that have been lost, but rather to learn and to utilize the tax benefits that today's laws provide for all real estate owners.

In 1984, when there was some talk about making interest payments on primary residences not tax-deductible, there was such a national uproar that within three days President Reagan reversed his stance. The mortgage-interest tax deduction is so ingrained that it's here to stay as long as the whole current economic system is in place. And it's easy to see why. Interest payments on housing make such a terrific tax deduction that everyone who can afford it feels he has to own a home. Every home owner in the United States has interest to pay, and every home owner demands that it be taken off his income tax, as it always has been. If you own a home, you're just not going to accept less than the right to deduct the interest payments on your mortgage.

This particular benefit to home owners helps support the entire real estate market and makes us want to join and stay in the real estate game as long as possible. As long as the game exists, it continues to be self-perpetuating, an enterprise in which everybody —all current owners and all future owners—has a vested interest.

The tax changes of 1986 (effective January 1, 1987) have reshuffled the deck, but they haven't changed the game. The major effect of this tax reform over the years should be to take the emphasis off buying real estate *primarily* as a tax deduction and to switch the emphasis to buying real estate for its current and future profitability, with tax benefits as simply the icing on the cake. As a result, we will base our purchasing decisions on the economic merit of a property (which I will begin to show you how to evaluate in the next chapter, and which I will show you in detail for different types of properties in chapters 7, 8, 9, and 10).

In the next few years, if, as economists predicted when the tax reform of 1986 was being debated, the tax reform results in keeping interest rates relatively low, then real estate owners will benefit with increased profits on income-producing properties, because savings on mortgages will increase their properties' yield. Rents should go up, too, as a result of a decrease in construction. Construction will decrease because now, after the 1986 tax changes, developers will not be inclined to anticipate and build in advance of actual need because the federal government has taken away the tax benefits which subsidized this approach. As a result, owners of existing buildings will profit from a firm rental market. Thus, the net effect will be even higher yields on existing properties. When compared to yields on other investments such as stocks and bonds, real estate should continue to be America's prime investment vehicle.

So far we've talked only about how strongly everyday people support the regulations that govern real estate. Politicians, too, generally own real estate. This means that they, like so many of the constituents who voted them into office, also have a vested interest in real estate's rising in value. The result is that an impressive—and an impressively vocal—number of Americans are rooting for real estate to go up. Thus, the human element involved in the observation that it's un-American to lose money in real estate is very powerful.

CHAPTER 3

HOW TO USE MY METHOD: A SCENARIO

In the last fifteen years my friend and partner Howard Banchik and I have assembled a portfolio of properties across the United States worth over $300 million and put together a staff of twenty to look after the properties and support us in continuing our company's expansion. In looking back at how we did this, I see two things: our company does everything that large corporations do, and we figured out how to do it all ourselves.

You can do the same thing as long as you have the motivation. It's just putting the left foot in front of the right and walking; it is seeing a problem and solving it; it is seeing a need and fulfilling it; it is throwing your hands up and saying, "I don't know what to do!" and then finding out what to do and doing it.

Let's take an example. Say you have a vacancy in a property, and that the vacancy is causing a loss of money. What do you do? Either you clean up and mend the vacancy by finding a tenant or you let the lost income bleed you to death.

Your first resource is your common sense. The very fact that a problem exists, that you know it needs attention, and that you're committed to taking care of it puts you in contact with your own resourcefulness, revealing problem-solving capabilities that you may never have known you had.

It was in exactly this way that I built my business with Howard. I didn't know beforehand what problems and needs would arise, nor did I know how I would deal with them when they did. I simply went ahead; realizing that I was ignorant didn't stop me. When problems came up I was motivated to find solutions so I could stay on track toward my goal. And I'm far from alone in being able to do this. All successful businesses grow out of this same process.

This is also how many accomplished people train themselves for their careers, and it explains why frequently those who are most successful in a field have received their education "on the street" rather than in graduate school. All you need for this training is what you will learn about real estate from these pages—a knowledge of how to use commonsense techniques to endorse or overrule your own intuition.

Let me show you how these elements interact in your new career.

Think of the process of investing in real estate as being analogous to taking a trip. In real estate, the map is the formal set of procedures for buying and selling properties: contracts and negotiations. Yet these formal procedures are worthless unless you know what type of property you want to buy, where you want to buy it, and what price you are willing to pay for it.

I'm going to outline how a person might go about finding his first real estate investment, knowing little or nothing about the market. Although this person can be a man or woman of any age, with a bank account of any size, I'm going to make him a man named Joe, and, to emphasize that he's a beginner, I'm going to make him twenty-four years old, out of college for two years, and earning $24,000 a year in a salaried job. Although he could live anywhere, I'm going to make him from my hometown, Los Angeles.

I'm going to take Joe through his first real estate deal from beginning to end, showing, in broad strokes, each step involved in the purchase of a property. Later in the book, I will expand in detail on how these broad strokes are accomplished.

Before getting down to the specifics of Joe's search for investment property, I'm going to introduce the general concepts he will use in the first stages of his search for value.

FINDING THE RIGHT PROPERTY

The first step for anyone approaching an investment in real estate is to look at properties. This means not just reading the newspapers, but getting out of the house, discovering what properties are available, and looking at as many of them as possible. It also means allowing yourself to start fantasizing about different possibilities: What if I bought this? What if I bought that?

In deciding *where* to look you must ask yourself many questions including what your favorite areas are, and why. This is the traditional way of calling upon your inner intelligence. Another form of the same guidance is to start asking other people about these various locations and listening carefully to what they tell you.

Although I live in California, I've bought property in sixteen other states. I am always amazed by how much valuable free information people will provide. By combining your own sense with the information provided by others, you will get a strong feeling about where you should invest.

For instance, if you learn that a major high-rise office building is going up where currently there are no high-rise buildings, common sense says, "This would be a great location for a coffee shop or any other business that relies on pedestrian traffic." With two thousand people working in the new building, there will be a need for other support businesses, which in turn will make all the real estate in the area more valuable.

I've always found that the best way of discovering my spot to buy real estate is to start asking people the simple question, "What's happening in this area?" In real estate, finding your spot means finding a place in which you feel the kind of energy you need to excite you about buying property, a place where you feel your property will rise in value and where you'd feel good about owning it.

As you ask questions about the different neighborhoods to which your instincts draw you, and as people begin filling you in on "the action," your mind will begin producing hypotheses about the value of properties. These hypotheses will roughly take the form of: "I believe a rise in the value of this property will happen because of [something] that is occurring in this location." Example: "I believe it will be a good investment to acquire space for a coffee shop here because of the new high-rise office building."

Anywhere I go, I always ask questions about what's happening in the general area I'm visiting—and there is always an answer. Even more surprising, the answers I get always tell me that something important is going on. It could be a new gambling casino in Atlantic City or a new Pizza Hut in Albion, New York. Big or small, these are clues pointing toward a potential spot for investment.

I had an experience that serves as a perfect model of how everyone is automatically locating his spot just in the process of living his life. While I was on vacation in Puerto Vallarta with my wife we decided to take a speedboat ride. The driver, Raul, a twenty-one-year-old native of the area, took us cruising down the coast in his speedboat, past miles of gorgeous deserted beaches accessible only by boat. Fifty minutes into our trip, Raul moored the speedboat and led us onto a beach where a local family was selling soft drinks from a shack. It was a typical tourist experience: we paid three times what the drinks were worth and silently chided ourselves because we suspected our guide was getting a kickback for bringing us there. But that day, we didn't care. We were enjoying the surrounding beauty, and I remember saying to myself, "Life doesn't get any better."

Raul took us for a walk on the beach, and told us there was nothing around for miles except five or six one-room shacks. The ones we could see looked like slum dwellings by American standards, though the setting was right out of *Fantasy Island.* As we walked, Raul, whom I considered a very sharp street hustler, remarked, "I've been coming to this beach since I was a kid. I can't believe how this place has grown. This is going to be the next Puerto Vallarta! When I first came here, there weren't any houses —now look at it!" It turned out that Raul expected a hotel to be built on that spot, and he was trying to persuade us to help him buy part of the beach.

Raul used the same method for finding his spot that I've described: his intuition led him to frequent the area because he liked it, and once there, he saw that there was an opportunity for investment. Seeing this, he was determined to get a piece for himself! And I have no doubt that he did.

Each of us is the *only* person who can feel whether something is right or wrong for us. If an area feels negative to you, that's your intuition talking, and you should listen to it. Even if it turns out that there are very solid reasons for investing in a particular location, if *you* aren't comfortable with it, it's not the right place for you. It is not *your* spot. Fortunately, there are a multitude of "right" places to invest. That's what makes the opportunity in real estate so vast!

The price range we choose to invest in is also a major factor, for it helps us decide which locations are practical to investigate. Obviously, the area we choose can only be one in which properties sell for prices we can afford. But what determines one's price range for real estate is *not* solely the size of his pocketbook. In fact, that may have nothing to do with it at all. With the method I'm about to show you, the way to make a decision about the price of your first real estate investment (and every investment after that) is not on the basis of your financial statement, but on the basis of the objectives you set for yourself and your perception of your abilities.

SYNCHRONIZING GOALS AND EXPECTATIONS: HOW TO DECIDE WHAT PRICE RANGE YOU CAN AFFORD

Whether you have a great deal of money or none at all, the first step toward deciding the price range of the property you will look at for investment is to examine your goals and expectations.

People generally reach their expectations, but they rarely reach their goals if their goals are greater than their expectations. Ask somebody, "What is the ultimate car you'd like to own?" She might say, "A Rolls-Royce convertible." Then ask her, "What is your expectation of the finest car you're going to own?" She might say, "A Honda." Based on the observation that people arrange their lives to meet their expectations but not their goals when their goals are greater than their expectations, this person is going to get a Honda, not a Rolls-Royce.

Every aspect of real estate investment—from what kind of properties you are going to buy to where you are going to get the money to buy them—comes back to the questions: "What is your expectation?" and "What is your goal?"

The trick is to make your expectations match your goals—in other words, to synchronize them. If you take the time and care to make an accurate observation about what is required to accomplish your goals, and you make a commitment to fulfill these requirements, then you automatically bring your goals and expectations into alignment. The goals then become possibilities; once they are possibilities, they can then become expectations. By bringing your goals and expectations into alignment, you can begin to achieve your fantasies.

Let's apply this to real estate. The most critical element in determining the price of the property you can afford is the *down payment,* the percentage of the overall purchase price that is required to transfer the property's ownership. Usually the balance of the price is financed. To see how the process of synchronizing goals and expectations can be applied in deciding how much of a down payment you will be able to make, we will return to Joe.

Joe has saved $2,000 in the two years since he's been out of school. He figures that in the next four months he can probably get together another $3,000 by working overtime and scrimping on luxuries. He doesn't know very much about real estate. He's been a renter since he's been on his own; his parents own a home, but they've never explained how they purchased it. He's heard that he will need as much as one third of the total selling price as a down payment for any property he buys. If this is true, then with $5,000, he can afford to look in the range of $15,000.

Joe would be ridiculed if he were to ask, "Where is a $15,000 piece of property?" because very few properties, if any, cost $15,-000 anymore. But if he raises his sights to a $100,000 property, every city and town will present him with opportunities. The question Joe must now ask himself is, "How am I going to get $33,000 (approximately one third of $100,000) for a down payment when I only have $5,000?"

Clearly, he will have to raise the additional money. The next question is "How?"

To make sure that he doesn't overlook any possible answers to this question, instead of playing a closed hand and figuring he has to keep his ideas to himself, Joe will ask the question of the world at large. He'll ask his friends, fellow workers, and family members for ideas. Some people will say "Borrow," some, "Find partners," some, "Rob a bank," and some, "It's impossible." Putting a question out into the world is the only way to find an answer.

Once Joe hears an answer that his heart knows is right for him, he will be able to plan exactly how he will get the $33,000 down payment he needs. Once he has this plan, the $33,000 will be his expectation as well as his goal. For now, the $33,000 is only his goal; he's heard two suggestions that appeal to him—borrowing or finding partners—and he's not certain which will be more appropriate. But because Joe has the expectation that by sheer determination and commitment he will be able to create the $33,000, he is prepared to look at $100,000 properties.

As Joe reads the real estate ads in the papers and looks at properties with brokers, he finds out that, in Los Angeles, a $100,000 piece of property is going to be in a working-class neighborhood, not in a prime business or residential location.

To narrow his search, he starts with his own intuition, asking himself, "Is there a place I'm comfortable with where I could get a property for $100,000?" He immediately realizes that the answer is Van Nuys, a suburb in the San Fernando Valley. He knows it's comfortable because he grew up there.

Having made this decision, Joe is ready for the next step. He will research Van Nuys in detail by studying it on a map, driving through it, and reading the real estate section of the newspaper every day for properties in Van Nuys. He talks to all the real estate brokers in Van Nuys, contacting them by phone and seeing them in their offices, asking them about what's happening in Van Nuys. He also talks about Van Nuys to people he knows, and constantly drives through the neighborhood scouting out "For Sale" signs. By doing all of this, Joe becomes an expert on Van Nuys.

His next decision involves what kind of property to buy. He has to consider what kind of property he would like to own, given his own personality and preferences as well as his expectations of how much he can afford. Theoretically, it could be a house, an apartment building, vacant land, an office building, or a commercial or industrial property.

From his research on Van Nuys, Joe sees that he is likely to find in his price range a small house or duplex, a small storefront, or vacant land. Because this is his first investment, and he believes that simplicity is an important priority, he decides on a small house.

Joe is now ready to start learning how to appraise properties.

His first step is to go with five to ten different real estate brokers to see every available house in his price range in Van Nuys. It's important for him to get many different opinions on value in that area, and seeing ten real estate people will give him the opportunity to hear all their points of view. It will also help sharpen his real estate acumen. He may seem naïve and foolish with the first broker; by the tenth, he will know the ropes and have confidence. He will be able to separate fact from sales pitch.

After he has seen about fifty houses in the $100,000 range, they will start looking pretty much alike. By this time he's stopped looking at their colors—stopped looking at the cosmetic details altogether—and has begun to look at each house as a complete package. We've all been in small houses that are so cleverly decorated with mirrors that at first glance they seem large. When you see six small houses in an hour and a half, this illusion disappears. The eye gets trained to see beyond appearances to the broader picture. It is through this process that Joe starts to understand how to appraise properties. *For a buyer, appraising properties simply means discovering which house is a better value for its price than comparable houses currently on the market or comparable houses that sold in the recent past.*

Few buyers take the trouble of going through this process. They get sentimental about tiny details and forget the more fundamental aspects of value. They are led by emotional need, not business sense. After seeing fifty houses with approximately the same amenities, it's easy to notice that one two-bedroom house listed for $95,000 is not very different from another for which the owner is asking $110,000. The only differences are cosmetic: The landscaping at the less expensive house was planted twenty years ago, and it's overgrown and hides the house, while at the more expensive house the owners have cut back the bushes and added flowers. At first glance, the more expensive house is a turn-on, and the less expensive house is a dud. Adding to the turn-on quality of the more expensive house is the fact that it's been newly painted in a contemporary color, while the other house hasn't been painted in years. The less expensive house has an old toilet and the more expensive house has a new toilet. What do all these cosmetic differences add up to? Toilets cost only $100; add to that $1,500 for landscaping cleanup and a new paint job and the houses are about the same.

As Joe makes these observations, he is looking at the bare bones of houses—mortar and stone—and judging which is the better value. It becomes simple for him to figure out that the house that needs to be cleaned up is a much better value than the other one.

One aid that will help Joe differentiate between what is important and what is not, and recognize which house is a better value than another, is for him to keep a diary from the first day of his property search. This diary should include each property's address, square footage, unique features, asking price, and the broker's assessment of its true selling price as well as Joe's own feelings about the property. Joe should be particularly aware of how the house is oriented on the lot and to the neighborhood as a whole: Does it have curb appeal? A view? Does the elevation of the house make it difficult for handicapped, elderly, or toddlers? Is it near such heavy traffic that noise and safety are considerations? Do huge trees with large roots threaten the sewer or are they dead, requiring expensive removal? Is the school system desirable? Joe wants to think in terms of marketing the house in the future, so he'll look at it from a future buyer's point of view in addition to his own.

Once Joe goes through the process and is convinced he likes the house, he decides to make an offer.

MAKING THE DEAL

To figure out what offer he wants to make, Joe goes back to his notes. He has now looked at and priced fifty houses in the neighborhood. Comparing the prices and the features of each house, Joe concludes that the house he is considering looks like a bargain even at the $95,000 asking price. Cleaned up, Joe is convinced he could get $105,000 for it if he sold it right away. Since he plans to keep it and rent it for a while, Joe expects the house to appreciate even more before he sells it. Consequently, he feels it's everything he wants it to be for his first investment.

Recognizing that the less he buys the house for now, the more profit he'll make when he sells it—and the more profit he sees as built in when he sells it, the more confident he'll feel about raising the money for the down payment—Joe tells the broker he can't pay a penny over $85,000, and he asks the broker if this is possible. The broker suggests that it would be foolish not to try, and he begins preparing a formal offer on Joe's behalf for $85,000.

Joe tells the broker that he's nervous, because this is his first deal and he wants to make sure he has the right for further inspection of the house as well as an escape clause in the event he cannot line up acceptable financing. So the broker writes up the offer *contingent* upon Joe's approval of these items, allowing Joe ten days after the seller's acceptance of his offer to make a final decision, and then ninety days before Joe has to consummate the transaction, or close the escrow.

For the next three days, the broker goes back and forth between Joe and the seller, and ultimately brings back to Joe the seller's final asking price: $87,000. The broker tries to get Joe to accept this, but Joe remains firm. The broker then comes to a common but painful conclusion among brokers: he'll either have to reduce his commission or lose the deal. So the broker, deciding that half a commission is better than none, lowers his commission by $2,000, and the deal is struck at $85,000. (Again, we are looking at broad strokes in this example. The art of negotiation and working with a broker are covered in detail in chapters 12 and 13.)

With a check for $1,000 as a *binder* or refundable *good-faith deposit,* Joe has the house tied up for the price he wants it, time to check out if it's really as good a deal as he thinks it is, and time to bring in a plumber, an electrician, a geologist, engineer, termite inspector or any other expert he chooses to make an inspection. The contingencies the broker has put in the agreement on his behalf give him ten days to walk away from the deal if he decides it really isn't good after all.

THE SARDINE JOKE

There is another set of factors Joe must evaluate, too, during this ten-day contingency period, to make sure this investment is all that he feels it is. Since he plans to rent it out, he must consider the demand for rentals in that area and determine whether the rent he will collect will cover the mortgage payment, taxes, and upkeep. With this information in hand he can make a crucial determination: whether in buying this particular house he will be buying "sardines for eating" or "sardines for trading"—and whether or not the deal makes sense on either basis. This is one of the most important concepts for anybody going into real estate investment to understand. In fact, it is the context within which *all* deals must be judged prior to purchase.

The expression "sardines for trading" and "sardines for eating" comes from an old joke, using as the major characters two wealthy Saudi Arabian men who haven't seen each other in ten years. Their names are Abdul and Yassar, and they meet at an embassy cocktail party in Washington, D.C.

"What have you been doing, Abdul?" Yassar asks after a warm greeting.

"I've been here in the United States for two or three years now, and it's the most fun I've had since the oil embargo," Abdul answers.

"Abdul!" Yassar cries. "Where did you get that beautiful fifty-carat ruby ring on your finger?"

"Oh," Abdul replies, "I bought that for myself with a little of the money I made on sardine commodities."

"What are sardine commodities?" his friend asks. "That ring must've cost two million!"

Abdul laughs. "Yes, I made that easily last week."

Yassar smiles. "Well, tell me about it."

"It's simple," Abdul responds. "You buy these commodities from the stock market—it's something Americans do. You put down a hundred thousand and you buy five hundred thousand worth of contracts on sardines, and two weeks later you sell them for one million dollars."

"Hey, that's really something!" Yassar exclaims.

And they go their separate ways.

A year goes by and again they meet at the same embassy.

"Yassar, what have you been doing?" Abdul asks his friend.

"You know, it's funny," Yassar answers. "I did what you've been doing with sardine commodities, and it's wonderful."

Just then, a butler comes up to them with a tray of canapés. "Would you like an hors d'oeuvre?" he asks.

Yassar takes one and bites into it. Instantly he starts retching and spits into a napkin in disgust. "What is this?" he demands. "It's revolting!"

"Sir," the butler responds politely, "these are the world's finest Norwegian sardines."

"Oh my god!" Yassar cries. "These are horrible!" He turns to Abdul. "All of my fortune is in these sardines! I'll lose everything! What shall I do? I'm going to kill myself!"

"Yassar, don't worry," Abdul reassures him. "Sardines are for buying and selling. They're not for eating."

Joe has to see how this joke applies to the $85,000 house. If a piece of property provides a profit from its rental, it is said to have a *positive cash flow;* it has the nature of a bond or an annuity. Looking at it from the perspective of the sardine joke, I consider the property "sardines for eating"—since the positive cash flow is "feeding" you. If it costs money out of pocket to meet expenses, it is said to have a *negative cash flow.* Since this type of property won't "feed" you now but still may be profitable when it is sold, I place it in the category of "sardines for trading." Of course a "sardines for eating" property can also be traded profitably at the point of sale.

Thus, a "sardines for eating" property gives you two benefits: it carries itself at a profit and it has the potential to generate more profit when sold. You may wonder, then, why anyone would buy a "sardines for trading" property. By the time we finish following Joe through this example, you'll see that "sardines for trading" properties are also often attractive investments. They can produce profits that will exceed the losses accrued while owning them, and the losses themselves may be reduced by certain financial benefits that come with owning real estate.

Your Free Board of Directors

With the sardine joke in mind, we pick up Joe where we left him. The house is tied up in escrow with contingencies that, in effect, give him an exclusive ten-day free option to buy it at $85,000, and he's begun to tell his friends and associates about the deal. He is also shopping for the best mortgage available so that he can present the most favorable terms when he tells people about the investment.

Joe knows that he must tell the world exactly what he's doing and ask any questions he might have. He knows that talking to people will help him prove or disprove his hypothesis that the house is a good investment; he knows that asking people how he can create the down payment he needs will provide him with possible answers. He already had some suggestions before he went out to look. Now that he has the deal in hand, and he believes his hypothesis that the house is a good value for $85,000, he begins to talk about creating the down payment.

"Of all the advice I've been given so far," he says, "I've narrowed it down to borrowing the money or taking in partners. I can't borrow the money from a bank, because I don't have enough assets for them to lend it to me. That leaves relatives, friends, and associates. So I expect I'll either borrow the down payment from them or bring them in as investing partners."

As Joe goes about acting on this expectation, he continues talking about how he sees the deal, reviewing it with everyone who will listen. Through this process, he discovers a whole network of people to tell him if he's right or wrong in his estimation of the deal. The home will be appraised by a lender, the real estate broker, a plumber, an electrician, and other experts, who will look at it from their special points of view, as well as family, friends, and associates, who will look at it from theirs. Before the contingency period is over—while he can still walk away from the deal—Joe may talk with as many as a hundred people who lead him to the correct decision about the value of the house.

When he verbalizes his investment plan and takes a stand on it, a network of people will form for Joe—and for you, too, in your real estate transactions. I call these people your Free Board of

Directors. Their advice doesn't cost a cent, and it's some of the most valuable advice you can get.

Some Board members will be experienced investors, some will not. Let me show you why it's valuable advice even if your Board members don't know the first thing about how to evaluate a real estate deal.

Joe's hypothesis is that the house he has tied up to buy for $85,000 is similar to other houses that are selling for as much as $105,000. This represents a little more than a 20 percent spread in value between the top and the bottom of the market on similar houses, which is realistic in most real estate markets.

The way for Joe to determine accurately what his property is worth is to test his hypothesis by putting it before his Free Board of Directors and asking them to respond. He must state all of his reasons for believing in the value of the house and then ask them: "Is this house really a good value for $85,000?" Inevitably, some people will tell him he's really stupid for buying the property, and others will say he's smart. Joe's job is to listen to what everybody has to say and sift through all the opinions until he is confident about the truth.

To get the most out of one's Free Board of Directors, it's helpful to become familiar with the concepts of "agreement machines" and "non-agreement machines."

We all know from experience where we can go to get positive reinforcement and where to go to get negative reinforcement. Joe knows, for example, that no matter what he proposes to his paternal grandmother and grandfather, they'll respond, "Don't do it. It's too expensive. It's too dangerous. Why take a chance?" They are his "non-agreement machines," always afraid of a risk. He also knows that his maternal grandparents are adventurous optimists and big spenders, and they're always going to tell him, "Anything you do will work out. Do it!"

Between the grandparents on each side there are a million other people. Some of them will tend to tell Joe yes, and others will tend to tell us no. In part, Joe has to disregard what both groups of people say while at the same time asking himself and them *why* they are saying what they're saying. Is it just a reflex response, or do they have sound reasons?

In a sense, "agreement machines" and "non-agreement machines" represent the two parts of your mind. They perform a vital function in bringing up all the pros and cons you can think of and some you may not. So ask questions about the deal of *all* the different groups on your Board and *make them validate their positions.* You'll find that most people enjoy demonstrating their knowledge so much that eventually you'll have to quiet them down.

Once all the opinions and explanations come in, you must put everything that has been said to the test. For me, there's only one ultimate test of any opinion or piece of information: the duck test.

THE DUCK TEST AND HOW TO USE IT

The expression "duck test" is derived from applying the age-old battery of questions, "Does it swim like a duck, look like a duck, walk like a duck, eat like a duck, quack like a duck, and fly like a duck?" in order to determine if the "bird" in question is actually a duck.

As I'm about to show you, almost any property can be evaluated with the duck test.

The duck test consists of evaluating every assumption and piece of information about a property by checking it against the hard facts. If facts are not readily available, performing the duck test means ferreting out the facts and seeing if the assumptions and information prove to be correct.

The duck test assures that you are not going to make a decision about a property based on what the seller tells you, what the real estate broker tells you, what you've heard through the grapevine, or what you *hope* and *think* might be true.

For Joe, using the duck test means asking himself questions such as: Is the house rentable? Is it resalable for a profit? Is it the right size for the area? Is the school district attractive to people with children? He must ask himself any question that occurs to him or any question that anybody else raises about the property, and then he must research the questions as thoroughly as possible to find the answers.

When I refer to the duck test, it is my shorthand way of saying that the process of verifying a hypothesis should be accomplished by looking at the questions raised by that hypothesis from a number of different vantage points. Then it must be investigated independently from each vantage point to see if it is still plausible.

The duck test means validating your intuition with research.

Since Joe plans to rent out the $85,000 house, one of his first questions must be: Is there an active rental market in the area? To get his answer, he will talk to realtors who handle rentals; he will check out every comparable rental in the neighborhood, whether apartment or house, to determine what price his prospective house will rent for and how quickly it is likely to rent; he will talk to landlords and managers of apartment buildings to get as much specific information as he can about the demand and turnover rate for apartment rentals, and he'll do the same with the brokers and rental agents who specialize in house rentals.

After Joe's satisfied with the answers he finds, he can then go to his paternal grandfather and say, "I think this is a good deal, and here's why." Being a "non-agreement machine," naturally his paternal grandfather will say, "Don't do it, Joe. You won't be able to rent the house out, so it's a bad idea from the start."

Now Joe has to ask himself honestly if the facts support his paternal grandfather's advice. "The broker said there aren't enough houses on the market to go around as rentals," Joe reminds himself. "I called five brokers and asked if they had this size home for rent, and they all said they have a waiting list of people who want to rent them. What the landlords and managers of apartment houses told me also confirmed that there was a demand for rental units in this neighborhood." The information Joe gathered from his research is also backed up by his own experience: he's never seen rental properties in Van Nuys stay vacant for long. So Joe concludes that Grandpa's theory collapses under the weight of the evidence he has collected. But asking Grandpa has made Joe go over his facts thoroughly, and it's convinced him even further that he's right about the house's value as a rental!

Now Joe goes to his maternal grandfather, the optimist, and asks, "Do you think this house that I'm planning to buy and rent out is going to be worth more in the future?" Grandpa number two responds, "Of course it's going to be worth more in the future. It's a good neighborhood. Look at how prices and rents have zoomed in the last twenty-five years. Buy it!"

Joe must evaluate what his maternal grandfather has said by asking himself, "Is Grandpa's opinion that the house will rise in value supported by the facts?" From his research in newspapers and from talking to brokers, landlords, managers, and residents in Van Nuys, as well as everyone else he knows and has met in the process of going into real estate—all members of his Board—Joe can answer with total integrity, "Yes, Grandpa's opinion is supported. The facts suggest that the house will rise in value for just the reasons that Grandpa said. It's a good neighborhood. Historically, the houses were cheaper. When they were built twenty-five years ago, they sold for $10,000! Rents were cheaper. Rents that were $100 per month twenty-five years ago are now up to $1,000 per month."

In continuing to evaluate his hypothesis that he can sell his house and make a profit, Joe next asks himself, "What factors could make the house more valuable?" It occurs to him that the house is likely to become more valuable if builders can't construct any more houses to satisfy the demand to live in that neighborhood. So he asks the question "Is this house going to be more valuable because as the demand grows, the supply must remain constant?" He concludes from his investigation that there isn't any more vacant land in that area to build on, and therefore additional houses can't be built.

By broadening his research base and bringing into his Free Board of Directors additional people with specialized knowledge, such as a building contractor, Joe can also find out that even if there were vacant lots in that neighborhood, it would cost substantially more per square foot to build a new house today than he would be paying for his prospective house. Thus by asking if the replacement cost of the house would be more than the asking price of the house, Joe discovers another factor that will make the house even more valuable in the future.

Joe comes up with all these facts just by searching for answers to questions, by conducting his search in a very commonsense, layman's manner. Through this process, Joe has found that the house, including plumbing and wiring, is in good condition, that it's situated in an active area with a lot of buyer and renter demand, that his price is substantially below what it would cost to reproduce a comparable house today on the same lot, and that by comparison to other houses in the area, it's a bargain. Every answer he finds convinces him that the $85,000 house will, indeed, find a tenant and that it will be resalable at a higher price in the future. Since it swims, looks, walks, eats, quacks, and flies like a duck, Joe has decided that it is a duck.

COMING FROM THE TRUTH

The cornerstone of my method is discovering the truth and telling the truth.

Telling the truth begins with telling the truth to yourself. If you don't tell the truth to yourself, you're going to end up cheating yourself. Only by telling the truth to yourself and to other people can you use your Free Board of Directors to its full potential.

Pretending the truth isn't the truth in order to make a deal "work" makes a deal that in the long run really won't work. The truth doesn't change because you don't acknowledge it. *Remember: you can't cheat other people by withholding the truth without also cheating yourself.*

If Joe makes a thorough investigation of every available fact related to his deal during the contingency period, tells the truth to his Free Board of Directors, finds out he is wrong about some aspect of the deal, and therefore decides against going through with it, he can still walk away with integrity. In doing this, he is merely taking advantage of a self-correcting mechanism, the built-in system of checks and balances.

Even if Joe decides against a deal, just going through this process —the exchanges with his Board members and the research he undertakes to substantiate or disprove their opinions and his own— not only teaches Joe more about real estate investments but also proves him to be a responsible person. Consequently, he is that much further ahead in putting together his next deal: his skills have been sharpened, his Free Board of Directors is already in place, and they have an impression of him as a person of integrity. This positive impression is itself a substantial asset to his career as a real estate entrepreneur, because, as you'll soon see, Joe's Free Board of Directors may ultimately become his network of investors.

GETTING DOWN TO FIGURES

Now that, in this example, Joe has decided to go ahead with the deal, what remains is for him to see exactly how the financing will work and to test its feasibility with his Free Board of Directors.

Let's say he's made the deal so that he can buy the house not with one third down as he'd planned, but with only 20 percent down, which is realistic. This means that he will need about $17,000 for the down payment. If he makes a down payment of $17,000, then the loan (or loans) he will take out to finance the balance will total $68,000. Talking to various lending institutions, Joe anticipates a 10 percent interest rate, which means approximately $6,800 in annual mortgage payments. He estimates that with these payments, plus closing costs, property taxes, insurance, and the money he will need for the cleanup he plans to do (a new toilet, a paint job, and landscaping), the total expense for the first year will be $9,950.

Because the house has two bedrooms, Joe thinks it's realistic for it to rent for between $800 and $900 per month in the current market. He bases his logic on the fact that two-bedroom apartments in the area rent for about $700, while two- and three-bedroom homes of similar quality to the one he's planning to buy rent for between $800 and $1,200 per month. If Joe is able to rent the house for $900 per month, he figures he will be able to collect a total of $10,800 for the first year's rent (12 months × $900 = $10,800). Based on this, he figures he's going to have a positive cash flow of approximately $850 for the first year:

$ 10,800	total first year's collected rent
−9,950	total first year's expenses
$ 850	positive cash flow

There's no question in Joe's mind that that would be a good investment.

But what if he can get only $800 per month for the first year's rent? Then he will have a total of $9,600 in collected rent (12 months $\times$ \$800 = \$9,600), and he will have a negative cash flow of approximately \$350 for the first year:

$ 9,950	total first year's expenses
−9,600	total first year's collected rent
$ 350	negative cash flow

With the positive cash flow based on \$900 per month rent, the house would be "sardines for eating." With the negative cash flow of \$350 per year based on \$800 per month rent, the house would be a "sardines for trading" property. Looking at the worst-case rental scenario—that it would cost \$350 per year out of pocket for the first year to own the house, making it a "sardines for trading" investment—Joe has to consider whether it's worth losing \$350 for this first year in order to sell the house a year later for substantially more than he paid for it. His new question thus becomes "Does the future upside of the investment—the price the house could sell for through appreciation—make it worth feeding money for expenses until the point of sale?"

To answer this question, Joe looks through the huge free network of people he's created for someone whose opinions he respects about financial affairs. When he finds this person, he asks, "Is buying this house and losing money on it the first year really a good idea?"

Once this proposition has been put before a financially sophisticated Board member, Joe is likely to hear the following: "You ask me why you would want to lose \$350 on expenses for the first year of owning a piece of property? One reason would be the potential profit you might earn from selling the house. You're buying with 20 percent down, and you're buying it for about 20 percent under top market value," she continues. "So if you bought it and sold it immediately for 20 percent more than you paid for it—which would be \$102,000—you'd double your money. You'd make 100 percent on your original investment."

If Joe made 100 percent on his money every year—even starting with an investment of \$5,000—and he did this for fifty years, he would end up being one of the richest people in the world.

What happens if, once Joe gets the house, he decides not to sell it in a year, but to hold it longer in the hope of an even better profit in four years? Are there any benefits to owning it that would help absorb the cost of holding it and would make the deal attractive to an investor?

"Yes," his Board member will tell him. "Thanks to the government, there may be tax benefits that offset the losses you'll have while renting out the house. There also may be tax benefits when you sell it." Joe's friend explains that for tax purposes the house, when rented, becomes what is called a depreciable asset, which, depending on Joe's income, may allow him certain yearly income tax deductions. There's also a writeoff on the cash loss, including the interest payments. "These are some of the things that make real estate the best investment vehicle around."

This is very important information for Joe in terms of raising the money for the down payment, his adviser continues. Since Joe doesn't need all these tax savings himself, he may have an excess of tax savings to pass along or share with others, depending on their tax brackets. These are attractions Joe can offer the potential investors to help him complete the deal.

There's another point Joe has to keep in mind in terms of holding on to the house for more than a year. It's a pretty good bet that if he has to rent out the house for $800 per month for the first year, he will be able to raise his tenant's rent during the second year. If he raises the rent from $800 per month to $1,000—which seems reasonable since the top-of-the-market house rentals in that area are already $1,200 per month—Joe will more than keep up with his expenses. Given this potential to raise the rent, Joe's negative cash flow would disappear in the second year of his ownership and he would have a positive cash flow made up of the increased rent ($12 \times \$200 = \$2,400$) and the money he would save on expenses (property taxes and insurance would continue as expenses in the second year, but closing costs and renovation were only first-year expenses).

CREATING THE INVESTORS

Now Joe is ready to transform his Free Board of Directors into his source of funds for the investment. If he is right about the investment, and if he presents his case truthfully and enthusiastically, someone in the network is likely to respond by lending him the money or investing with him as a partner, just as my friend invested with me when I told him about the house I was going to buy in Playa del Rey. Even members of his Board who don't personally invest with Joe may recommend other people who they think might invest.

Now Joe is ready to act, going first to those candidates for partnership who his intuition tells him are most likely to make the commitment he seeks. Armed with the financial facts of his overall game plan as well as the tax benefits of the deal, Joe can find a family member, friend, or associate and say, "I've got a fantastic deal. Here are all the facts about the house that show why it's a terrific value at this particular price." [He gives them all the facts he's researched about current and past comparable sales.] "Here are the facts about the neighborhood and why property values are going to rise." [He gives him all the facts about Van Nuys and shows what the trend in real estate sales has been in the last ten years.]

Now Joe tells the potential investor exactly what he is proposing, "Let's buy the deal together; I'll take care of running it, you get any tax benefits, and I'll get a share of the profits."

Everybody in this scenario ends up happy. Joe's business associate, aunt, uncle, or family friend gives him $17,000 for the down payment plus the $1,600 for repairs and cleanup, takes any tax benefits, and funds the loss for expenses, if there is a loss, until the property is sold. This investor may even have a newly wedded daughter or a mother-in-law who would be a perfect tenant for the house. When the house is sold, the investor makes back the initial investment, and then he and Joe share in the profit according to a mutually agreed-upon formula.

Once Joe has found his partner—or partners—his next step in putting together this hypothetical transaction will be to conceive and draw up a fair and binding partnership agreement. Since Joe is not a legal expert, he's faced with a new question: How should he go about drafting this agreement? What would be a fair distribution of profits. What would be a fair distribution of losses? If more money is needed, who's going to put it up? What would be a fair division of responsibility? By questioning his network, he will find how others have done it or think it should be done. He will get people's reactions to what sounds fair to them. Then he must consult with an attorney.

YOU DON'T HAVE TO DO IT ALONE: HOW SYNDICATION OPENS YOUR VISTAS FOR SUCCESS

For Joe, the deal I described in the example is a vital move to establish himself as a real estate entrepreneur and begin building an estate for himself. The reason I used him as an example is to show that it's entirely possible for someone with an average twenty-four-year-old's limited financial resources and narrow experience of the world to put together a successful real estate deal. As you begin your career in real estate, it's important for you to realize that there are larger and more profitable deals that you can make using the exact same method.

My suggestion is to use the method I'm teaching you to put together deals for $300,000, $400,000, even $800,000 or more. The reason you can buy even a $1 million building even if you don't have a cent of your own to invest is that you don't have to do it alone. Putting together deals with investors is what I do every day, and more and more people who have never invested in real estate before are beginning to act on this opportunity.

Syndicated real estate—property ownership by partners—has grown in the last ten years from a small occupation to a multibillion-dollar-a-year business. Real estate has become so valuable that it's caused a shift in the American dream. While it's still very much the American aspiration to own your own home, today many people have modified it to owning their own condominium. The dream of owning real estate as an investment has shifted, too. While ten years ago the goal and the expectation of people who wanted to invest in real estate was to own an apartment house or a shopping center, today the dream has changed to owning a part of an apartment house or a shopping center. That's why forming partnerships to buy real estate is an idea whose time has come.

This may mean raising your goals and expectations to a higher level than you've ever anticipated. Once you synchronize your goals and expectations so that you are looking for an investment even in the $300,000 to $400,000 price range, you will be able to consider buying a large variety of office buildings and commercial properties as well as apartment buildings.

I did it exactly the way I'm telling you to do it. That's why I know it's possible and realistic to become a multimillionaire in real estate, whether you have working capital or not. There's always a way. With these guidelines you can transform yourself into a real estate entrepreneur and raise yourself to whatever level you can envision for yourself, regardless of how much or how little money you have at this very moment.

The next three chapters will help you to expand your own horizons to include the possibility of more sophisticated real estate transactions, and will introduce you to the concepts you need, on both a personal and a business level, to help you begin finding the right investment for you.

CHAPTER 4

REFLECTIONS FROM MY MIDLIFE CONSCIOUSNESS SEARCH: WHAT IT TAUGHT ME ABOUT REAL ESTATE

I mentioned that I first recognized my method in retrospect. To be more precise, I began to see it clearly about ten years ago, as I was approaching middle age. I felt discontented with my life and wanted to learn more about myself, my relationships with other people, and my chances for making my life more enjoyable. I seemed to have no trouble creating money for myself, but good feelings not connected to business were rare.

The search for self-knowledge brought me to participate in a good many self-realization processes and experiences, including psychotherapy, est, Mind Probe, and bathing in the hot tubs at Esalen in Big Sur. I also began to read books on human potential and psychology, anything that would help me to improve my life. I tried to approach each new experience with the same diligence and commitment with which I approached my business.

With my new awareness came a personal introspection that soon overflowed into my business life. Instead of acting on automatic, I began to be conscious of my actions and feelings. This is how I began to see what my method was—and as I focused this awareness in my real estate activities, I became even more successful there than I had ever been.

This book was born of that awareness. I saw that *the first require-ment in succeeding with real estate investments is to be able to see value.*

I define "seeing value" as seeing from the start how I can make a profit on a deal. I always say that I make my money when I buy, not when I sell, because when I buy a property at the right price —and I buy *only* at the right price—I know that the property I'm buying may be sold at a higher price at that very moment. That's what makes it the right price; that's what gives it value. I *see* the value because I know the marketplace. And "seeing value" has everything to do with learning the market.

Remember: buying real estate isn't like going to the store and buying a loaf of bread that costs exactly ninety-nine cents. There is no standardized price in real estate. Three people, all sophisticated investors, will have three different opinions of value. One may think a property is a steal at $100,000, another person may feel it's perfectly priced at $95,000, and still another may feel it's over-priced at $90,000. *"Seeing value" is being able to understand and evaluate the other person's logic in his evaluation of the deal.*

There are some people who want only certain kinds of diamonds —the kind a jeweler would grade flawless—and are willing to pay market value for them, even if the market value is $50,000 per carat. There are other people who don't care about the type of jewel or its quality but will buy only if the price is what they consider below the market. If you have a particular jewel to sell, which buyer will you take it to? When you buy with that question in mind, you are "seeing value," because you are looking at the property within the context of what the next buyer wants.

Seeing value also means knowing whom to ultimately sell a property to: knowing what kind of a jewel, and at what price, a particular buyer is likely to want.

If you believe a property is a good deal at $100,000, it's because you think that there are other people who will pay $110,000 for it.

When Joe's $85,000 house is fixed up (new toilet, paint job, landscaping) and priced for sale, at say, $105,000, a frugal accoun-tant with an interest in home improvement may consider it over-priced; it is no longer a "fixer-upper." But a movie producer who wants a house for his new ladyfriend might prefer Joe's house to a fixer-upper because it is precisely the right kind of jewel already in the right kind of setting.

This awareness has to go into Joe's thinking as part of his learning to see value.

The second requirement in succeeding with real estate investments is the willingness to do whatever is necessary to accomplish your goal. This is true whether your starting place is a particular piece of property and your goal is to buy it below market value, or whether your starting place is a desire to become wealthy and your goal is to make $10 million. Only the willingness to form a practical plan and then do whatever is necessary to carry it out will bring you to the achievement of your goal.

What can stop you? Many potential obstacles may arise as you move toward your goal, but it always comes down to the fact that you and you alone can stop yourself. How? By giving in to fear, by lacking clarity, by not dealing responsibly with power, and by submitting to the feelings of limitation and fixed thinking we associate with being old. Fear, clarity, power, and the liabilities of feeling old are four qualities I was introduced to very powerfully in Carlos Castaneda's *The Teachings of Don Juan.* [1]

Certainly a person entering the field of real estate investment with the goal of succeeding does not begin without fear; he or she is willing to learn and to move ahead despite fear.

There are many fears you might face in approaching a commitment to real estate investment, especially for the first time. There is the fear of the unknown, the fear of failure, the fear of success, the fear of showing ignorance, the fear of asking for support, the fear of taking responsibility for your own money, the fear of taking responsibility for someone else's money.

In saying that you must move ahead despite your fears, I'm not telling you to disregard them entirely. In fact, fear can be a wonderful instructor, because it helps you thoroughly investigate the deal before you make a final commitment. If you are fearful about some aspect of the deal you are putting together, research it and find out if your fear is pointing you toward a trouble spot or if it's just obstructive chatter in your mind. The way to determine if your

[1] Carlos Castaneda, *The Teachings of Don Juan* (New York; Ballantine Books, 1978).

fears have a basis in fact is by asking aloud all the questions to which they give rise. Play detective and bookkeeper to find out what the real financial facts of a deal are (What are the expenses? What is the income? How much will it cost to make necessary repairs?). Use the duck test. See exactly what is required to complete the deal and run the property successfully, then plan how you will do it. Once you find the answers to all the questions, you'll discover if you have reason to be afraid or not. If you are afraid that you are incapable of doing the necessary work to make the deal successful, write down the specific things you fear doing and see if these fears are worth stopping you. Are you willing to make a commitment to act despite your fears? If you are, then you are responsible enough to complete the deal successfully.

After you find out the facts, you have graduated to *clarity*. If you're considering purchasing an apartment house, for example, and you're estimating its income and expenses, it's important to realize that whether I own the building, you own it, or the worst businessperson in the world owns it, the truth—in terms of the financial facts—is the same for all of us. We're all going to pay, give or take a little, the same amount for the carpets, electricity, gas, and other goods and services the building requires. If the seller or broker tells me it's going to take only 30 percent of the rent to pay the expenses, and I know from a careful study of the figures that the expenses will be 40 percent, they're not crazy and I'm not crazy. They're just misleading themselves and I'm not. I've probably seen twenty thousand sales brochures or fact sheets on various properties; not 5 percent of them have truly reflected every possible item of expense. That's why it's necessary to protect yourself by doing careful independent research to gain clarity.

You can't assume that because of the exhaustive research you've done for one deal, or two, or three, you have just "become clear," and therefore automatically have clarity about every deal. You must engage yourself in the research process for each property— that's the only way that clarity works for you. It's something you always strive to attain, not something you attain and then stop striving. Even when you think you have clarity, you still must test it.

When you constantly test your own clarity and act on it neither too quickly nor too slowly, then you have come into your *power.*

The funny thing about knowing one's power is that when all the layers of the onion are peeled away, and we see how things truly are, we realize that each of us *always* has power. We all have energy; we all have the potential to perceive options; we all have the potential to act. Even the person behind the eight ball has power. He has the power to make certain choices, and even if these choices are very limited, some of them are better than others, and some may lead him out from behind the eight ball. If you don't feel a connection to this power yourself, you may be wearing blinders and seeing things only one way (a way that says, "I have no power"), instead of using your power to see your options clearly and then to act with commitment.

Making choices from clarity is exercising your power and getting out from behind the eight ball. Making these choices begins with *seeing* that you have choices to make; that is, in itself, a connection to your power. *The next step is acknowledging your connection to the power within you, learning to tune into it, and knowing that when you have tapped it to create success for yourself, as long as you respect the power and appreciate it, you will also have the power to handle it responsibly.*

Handling power responsibly means not using it cavalierly or with cruelty. As long as you know when and how to use your power, you will be able to make your own life creative and joyful, and you will be able to be responsible and positive in your relationships with others.

Next we come to the fourth quality, developing a *mind-set that fights old age.* My personal definition of aging has nothing to do with years. Old age sets in when you stop creating your life anew each day and continue living off the energy and ideas of yesterday; when you behave as if your "warrior" days are gone. As Carlos Castaneda points out, one has to fight every day to be a warrior—and the enemy in this context is not only apathy and the feeling of aging, it is also feelings of omnipotence. The battle against an attitude of old age is a constant challenge, full of vitality and joy and continual renewal.

In terms of real estate, chronological age doesn't count the way it does in other professions. While most fields rarely produce new stars over forty, a real estate entrepreneur can be a prima ballerina or the fastest player on the court at any age. Again, it all depends on your willingness to fight the mind-set of old age. If you are rigid in your thinking, willing to rest on past glories, or prone to inaction because of past failures, you have entered "old age" even if you are twenty-four.

One part of fighting aging is a sense of optimism. Although optimism is often associated with youth, it's an asset at any age, provided it isn't acted on blindly. Flexibility, which I define as the capacity to respond to new situations despite anxiety, is another quality that helps to fight aging. Flexibility is particularly important in real estate, where there are always new trends. In the real estate marketplace, trends always present opportunities to dogs flexible enough to learn new tricks, but they consign rigid, unwilling dogs to inactivity.

I have discovered from my own experience that if you are willing to overcome fear, reach clarity, handle power responsibly, and fight old age, you will have the qualities you need to expand your economic opportunities through real estate investments.

CHAPTER 5

RAISING YOURSELF TO THE POINT OF OBSERVATION AND SEEING VALUE

Up to now I've talked about seeing value in terms of knowing what kind of a property a buyer wants and at what price. I've pointed out that seeing value is essential in learning the market.

The classic definition of value in real estate is what a willing buyer will pay a willing seller for a piece of property that is properly exposed to the marketplace.

Ultimately our main goal in buying property is to sell it at a profit or to bring it to someone who will lend us money on it. In either case, we want the property we buy to be what the other person wants. *In buying a property, ultimately we are packaging it for another buyer.* The spread between what we buy the property for and what the next buyer will pay for it is our profit. The big variable in this equation is that many people who look at the same property we are looking at will not see the property as we see it. Our job in buying real estate may thus be defined as *recognizing* the value of a property by seeing in it what somebody else doesn't see. Although this may sound difficult, it's really quite easy.

Value in real estate is fully realized when the property is being used for its highest and best use. So if you perceive that a particular property is not being used for its highest and best use and you see what the highest and best use is, then you are seeing the true value. If you can buy the property at a price that reflects its current use, which isn't the highest and best use, then you know the moment you are purchasing it that it is worth more than you're paying for it.

It could be that in looking at an apartment building you see that the tenants are paying low rents compared to what the rental market in general is charging, and the current landlord doesn't see this. The building is worth more than its negotiated price because the income produced from the building can be increased by raising the rents to the current market level. Or you may see that there are better available tenants for a group of stores in a piece of commercial property, while other potential buyers don't see that; you may see that a low-end industrial area may be just on the brink of converting to chic boutiques and art galleries, which another investor doesn't realize. Seeing value may be as simple as buying the work of a young artist and holding on to it while the rest of the world discovers her. Or it may be buying a building in the low-end industrial area just as it starts conversion and holding on to it while the rest of the world discovers the area.

Bringing a property up to the level of its highest and best use will increase its true value. With this knowledge, you can buy a property and bring it up to its highest and best use, or you can simply buy it and sell it to someone else who sees a little later than you did what the highest and best use of the property can be, and is willing to buy it from you at a profit to you. Either way, your being able to see that the property is currently not at its highest and best use, as well as being able to see what the potential for the highest and best use can be, automatically creates a profit for you. That's seeing value.

About six months ago, I bought a thirty-unit apartment building in Los Angeles. Until one month prior to my purchasing it, it had been owned by the original builder. It's in an area where the ethnic mix has been changing for a long time. Even though it's two blocks from a prime office-building financial center, racial prejudice made the building's value rise far less than the values of buildings in other parts of town. When the owner constructed the building, the neighborhood population was nearly all white; then the ethnic mix became half white and half black; now it is becoming primarily Korean. The builder-owner was a middle-aged man twenty-seven years ago, and he never gave up his prejudices. His point of view was that the highest and best use of his building was to keep it segregated, not to let it change to reflect the ethnic changes of the seventies and eighties. He kept minorities out of his building, and thus maintained it as a lily-white building. In order to do this, he employed managers who covertly kept everybody out except for the tenants the landlord and the managers thought would be "best" for the building. The managers found this a difficult task, and had to induce the "special" tenants to live there by giving them bargain rates over a period of time. The owner didn't realize that eventually his rents were 30 percent below market.

We bought the building and changed it only by hiring a manager who had no racial prejudices. Since then many of the thirty tenants have moved, and new ones have come in at a substantially higher rent—the same rent the other buildings on the same block charged. The building is already worth more than we bought it for, and we've owned it for only six months. The highest and best use we saw for this building was renting it "eighties-style"—in other words, to any responsible tenant who met our financial requirements, without prejudice.

Everyone in his situation wins: we surely did, the American melting pot system did, and even the old owner did because he made a great profit when he sold his building to us. It's interesting to note that if he hadn't succumbed to "old age"—in the sense of letting his fear block his clarity and power—by keeping up with the times, he would have made another $200,000!

WHAT IS THE POINT OF OBSERVATION IN REAL ESTATE AND HOW DO YOU REACH IT?

When you get to observation in real estate the "seeing" can start. *The point of observation in real estate—which is exactly the same as the point of observation in life—is the point at which you can stop being involved in your own personal pictures and ideas of things and just look at what's there, without adding to it your own point of view.* Using this thirty-unit apartment building as an example, we didn't have a point of view that one ethnic group of tenants was better than another. We had a building in a neighborhood that had changed, and all we had to do was to let it adapt to the neighborhood.

The key to seeing value and being at the level of observation is to abstract yourself from the situation and look at it as if you're in a helicopter flying above it. Reach that point of overview and say to yourself, "Now let me look at all of what's below as a whole; what's going on there?"

The technique of observation has to be constantly renewed so you can keep being able to look with a fresh eye every day. A perfect example to illustrate this involves a couple buying their first house, built twenty-five years ago, a two-bedroom colonial. Once they own the house, they do it over in the style of the moment. They furnish it, they paint it with current colors, they fix the landscaping, and when they think they've done the job, they shut off all progress on the house from that day forward. Ten years later the property hasn't changed from the day they "finished" it. The couple who buys it from them ten years later may get it for a bargain price: they see value in it because they look at it as what it should be at the moment they are buying it; the sellers have grown older in their observation and may unknowingly see it below its value. They're not changing with the times; they're not swimming with the current. They don't even observe the changing direction of the stream.

Once you own a building, as long as you stay on top of things and keep it going in the direction the world is going, you are at the point of observation, and you are making active choices that are likely to increase the value of the property.

Seeing value is just knowing what's going on at a broad level, accepting it, and applying yourself to stay with it.

If the previous owner of the thirty-unit apartment building had been willing to see what was going on in the neighborhood and say, "That's good," rather than judging it and saying, "That's bad," he would have gotten more money for his property. Not only did his lack of observation keep him from knowing the rental market, it kept him from knowing the value of similar buildings. He would have been able to see both of these important factors for himself if he had seen what everyone else was doing instead of holding on to his point of view.

SEEING THE RHYTHM OF THE REAL ESTATE MARKET

To reach the point of observation, it's necessary to bring that helicopter high enough so that your overview includes more than just the one block a particular property is on; you want to get an overview of the *entire* real estate marketplace. Most people don't look at the marketplace as a whole: they look only at segments of it. It is very common for a person to say, "Okay, if my house is similar to the house next door and the one next door is priced at $125,000, that's probably the value of mine." Most likely, the person won't look to see what houses in neighboring blocks are worth, and what houses in other neighborhoods are worth. He probably won't look to see the trends in housing.

When you look at the whole market instead of just the individual segments, trends appear. And out of the trends, one begins to perceive the rhythm of the marketplace. Continuing with the previous example, if that person sees the whole marketplace in his area he may discover that the $125,000 house next door is overpriced or underpriced; he may discover that there is a shortage of houses for sale right now and those that are being offered are selling quickly, or he may discover that there is a glut on the housing market right now and houses are moving slowly. The asking price of the house next door is only one factor; only a combination of factors will tell him the value of his house at any given time.

Seeing the rhythm of the marketplace gives essential information about any property being considered for purchase.

When I started to invest in real estate in the mid-1960s, apartment houses were the popular real estate investment in and around Los Angeles. Three years later, apartment houses were declared "overbuilt," and the real estate community decided that land for new subdivisions was the popular investment; from subdivisions, the popular real estate investment became nursing and convalescent homes, then office buildings, then apartment houses again, and then shopping centers. During all of these periods, the rhythm of the marketplace was moving to the beat of one of these investments more than to those of the others, and this rhythm affected the values in the marketplace as a whole. People who bought at the beginning of the trends made fortunes—a result of their abilities to see value in terms of trends and rhythm.

Recently a man asked to see me in order to renegotiate a note on an apartment building he had bought from someone who had bought it from me. It was an old building in downtown Los Angeles. We took it in trade and sold it two months later because I unhappily felt like a slumlord owning it. The reason the new owner bought it, he explained, was that he raised himself to the level of observation and observed that a major new hotel was to be built a quarter-mile away from the building, and he reasoned that the spillover of this first-class hotel being built had to affect the whole area.

I knew the same facts, but I didn't care: that wasn't my way of looking at it. To me, it was a matter of my not liking to own the building and knowing that there were equally good investments on the market that I *would* like to own. So I turned it over quickly and moved on to another investment. To the man who came to see me at my office, it was simply common sense that magical things were happening near that building, and that the magic would have to rub off on his building because of its location. "If I take this garbage building and just hold on to it," he said to himself, "it has to skyrocket in value." And he was absolutely right: he held on to the building for three or four years and then sold it for $2 million more than he had paid for it.

My dislike of being what I considered a slumlord stopped me from feeling the strength of the change coming; my emotions blinded me. Had I known I was leaving $2 million on the table, I would have dealt with my feelings by upgrading the building and held on to it longer. Yet even though I had kept the building for only two months, I did see—even in my emotional state—that the construction downtown would have a positive effect on the marketplace, and I was able to see new value in the building to the extent that I was able to sell it for a sizable profit.

When you're at the level of observation you see that you have choices. In real estate you can choose property that will obviously rise in value.

Newspapers and magazines are among the best sources of information to investigate to help you raise yourself to the level of observation about the marketplace. Note that I said "sources of information to investigate," not "sources of information to be taken literally." As an investor, you have to raise yourself to the level of observation about any information you read in an article; the direction you decide it may point you for an investment may be very different from the direction in which the author thinks he is pointing you.

An example of this is an article about Hollywood High School I recently found in a national news magazine. It basically said, "Look at this wonderful high school that years back had Ozzie and Harriet's kids in it, and where Lana Turner was discovered, and where the students had the highest grade point average and the best football team. Now, because Hollywood has turned into an American melting pot, and the students speak so many different languages, the only thing the school gears itself up for is to teach these people to cope." The point of this article, like that of many others published in the last year, is that for many new immigrants Los Angeles has become what the Lower East Side of New York was for European immigrants in the first part of this century.

But think about the article from the perspective of observation —about what the information it contains means in terms of real estate investment. Then what you'll see is what the article *doesn't* say. It tends to look at the area it describes as going down. It says, for example, that the neighborhood is plagued by crime. What it fails to look at is why that area attracted the new refugees to begin with. The reason is that it was already inexpensive, so it gave new people an opportunity to live comparatively cheaply. The article also fails to mention that crime was already in evidence there.

I had stopped buying buildings in Hollywood some years back because I thought it was becoming a rundown area as a result of attracting more and more of what I call "glitter people"—people from all over the country who were looking for something for nothing. They didn't really have jobs. Hollywood was a haven for runaway kids, dope pushers, and prostitutes; it was becoming a colony of lost people.

When I read that article from the level of observation, I saw that the new people pouring into Hollywood who don't speak any common language are people who cannot afford glitter; they're not moving to the area because of the myth of Hollywood, but because they can afford its reasonable rents. These new Americans are displacing the "glitter people." Even though they have their own problems, they are carving out a niche for themselves and making the neighborhood better. So in an area where I once avoided investing because I believed it was being ruined by crime, I now see a potential upgrading because the new arrivals are going to make a good place for themselves to live. And the very process of their doing this will raise the value of everything in the area. At the level of observation, I can see opportunity there. Trends, whether they are considered positive or negative by others, must be evaluated carefully.

Trends come at all levels. On the broad level is the country's economy. When economists are predicting good times ahead, common sense suggests there will be business expansion, which creates a demand for real estate at all levels. The opposite forecast could portend vacancies and bankrupt tenants. The problem in looking to prophecies about the national economy as an index for real estate investments is that economists often disagree among themselves; moreover, they are often wrong.

Trends at a local level are much easier to read. This is where we can see, hear, and even feel the movement in our own areas. Are businesses opening or closing? Is there new construction? Is there too much new construction? How fast are properties being rented? Are people feeling negative or positive about their economic future? Any specific area can be out of step with the economy in general: it can be a boom or bust climate locally regardless of what the national economy is doing. Read the local papers, subscribe to the *Wall Street Journal,* ask friends and associates what they think the trends are.

DIFFERENT LEVELS OF OBSERVATION FOR DIFFERENT PEOPLE

At the level of observation one can generally see the rhythm of the marketplace and the value of properties in that marketplace, and one automatically knows how much should be paid for a particular property. For someone like Joe, who is a beginner with limited funds, the level of observation will reinforce his belief that he has to buy a property at exactly the right price, to within a few dollars of the low end of the market. For someone who is very wealthy, with a lot of staying power and the ability to hold on to the property for many years, it hardly makes a difference in the long run whether he buys the property for its exact rock-bottom price—whether he pays one thousand dollars more or less or 5 percent more or less —because his expectation is that by the time he sells, his profit will be tenfold. Thus, a person's resources may influence what he sees —as well as what he looks at—from the point of observation.

For example, it's common knowledge that there is a national oversupply of commercial office space. Nowhere is this more evident than in parts of Texas where a massive building boom was fueled by overoptimistic predictions of growth space needed by the energy and high-technology industries. This resulted in "see-through office buildings" (transparent from lack of tenants) with millions of square feet vacant. A new kind of investment scheme, which real estate insiders have dubbed "vulture funds," has been created with the sole purpose of buying these buildings at tremendously discounted prices, and holding on to them for as many years as it takes until the rental market can absorb them.

These vulture funds are an example of seeing opportunity where most of us see failure, and this brings us to the next point about seeing value.

DIFFERENT REALITIES

Obviously it's fine for companies like the vulture funds to bet on the future at a high level, because they have the staying power to do it. Most people's attitude would be "I don't have the luxury of doing that, so why should I care?" That observation is appropriate, but I want to point out that in order to observe the marketplace, one has to see that other levels are working at the same time as your level, and that all levels influence each other.

The operators of vulture funds realize that their profits will come years from now; they are buying the buildings at a fraction of their replacement cost because there is little demand for them now. As new owners of these distressed properties, they have the advantage of being able to rent them at a fraction of the cost that their predecessors asked and still make a profit. This will be their strategy, and they will market the space to potential users from all over the world, who will be attracted by fabulous office space at fire-sale prices.

This is a fine example of how different realities work at the same time. The idea that vacant buildings in a depressed economic area just didn't work is one reality. The idea that these same buildings discounted at pennies on the dollar and held for the future or rented at giveaway prices is a different reality.

As a beginner in real estate you may ask, "What does this have to do with me? What does this reality have to do with my reality?" A lot.

First, it shows that in any situation, no matter how hopeless it may appear, there is opportunity for someone.

Second, it shows that investors using the contrarian approach to real estate, such as the operators of vulture funds are using, are simply raising themselves to the point of observation where they can see problematic situations turning into grand opportunities.

The real point is that in reaching the level of observation, we can see that the very same rules for seeing value apply to large properties as well as to your own real estate investments.

CHAPTER 6

EVERY PROPERTY HAS A STORY

Every property for sale in the world has its own story. This is part of what a potential buyer is buying: it is romance; it is information; often, it is an appeal to greed; just as often, it is total fiction.

Since most of the time real estate brokers will be acting as intermediaries between you and the sellers, they will generally be the ones telling you the stories. A broker might say to you, for example, "You know what makes this building a great deal? Sam, who owns it, is an old man and he's been sick, so he just hasn't wanted to raise the rent for years." Another story you often hear is "Oh, the owner kept everything up so well that the building is in perfect condition. You can buy it today and you won't have any trouble with it at all." Or the contrary: "The owner is so damned cheap he wouldn't fix anything. Because he wouldn't, he kept getting bottom-of-the-barrel tenants who would only pay half the rent. All you have to do is come in and make the repairs and raise the rents and sell it for a profit."

You can always learn something, some information that suggests where the value of a particular property may be, from every story you hear. To test the truth of this proposition, all you have to do is find the facts that would support it and give them the duck test.

I've never walked into a house or an apartment building where I haven't immediately heard a story. With a house, either the person has been transferred and wants to get out quickly, or the family outgrew the house and has already bought another one they want to move into right away. Or there's a remarriage, and the wife doesn't want to live in the old house with her new husband because her former husband lived there. All of these stories would support the proposition that in order to make a quick sale the owners would be willing to sell the house at the low end of market value.

It doesn't make a difference if the story is true or not; either way, the story attracts you to a property or repels you from it and helps you decide whether to buy the property. Follow the threads of the story and find out if the deal is sound. Set yourself up as a devil's advocate regarding the story. Keep trying to invalidate it by asking the storyteller questions. In this way you will uncover the true value of the story and the value in the seller's logic. Ask your Free Board of Directors what they think. If the story is false, following the threads and seeing where they lead will show you if you should explore the deal further or stay away from it.

If you discover that the story is a lie but you have a good feeling about the property anyway, you've gotten a valuable negotiating chip. You can now walk into the broker and say, "Well, the story you [or the seller] told me isn't true because . . . so I can't feel good about the price we were originally talking about. It isn't worth it. But I will pay twenty-five thousand dollars less for the property. That's all it's worth to me." If, on the other hand, discovering that the story is a lie tells you the property simply is not a good deal or that you should be totally mistrustful of the broker and the seller, then it's time to move on to another potential deal.

Sometimes listening to a story provides you with a valuable strand of information about the sellers, and thus about the total integrity of the deal.

A friend of mine, a skilled tax attorney who is chief operating officer of a large real estate syndication firm, mentioned to me that he was in the process of buying a major office building under construction in New York. The negotiations had been going on for a long time, and my friend had a sense that the seller was not entirely trustworthy. During a break in the negotiations, the seller came up with a story about his own life. In telling it he mentioned that he had been involved in fixing some horse races. My friend immediately thought, "Aha! The guy's a crook!"

But my friend didn't stop the negotiations. In fact he was continuing them at the time he told me the story.

"Okay," I said to him, "you're already on notice that you're dealing with a crook. How do you think you're going to come out?"

My friend responded, "The only way that I'd do the deal with this guy, knowing he's a crook, is to get a letter of credit from a bank guaranteeing he will do everything he says he will. A contract wouldn't be enough in this case."

I have two points to make about this. One is that by listening carefully to what the other person in your transaction says—every word he says, not just what he says about the property under discussion—you hear the story. It's as if the story leads to the center of a spiderweb. My friend knows he's going to get bitten at the center of this web because he knows the man he's dealing with is a cheat. I would have asked, "Do I have more to lose or more to gain by getting involved with a crook?" Generally, you have more to lose. My guess is that my friend was wasting his time. I think when push comes to shove, the bank will find out that the seller is a crook and will not give him a letter of credit that will protect my friend. And that means the deal won't go through. So why waste your time?

Probably one in every fifty deals I work on comes through. So, in a sense, wasting my time is part of the process, and I don't mind it. But on the other hand, I don't like to waste time by working on a deal if I know it probably will never be consummated. My solution is to work quickly on every deal. As soon as I see a red flag, I confront the problem and decide if it will ultimately kill the deal. If so, I stop working on that deal. The red flag in the deal my friend was working on was the fact that the seller was dishonest.

GETTING TO THE CENTER OF THE WEB

Imagining a spiderweb is a helpful way to visualize a real estate transaction. The story isn't the only way to get into the web; another way is to talk to members of your Free Board of Directors who are experienced in real estate. Ask them, "Where is the center of this web? What is this deal about? Can we make money on this property?" One way or another, everything *can* be checked out.

As you begin to look at properties, you may hear some of these stories:

- Divorce forced the sale.
- Bankruptcy forced the sale.
- The owner died and none of the heirs wants the property or knows what it's worth.
- Foreclosure forced the sale.
- The owner's transfer forced the sale.
- The tenants are driving the owner crazy, so he's decided to sell.
- The owner needs cash desperately.
- The owner is retiring and wants out.
- The owner is terminally ill.
- The owner has gotten so friendly with the tenants that he can't collect the rents.
- "Keep it quiet—I bribed the portfolio manager of the insurance company that used to own this building, and he sold it to me for fifty percent of what it's worth, so I can sell it to you for a bargain."
- The place looks so bad that most people won't consider it, but they don't realize it's not as bad as it looks.
- The owners don't need the money—they'll carry 90 percent financing at 10 percent because they like you.
- The area's going to be rezoned, and this property will be worth a fortune.
- "A new intergalactic rocketdrome is going to be built next door. It will be totally silent, it will create twenty-five thousand new jobs, and there isn't enough housing in the community, so the value of this property is going to skyrocket."

As you go through your daily routine, listen for stories about properties in your area—and begin to think about how you would go about checking them out for yourself. You may find a road map to a good deal just by hearing a story someone casually tells you.

In the third part of this book, I'll take you step by step through the process of actually buying your own first property. But first I want to teach you the general rules for investing in apartment houses, office buildings, and commercial and industrial properties. Once you're familiar with them, you'll be able to make a decision about the type of property you want to look for as your first investment.

Part Two

CHAPTER 7

APARTMENT HOUSES: EVERYTHING YOU NEED TO KNOW TO BUY THEM

Everybody who is even marginally interested in real estate has heard that "apartment houses are a great investment," yet few people ever ask anyone to tell them exactly how investing in apartment buildings works. When people do run across someone they feel could answer this question, they often feel it would be too much of an imposition to press for an answer. For many people, talking about how to make money is considered as impolite as talking about sex.

In order to alleviate this problem, I'm going to become a member of your Free Board of Directors and explain the rules of investing in apartment buildings. I'm also going to show you how I play by these rules and win.

WHY BUY APARTMENTS AT ALL?

Apartment houses are so well regarded as investments because:

- They go up in value—they *appreciate.*
- Even mild inflation will create greater and greater profits.

- As current building costs rise, existing apartment houses become more valuable, since they would cost more to replace today.
- People expect rents to go up, and most economists expect a shortage in housing units.
- Apartment rents generally outpace rents on other forms of real estate.
- Apartment houses have their share of headaches, but these headaches are often less problematical than the headaches that may accompany other types of real estate investments.
- They are excellent trophies or status symbols.

LOCATION, LOCATION, AND LOCATION: WHAT DOES IT MEAN?

One of the first things people hear about real estate is that the three rules to buying a property are location, location, and location. *This means that the location of a property is paramount in determining its value.* The same building on the best block in town is obviously worth more than that building on the worst block in town; conversely, the worst—and smallest—building on the best block in town may be worth more than the best—and biggest—building on the worst block in town.

The reason for this goes back to the definitions of value: The value of a property is what a willing buyer will pay a willing seller when the property has been exposed to the market properly. A willing buyer is always going to pay more for a property on the best block in town simply because it is on the best block in town.

Picture an apartment building on the best block in town. Its rents are much higher than those for apartments in a similar building in a less prime part of town.

Contrary to how it may at first appear, this doesn't mean that you should buy only a building in the best part of town. It does mean that what you pay for a building depends on the building's location: There will always be a demand for the best locations, and buildings in the best locations always command better prices than their less well located competition. One of the purposes of this chapter on apartment buildings is to help you choose the location in your area in which you want to buy, whatever type of investment property you choose, and to help you determine prices in that location.

UNDERSTANDING THE CONCEPTS OF THE APARTMENT GAME

The selling price of an apartment building is often expressed in terms of the building's "gross multiplier." The gross multiplier is calculated by dividing the *rent roll* (the yearly anticipated rental income from all the apartments in the building before allowing for vacancy and uncollected rents) into the building's selling price. Thus, a building with a $10,000 rent roll that's selling for $100,000 has a gross rental multiplier of 10, and its selling price is expressed as "10 times the gross." (The word "gross" in this context is the abbreviated form of *gross scheduled income,* another name for the rent roll.)

The gross rental multiplier (GRM) is a very important way of getting a thumbnail sketch of an apartment building's value. The primary use of the GRM is the quick comparison of one deal to another. If one apartment house is selling for ten times the gross and a similar building in the same area is selling for nine times the gross, the latter one *sounds* better at first hearing. Remember, however, that the GRM description should in no way be taken as the only criterion for judging value. I view it as a way of describing a blind date to a friend—"good-looking, intelligent, friendly." When my friend actually meets the person he may find her very unappealing. Still, the description goes a long way in the early stages of matchmaking!

When one is trained in seeing value and has become an expert on the various marketplaces, he knows what the GRM of each location should be. The GRM is an immediate reference by which he can sort out whether a particular project can make sense. GRMs vary from location to location and from property to property within each location. As I've said, it isn't the only criterion to base decisions on, it's just a way to help size up a deal fast.

As the owner of a building, you will have to pay your expenses and mortgage payments out of the building's gross scheduled income. Just as with Joe's rental house, whatever is left over—if there is anything left over—will be your positive cash flow. If it costs you money out of pocket to meet your expenses, the building has a negative cash flow. If the income exactly covers the expenses, then it has a *break-even cash flow*.

Your *expenses* as an owner of an apartment building (detailed later) include all costs for loss of income due to vacancy and uncollected rents, managing and maintaining the property, and financial reserves for repairing the property, as well as monthly payments on the loans you take out to purchase the property. The combined total loan payments are called the *debt service*. In some parts of the country these loans are called *mortgages;* in other parts of the country they are called *trust deeds*. It is common for properties to have first, second, and even third mortgages or trust deeds, meaning that the buyer has arranged or assumed up to three or more separate loans to complete the purchase of the property. All these loans may have different *terms* (that is, they carry different interest rates and have different lengths of time in which they must be repaid).

An ideal transaction on an apartment house is one in which you are able to buy a building in a prime location for a low enough price so that after you have paid all your expenses, including debt service, there is a positive cash flow and some *equity buildup* (reduction of your indebtedness on the property), and the loan you have on the building will take a long time to mature. The worst deal is one in which you buy a building in the worst location in the marketplace for such a high price that after paying all your expenses there is a negative cash flow, and all the loans are due next week! Between the best deal—which is seldom, if ever, available—and the worst deal—which also rarely, if ever, happens—lie a multitude of workable deals.

Some deals on apartment buildings have positive cash flows and some have negative cash flows. These are the two basic apartment building games—and there are good, solid reasons for making real estate investments with either of these variations, depending on your particular goals, personality, and financial resources.

A key factor in deciding which of the cash-flow positions merits the investment is *leverage,* the ability to purchase a property for a down payment that is only a fraction of its total purchase price while reaping economic benefits based on the entire purchase price. If a $1 million property appreciates 10 percent per year ($100,000) and you've put down 25 percent ($250,000) there will be an annual rate of return of 40 percent on your investment before adjusting for positive or negative cash flow and taxes ($100,000 = 40% of $250,000).

The same property using 50 percent down ($500,000) will show a return of about 20 percent ($100,000 = 20% of $500,000).

Therefore, even if the current cash flow is less or possibly negative, the more leveraged example (25 percent down as opposed to 50 percent down) may show a greater profit over the longer run, since the original investment (your down payment) on which the return is produced is smaller. It may also have additional tax advantages depending on your overall tax situation.

You will be able to make an initial quick evaluation of the cash flow of any apartment building from the *setup* or *fact sheet* that the broker or the seller will give you when you look at the building. The setup generally lists the asking price for the building, the number and types of apartments it contains, the current income, expenses, and financing, and a projection of what the income, expenses, and financing will be for the new owner. The setup may contain additional information as well, at the discretion of the seller and the broker. Once you've started working in your marketplace and you know the standard GRMs for properties in different neighborhoods, the setup alone may furnish enough clues to tell you if you want to bother seeing the building it describes. Again, this is only a quick way of sizing up a deal. I've probably missed many good transactions by dismissing them solely on the setup. On the other hand, this screening technique has saved me thousands of hours.

WHAT CAN YOU SEE FROM A SETUP

If you see a setup that tells you that the property can be bought for a reasonable down payment and that with the current income and expenses and your new debt service it would have a positive cash flow, you know that the deal is worth exploring further, even though later you may find the setup was wrong.

Even if the setup shows that the building would have a break-even or a negative cash flow, if you see that the GRM is low for that building in that location, the deal still justifies further exploration.

Another tool you can use to help evaluate a deal from the setup is the *cost per unit,* or *CPU.*

If a ten-unit apartment house consisting of ten one-bedroom apartments sells for $400,000, then the cost per unit is $40,000. The "seeing expert" will readily learn, just as with GRMs, that the per-unit price of one deal can be compared very effectively with the per-unit price of another deal. If a property under consideration is selling for $40,000 per unit, and similar units in the same location sell for $50,000, the property is probably a great deal even if it has a negative cash flow initially. But again, the CPU alone is not a sufficient indicator of a great deal. It is to be viewed only as a *part* of the buying picture. The CPU is a quick way of evaluating apartment buildings on a "cost-per-pound" basis.

In order to be able to calculate the cost per unit of different sized apartments, I've created a system of weighting the units by calling one-bedroom apartments (the most common type) 1 unit; single apartments (apartments consisting of a kitchen and living area with no separate room for sleeping) ¾ of a unit; two-bedroom apartments, 1¼ units; and three-bedroom apartments, 1½ units. Thus, for example, a ten-unit building with ten one-bedroom apartments equals 10 units. A ten-unit building with six one-bedrooms (6 × 1 = 6 units); two two-bedrooms (2 × 1¼ = 2.5 units); and two singles (2 × ¾ = 1.5 units) also equals 10 units. A ten-unit building with six singles (6 × ¾ = 4.5) and four one-bedrooms (4 × 1 = 4) equals 8.5 units.

Using this weighting system, you can sort through setups and compare the CPUs of various apartment house deals in the same location in a matter of minutes. Remember that even this can be misleading, because the buildings being compared must be adjusted for differences due to age, amenities (pools, dishwashers, fireplaces, etc.), and general condition.

LOOKING AT A BREAK-EVEN DEAL

Different types of cash-flow deals prevail at different times in each marketplace and at different locations at any one time in each marketplace.

Since all marketplaces experience cycles of change, you have to research your marketplace to see what the progression has been, where it is now, and what the trend for the future looks like. Once you see this, then you will know where your opportunities are.

A successful investor in apartment buildings will find a building at a price and with terms that are better than the average for comparable buildings. Once you see how a break-even deal works, it will be very clear to you how positive and negative cash-flow deals work.

When I first started buying apartment houses in the mid-60s, I could buy a building in Los Angeles for about 10 percent down. Typically, I could get a 70 percent first-trust deed, and the seller would lend me, in the form of a second-trust deed, the other 20 percent. There was also a positive cash flow of about 5 percent and about a 10 percent annual appreciation. With these parameters I could double my money each year! Today in the Los Angeles apartment house market, it would be a pretty good deal to break even on a yearly basis using 25 percent to 30 percent down, and arranging a 60 percent first- and a 10 percent to 15 percent second-trust deed. Given these financial facts, if the annual rate of appreciation is 10 percent per year, this investment will still show over a solid 30 percent rate of return in its first year. And that's on a break-even deal!

Let me show you how I calculate the income and expenses, and what I look for in appreciation on a break-even deal. As expenses, I include reserves for vacancies, lost rent, property taxes, utilities, insurance, gardener, swimming pool maintenance, and trash collection where applicable, overall building repair, apartment cleanup to prepare vacancies for rental, maintenance (for plumber and electrician, etc., as needed), replacements (for carpets, drapes, and appliances), and other miscellaneous costs, as well as a professional management fee. Some of these costs can be projected accurately from the previous owner's books and records, the rest can be projected on the basis of experience or according to industrywide standards. These standards can be learned from professional brokers, other building owners, or referrals provided by your Free Board of Directors. The expenses vary from city to city. Subtract the total of these anticipated expenses from the gross scheduled income of the building, and the remaining balance will be all that is left to cover debt service and profit (or loss).

In coming up with a model of a break-even building, let's say that 40 percent of the gross scheduled income would be just enough to pay all the expenses including a reserve for vacancy, and the other 60 percent of the gross would be just enough to cover the debt service. You would have neither positive nor negative cash flow.

Why would it be worth getting involved in a situation that was a break-even from a cash-flow point of view? There are five reasons:

1. leverage
2. appreciation
3. trophy value of the building
4. tax advantages
5. it's the best deal on a property available in the location you've chosen.

Let's look at these a little more closely. Let's assume that a certain building is selling for $800,000, and you are paying 25 percent ($200,000) as a down payment. Let's also say that the rent roll is $100,000 (that makes a gross rental multiplier of 8). It is a break-even situation. Furthermore, assuming that there is inflation—between 4 percent and 5 percent per year—in five years the building will be worth approximately 30 percent more than what you paid for it. Since leverage permitted you to buy the building with only 25 percent down, the effect of inflation will generate a substantial profit. This is because the entire building, including the mortgaged part (not just the 25 percent down payment) appreciates with inflation. If you held the building for five years, even without any reduction on the mortgage, you would more than double your investment when you sell it: from a $200,000 investment, you'd be getting back a minimum of $440,000—and probably a great deal more.

Why?

Because the new buyer will be paying a multiple of the rent roll just as you did, and the rent roll, having gone up 5 percent a year for five years, is now about 30 percent higher than it was at purchase. If it was originally $100,000, after five years the rent roll would be about $130,000. If the new buyer buys the building for the same GRM of 8 times the rent roll that you bought it for, the purchase price would be $1,040,000—instead of the $800,000 you bought it for. That means that with your $200,000 you made a $240,000 profit.

There's another reason to buy a break-even building: many of today's break-even properties are tomorrow's positive cash-flow properties. If the expenses and debt service on the building stay constant, that simple 5 percent annual inflation makes it a positive cash-flow building as soon as the rents are adjusted. If a building has $40,000 of expenses and $60,000 of debt service, and the rent roll when it is purchased is $100,000, then the day the rent roll goes up to $105,000 (which it would over a year with 5 percent inflation), you have met your expenses and you have $5,000 profits. At the same rate of inflation, the increase in five years would be about $30,000 in the rent roll, and the building would be running with a positive cash flow of $30,000 a year.

"BLUE-CHIP" LOCATIONS

Negative cash-flow deals are frequent when properties are in "blue-chip" locations. Blue-chip locations are the super-prestige areas in a community, and people pay a tremendous premium for properties within that area.

The blue-chip properties in the game of Monopoly are Board-walk and Park Place. In Los Angeles, Beverly Hills is blue-chip. In New York the blue-chip properties are on Fifth Avenue, Madison Avenue, and Park Avenue. In Chicago they are on Michigan Avenue and Lake Shore Drive. In Boston they are in Beacon Hill. Every city, town, and village has its Boardwalk and Park Place. Premium properties sell at a premium because they are considered the best trophies. The expression "pride of ownership" comes out of the status or trophy value of real estate. Consciously or unconsciously, people invest in real estate to acquire it as a trophy of wealth.

We rationalize paying a premium for a trophy by saying that it's acceptable to get a lower return on a blue-chip property because the next buyer will want it even more than we did, and will therefore pay a lot more for it.

A property in Beverly Hills, for example, sells at such a premium that a break-even situation can be an extraordinary deal, a small negative cash-flow property can be a fine deal, and a major negative cash-flow property can often be an acceptable deal. Remember that the negative cash flow often isn't permanent. Income will rise over time, turning the negative cash flow into a positive cash flow. And rents tend to rise rapidly in premium locations.

At the other end of the spectrum is a building in a deteriorated or ghetto area where the rent roll is high in relation to the low purchase price. Most people do not want to own these buildings because they do not want the management problems associated with them. Rent collections may be a headache, and even a well-managed building with responsible tenants will be subject to the spillover of problems from the surrounding properties.

Whatever your choice, it's important to know that people are buying buildings in both types of locations, the two extremes of any local marketplace, every day. Those who choose to own low-end buildings in deteriorated areas get the benefit of buying them for a comparatively low price with a comparatively low down payment and, on paper at least, they generally have a large positive cash flow. Those who choose to own buildings in blue-chip areas are willing to pay a high price for them with a comparatively high down payment and are willing to support the negative cash flow because they believe that over the long run their building will appreciate greatly. They will reap their reward when they find a buyer willing to pay more for this "trophy" than they did. This is simply the "sardines for trading" principle at work.

On the subject of trophies, it's important to keep in mind another fact: all buildings are trophies. When I began my career in real estate I had a friend who also started buying properties, but he bought properties in West Los Angeles, which is more of a blue-chip location than the areas I specialized in. All of my properties penciled out beautifully (which means that on paper they had wonderful returns); all of his properties penciled out with minimal returns—which is why I wasn't buying them. Twenty years have gone by, and I can now see which properties—blue-chip (his) or average (mine)—have done better. The difference seems to be that his properties are better trophies, while mine bring in more cash while I own them. Now that the score is in, it seems that they have worked out just about the same—fabulously.

What Makes a Building Work?

Let's remember that an apartment building with negative aspects can work as long as its positive aspects outweigh the negative. Bear in mind that a part in each of us wants to invalidate any purchase by creating barriers; we can't let a bad roof, poor plumbing, or faulty wiring invalidate an entire building. Any of these problems can be cured with money. When we evaluate a building we want to focus systematically on what problems exist, how much it would cost to solve them, and whether or not we want or can afford to take on that responsibility.

If our instincts tell us that the building is a good deal for the price at which it's being offered and our research confirms our instincts, and if our testing of the various components of the building proves to us that the majority of components is positive, then we know that the package works as a whole and that the deal is worth completing.

Let's start by checking the physical components. These include the structural elements of the building and the roof, the plumbing and electrical systems, and any other mechanical improvements, such as elevators. They also include the layout of the apartments and the design of the building. Another component is the apartment mix. Is the building the right kind of property for its neighborhood? Even if all these components prove to be 100 percent perfect—which would be rare—you will still have to decide if the building is the right property for you.

START WITH THE LAYOUT: MEDIOCRE IS FINE

In deciding if an apartment building is logically laid out it's important to make sure that all the apartments in it are comfortable for people to live in. If the apartment layout is inherently uncomfortable, the tenant will eventually become upset about it and move out. *Turnover usually means a less profitable apartment house.* Although turnover may present an opportunity to raise rents, it also means expense. If the turnover is exceptionally high, most times the landlord will lose more in dealing with vacancies than he gains in rent increases. If people keep moving in and out, you lose rent, you have to repaint and clean the apartment, you may have to replace items included in the apartment, such as rugs, draperies, or built-in appliances and, in general, you have a lot of aggravation as well as expense.

It's easy to determine if the apartments are comfortably laid out: just walk into every single one in the building—yes, every single one—and ask yourself if you would be comfortable living in it or if the layout somehow doesn't make sense.

If the apartments seem simple, plain, and mediocre, and the deal makes financial sense, the building may be worth buying. But if the apartments all seem awkward—poorly laid out—then don't buy the building (unless the economics of the deal are so favorable that you can't pass it up).

WHO LIVES THERE ANYWAY?

The next component to investigate is the apartment mix. Is the ratio of one-bedroom, two-bedroom, single apartments (kitchen facilities, no bedroom), bachelor apartments (no kitchen facilities and no bedroom), and whatever other size apartments are in the building a good ratio for the building itself and the neighborhood?

For the sake of this discussion, apartment tenants can be grouped into two basic categories: grown-ups and kids. A building with a lot of children has many more problems than a building tenanted primarily by adults. Because most buildings don't provide play areas, children play in the hallways and leave their toys and bicycles in public areas. The resulting mess makes the building unappealing to families without children, and tenants with more little kids move in, exacerbating the problem. So kids' buildings are okay—obviously children need a place to live—but the wear and tear on these buildings make them more costly to maintain. They also may cost more in emotional wear and tear, since most people love their own kids but don't necessarily want to put up with the demands of living close to their neighbors' kids. In kids' buildings, it's hard to rent out the single and bachelor apartments, which are designed for adults with no children.

Buildings with two- and three-bedroom apartments in working-class areas where people can't afford to waste money on rent will attract tons of kids. If a building full of two- and three-bedroom apartments is in an area with substantial unemployment, owners often find four, five, and six people living in apartments designed for one, two, or three. This situation greatly raises the utility costs, because more people take showers, need heat and air-conditioning, cook, and use other appliances.

For all these reasons I don't like to buy buildings that are comprised of mostly two-bedroom or three-bedroom apartments, or a combination of both. I know from experience that they are more difficult to run and result in less profit.

Would You Be Happy as Their Landlord?

I've found the old adage "Birds of a feather flock together" holds true for tenants. Invariably, the tenants in an apartment building all seem very similar. This applies to nice tenants and not-so-nice tenants. I know of twin buildings side by side, where one building is filled with mature, responsible tenants, and the identical one next door is tenanted by flighty, troublesome people. Often it's not so much the architecture or location of a building that attract tenants of a particular type as much as its other tenants. So when you inspect the layout of every apartment you should also try to find out what kind of people live in the building. If an apartment is neat and decorated with pictures of family and loved ones, the tenants are likely to be responsible; if the apartment is filthy, with nothing but clutter and tattered magazines scattered around, the tenants very well may be a problem.

Ordinarily you will make your apartment inspections during the day when people are at work, so there is no difficulty in browsing around. The information learned through this process is vital, and sometimes shocking. For example, I'm amazed at the number of apartments I've seen filled with guns. If I see an abundance of them, I say to myself, "Stay away from this building."

Another clue is the tenants' furniture. In today's mobile society many tenants have a mattress on the floor and use boxes as cabinets and suitcases as dressers. If you see this kind of makeshift furnishings, the tenants are probably transient, which means high turnover and high expense for the landlord. The opposite extreme is a preponderance of substantial furniture: Due to the expense and bother of moving, these tenants are not going to move out on a whim. Keep your eyes open and pay attention to these elements. You can get this valuable information simply by insisting on going into every apartment.

You can learn even more about the tenants by going through the garage area and looking at the cars. Out-of-state license plates mean it's a transient building. If the cars are all banged up, then it's a clue that the tenants may not be rent-paying, stable people. If the cars are recent models and in good condition, the tenants are likely to be the type you want to have in your building. Knowing what kind of people your tenants would be helps you determine what kind of building you're buying, and whether the vacancies and expenses will be high or low. Above all, make sure that the tenants are the kind of people you would feel comfortable dealing with.

CHECKING OUT THE OTHER PHYSICAL COMPONENTS

Eventually you're going to need an expert to inspect the building's physical qualities, but don't bring him in until your offer on the building has been accepted and you and the seller have written up a contract with conditions releasing you from the deal should you later decide it's not a good one. Your initial walk through the building will give you a gut-level evaluation of the physical components—roof, plumbing, electrical, and structural. You can bring in experts later.

The condition of the roof has a great deal to do with where the building is located. The roof generally will require a great deal more maintenance in a cold and snowy climate than if the building is in an area that is always warm and sunny. My company rarely has to make expenditures on the roofs of our Los Angeles properties. They can be ten and twenty years old and still not need major repair. But the roofs on those properties we own in the East, where the weather is often inclement and there are radical variations in temperature, need to be replaced more frequently, and they tend to be more expensive both to maintain and replace.

When you're ready to call in a capable roofing person, keep in mind that the roof is something that will cost money every once in a while. I often hire roofing consultants rather than roof contractors. Consultants are in the business of diagnosis, not repair. They don't mislead customers just to make a sale.

Check out the plumbing in the building before you bring in an expert. Look at the kitchen and the bathrooms in each apartment to spot plumbing problems such as leaks or cracked plaster from pipe problems. Check out the building's electrical system yourself by talking to tenants and asking if they have had trouble resulting from the wiring. Look for the "octopus" plugs that indicate inadequate wiring.

I have found that the plumbing and electrical systems in apartment buildings are rarely a major problem. At most, they are nuisances. Even major crises often turn out to be only minor emergencies. We once owned a building in Sherman Oaks, California, and hired an on-site supervisor to care for it. The building developed a plumbing problem about a month after we bought it, and the building supervisor became so upset by the plumber's assessment of how much work was needed that our property manager told me, "We've got to sell the building; it's going to be a total disaster." With some minor repairs, we went on to own the building for six years without ever substantially overhauling the plumbing, the "disaster" never showed itself, and the tenants were happy the whole time. I remember feeling terrific when we sold it because I had told the plumber and the property manager, "You may be right, but in my life's experience, this has never happened." And it still hasn't happened. I've owned about 5,000 apartment units—

65 percent of them over twenty years old—and we rarely have major plumbing problems.

Clearly, each of a building's physical components presents potential problems. All of these potential problems can be resolved with money. The task at hand in evaluating an apartment building is to find out how much money it would cost to solve these problems, and then to figure if it's worth it.

Don't be afraid to talk to the tenants about the building. Whenever I walk into a building I'm considering buying I tell the tenants I see that I'm interested in buying the building and ask them what they think about living there. People give you all sorts of useful information just because you've taken the time to include them in your evaluation process.

FIGURING OUT IF IT'S WORTH BUYING A BUILDING THAT NEEDS WORK

The cost to repair *deferred maintenance* on a building—work that must be done because it hasn't been done in the past—should be considered as an additional cost of purchase. If you buy a building for $500,000 and put $100,000 into it for deferred maintenance and then have a building worth $1 million, that's great! If you have to put up the $100,000 and the building is still worth only $500,-000, you're in trouble. Remember, too, that fixing up a building takes more than money: it takes quite a lot of time and energy. While there are drawbacks for you as owner, the tenants, on the other hand, will be pleased to have a new landlord take care of all the repairs, and the repairs should not come up again for a long time. They are also tax-deductible to the extent that they reduce the reported income.

In terms of taking care of future repairs and other expenses that may arise in the operation of a building I advise establishing a rainy-day fund, which I will explain in Chapter 8.

SOONER OR LATER, YOU HAVE TO TAKE A STAND

If you want to play the apartment building game, you can't spend a lifetime puzzling over a building, interviewing tenants, or checking pipes. You can't spend a lifetime puzzling over the component parts of a deal or figuring out reasons not to choose a building. Ultimately you have to decide if you are going to choose a building or if you're not. You are eventually left with your own intuition to decide whether or not you are going to choose a particular building and deal with the consequences. And you have to be clear about the difference between your intuition and your fear.

I want to stress again that most people find it so hard to take a stand—to choose at all—that they never do anything. When someone uses the poor condition of the roof or the plumbing to make the choice for him, and ignores the positive components, that person is choosing to say no—not based on the evidence before him, but out of the fear of choosing to act. Nothing will work for you if you refuse to be an active player. Remember: power comes from choice, from taking a stand.

In evaluating the components that make up any real estate transaction, my advice is to determine if all the components, taken as a whole, make the deal work, not to find ways to prove that the deal doesn't work.

Talk with your Free Board of Directors and whatever experts you bring in. Don't be afraid to show the building to your Free Board of Directors, to drive them by or take them in and hear what they have to say. Don't be afraid to hear what anyone has to say —just listen and check it out. Then act!

Here's the Formula You've Been Waiting For

Now I'm going to teach you how to figure out the market value of any apartment house in any location. As an example, I'm going to describe the model I use to purchase apartment houses in Los Angeles. You can modify it for your area—or for any area—so that you can evaluate the price of any apartment house.

I'm going to talk about a run-of-the-mill apartment building in an average area, not a blue-chip property. I first pick out a specific neighborhood, make myself an expert on it, exactly the way I said Joe would do, and familiarize myself with the prices of all the apartment buildings in it. Having taken these steps, let's say I've concluded that a good buy on a building in this neighborhood would be 7 times the gross scheduled income. (I'm defining "a good buy" in the same way that I did for Joe: It is a property selling at the lower end of the 20 percent spread in prices in a particular marketplace at that given time.)

I arrived at a gross multiplier of 7 by looking at the recent sale prices of all the buildings in this neighborhood, calculating their gross multipliers, seeing what the highest and lowest gross multipliers are, and determining the average gross multiplier. I researched these facts by talking to the local brokers. Many of the setups show a gross multiplier of 8 or 8.5. In rare instances, some have a gross multiplier below 7. So if a building in the neighborhood is priced at 7 times the rent roll or less, I know I'm interested in exploring the deal further. (I also might consider apartment house deals in this neighborhood with a gross multiplier over 7 if the deal has very favorable financing, has below-market rentals, or is clearly the best-looking property on the block.)

In addition to checking the gross rent multipliers (GRM), I also see what the average cost per unit (CPU) is of buildings in the marketplace so that I can compare any individual property's CPU against the average.

This average is calculated by getting setups from actual sales, checking out setups of current offerings on the marketplace, and especially by talking to owners and brokers. This process establishes for me that the average cost of a one-bedroom apartment in this model area is $37,000.

Thus armed with two formidable tools, my target GRM and my target CPU, I search the marketplace for deals that fit. Now I know what I'm looking for. All I have to do is listen to the stories. Let's say I hear about an apartment building in this run-of-the-mill neighborhood, and that this building has ten one-bedroom apartments, a rent roll of $52,857, and an asking price of $370,000. I can see immediately that the GRM is 7 ($370,000 ÷ $52,857 = 7) and the CPU is $37,000 ($370,000 ÷ 10 = $37,000). Since both the GRM (7) and the CPU ($37,000) are equal to my target GRM and CPU, I'm interested in the deal.

The marketplace will provide all the leads, and the refining process leads me to make an offer. Now my goal is to get the actual sale price below the target. I will find deals in the range of my target GRM and CPU, make offers below the target price, and see how much better than my target I can do.

I'll pay a premium if there is great financing or the building has above-average features (dishwashers, pool, elevators, fireplaces, etc.). Conversely, if the building demands immediate repairs (deferred maintenance), I should get a discount in compensation. In evaluating a deal, I also make an allowance for the leverage: the greater the leverage (meaning the lower down payment), the greater the potential return on the investment.

Let me show you exactly how this worked in an actual transaction that took place a few months ago.

A broker I had never met called me on the phone. He worked in a suburban office of Coldwell Banker and was representing a seller with an apartment building in an area I knew well. As soon as I heard the figures over the phone I knew it was a fabulous value on exactly the basis it was being offered. Over the phone I agreed to exactly the asking price, with no changes. One hour later the broker was sitting in my office with the contract. The offer was for $1 million even. The existing income on the building was $145,000. So the purchase price came out to 6.9 times the gross.

There were thirty-seven one-bedroom units, and so the per-unit price came out to $27,000 a unit ($1,000,000 ÷ 37 = $27,000). I knew that $27,000 per unit was $10,000 less than the average price for one-bedroom apartments in this type of a neighborhood. In fact, I hadn't seen similar units at $27,000 in a few years. So far the figures told me that the deal looked terrific.

Taking the annual rent roll of $145,000, I calculated that the average rent per apartment was $326 per month. I knew from owning many other units in the area that *any* one-bedroom apartment in that neighborhood was worth a minimum of $400. These simple calculations told me right off the bat that $326 per month was a bargain rental, not a high-priced rental—and that the building would bring in approximately $33,000 a year more in rent:

$ 400	market-value rent
−326	current rent
$ 74	rent increase per apartment
× 37	apartments
$ 2,738	monthly rent increases
× 12	months
$32,856	additional annual rent at market value

If I take the $33,000 and add it to the rent roll of $145,000, I get $178,000. If I multiply that by 7, the average GRM for that area, I get $1.246 million, which is $246,000 more than the $1 million I would have to pay for the building. So I knew I had at least a $246,000 profit built in at the time of purchase.

And how much would it cost me to make this money?

It's realistic to get a loan on the building for about 65 percent or 70 percent of the purchase price. So even if I put as much as $385,000 down and got a $615,000 loan at 11 percent interest, the total debt service would be about $70,000, which is less than 60 percent of the gross scheduled income. With the expenses just under 40 percent, the building would have a positive cash flow on paper of $17,000, even with below-market rents.

I knew my profit would be greater than $246,000 because I knew that two blocks away a similar building had just sold for $37,000 a unit. Therefore, the day I bought this building I knew I would make at least $370,000 on it because I was buying it for $27,000 a unit and could sell it for $37,000 a unit. And the person who would be buying it from me at $37,000 a unit would still be buying it at market value.

The point is that a broker—a total stranger—called me on the phone, told me about a deal, came to my office, heard my offer, and communicated it to the sellers; the sellers accepted it, the broker earned his commission, and I made a great deal—without having to negotiate a single point. And the deal came in exactly the way that I would have dreamed it: from a phone call. I knew it was a good deal because I had done my homework. Naturally, between the time we wrote up the contract of purchase and the close, I inspected the building thoroughly, went through the books and records, and, most important, brought in my partner and a few friends to listen to the facts and review the deal with me. This is all part of the debate process that double-checks the logic of the deal.

The important lesson is that I saw the value right away. The reason I saw the value was because I'm constantly looking at the marketplace. You will become an expert on your area the same way.

APPLYING THE FORMULA

It doesn't matter if you live in a large city, a small town, a suburb, or anything in between, the game is played the same way: find the average gross rental multiplier (GRM) in that location and the average cost per unit (CPU), and they become your targets to better.

Your first step in doing this is to read the real estate section of the newspaper where you live every day and see what the asking prices of apartment buildings are in every location in your marketplace. Also note how many units each building has. If an ad doesn't give the building's rent roll, call and ask. Now use the formula to determine each building's GRM and CPU. That will give you some idea of values in the marketplace; you can then determine the range between the gross multipliers in the blue-chip locations and the gross multipliers in the average and the low-end locations.

You're ready now to define the specific location you want to work in. You will base your choice on a combination of factors: asking prices, personal preference of area, and the amount of money you have as your goal and expectation to spend. Once you've chosen your location, make yourself an expert on what constitutes value in that specific location.

After you read the newspaper ads, start going to real estate brokers and ask them to show you every apartment house they have listed for sale in that location. Look at these buildings and compare prices and per-unit costs. Once you know the range, you'll be able to figure out a formula that constitutes a good buy in the location you've selected.

As you look at buildings and make comparisons, you are doing more than calculating what a good deal would be; you are also educating yourself. You do this by constantly asking questions of the broker, the seller, and anyone else participating in the process —"How did you figure out the rent roll? The expenses? What would my profit be? What would my loss be?" The brokers are trained, high-priced practitioners who will train you free of charge if you're clever enough to ask questions and listen to the answers. Ask the brokers to give you the setups (or fact sheets) on every apartment house you see. Go over the setups carefully and see what expenses they list. Building expenses are by no means a mystery; by formulating every question in your mind and by asking everyone you know for the answers, you will see that no fact about a building is a mystery.

To learn more about expenses for apartment buildings, go beyond the setups. Question property management companies about their services: "I'm going to buy a building and I want to ask you some questions. If I hire you to manage the building for me, what can I expect it to cost—and why? What will the money go for? Exactly what will you take care of? What services will you be providing?"

Going to see a property management company, even if you eventually decide to manage the property yourself, is part of learning the rules of the game. The way you learn the rules is by asking the players. Talk with other owner-managers to find out what's involved in managing a building. To determine what a property's taxes are, ask the seller to show you his tax bill and then call the city to ask if there will be an increase in taxes to reflect the new purchase price. To find out about insurance costs, call an insurance broker—or more than one—and say, "I'm going to buy a building. I'm paying X amount of money. This is the location. Can you tell me what the insurance will cost me?" He will tell you what the insurance is to the penny. You can use this question-answer process to remove any barrier that is keeping you inactive.

What Is the Building's Income and What Are Its Expenses: Separating Truth from Fiction

Once your offer on a building has been accepted and you have the contingency period to check and double-check any considerations, your job is to play detective. In analyzing any apartment building transaction you must first calculate what the actual income and expenses of the building have been for the current owner, and what they are going to be for you. Your initial source of information is, of course, the setup, since it enumerates the present expenses, giving a dollar amount for each, lists the present income, and projects the expenses and income for the next owner. (Remember that what you are getting is always an estimate, not a dollar amount etched in stone.)

Ask the seller about the utility costs. Ask about the costs for trash collection. Ask about the property's income. Ask the seller to show you all of his records so you can verify the figures he is reporting to you.

There is no need to buy a building without knowing everything that you want to know. It is standard practice to make your inspection and approval of the books and records a condition of purchase. And it is important to know that contracts for properties go beyond standard practices all the time; they can include *any* condition that will make the buyer comfortable as long as the seller agrees to it.

You should expect the setup to reflect some literary license on the part of its writer. Expect it to be an over- or an understatement for the same reason you expect a used car dealer to suggest he's never had a problem with the cars he sells. The practice is accepted as "fair" even if it isn't entirely honest. Along with used cars, real estate is also classified under the "buyer beware" category. That's the way the game is played, and once you know it's played that way you will be wary and not waste time or energy being offended.

When a property owner is considering whether he is going to sell, he thinks to himself, "I'm going to ask more for my building than I think it's worth; if I have to sell it for less, then I'll keep it." Since an apartment building usually sells for a multiple of its income, a seller has a tendency to exaggerate the income and minimize expenses. Sellers start by asking the highest price they think they can get, and in order to justify that price they feel they have to maximize the income and minimize the expenses.

Consequently, you have to expect that there's going to be an element of "puffiness" in the setup. We simply have to verify all the figures, and if we find something wrong, then we figure out a compromise in the purchase price to make it right.

EXAMINING THE RECORDS

Our main purpose in our detective work, verifying and expanding our knowledge beyond the setup, is to figure out if, when we own the building, its income will actually cover its expenses, and what kind of cash flow, if any, it will provide on top of that.

Once you've made your offer and the seller has accepted it, you're ready to move beyond the setup to the owner's records on the building. Although the seller may be overstating the income of an apartment building on the setup, you rarely have to worry about getting misinformation on the building's income if you look at the books, the records, and the owner's tax statement, because people seldom overstate their income to the IRS!

Expenses, on the other hand, may be understated on the setup and overstated in the owner's records and even in his tax statement. Certain expenses, like property taxes and insurance, are black-and-white and will therefore be stated truthfully. Repairs and replacements are a gray area, and some property owners may misstate them to obtain higher tax deductions.

The truth about expenses usually lies closer to the owner's records than to the setup. At worst, the truth is somewhere between the two; at best, you are dealing with an honest owner who is providing you with totally accurate information. In any event, going over the paperwork is crucial for you to make your estimate.

As you go down the list of expenses one by one and check them out in this way, you'll find that all the fixed expenses (utilities, property taxes and insurance, elevators, salaries, pest control, rubbish pickup, and so on) can pretty well be determined in advance. The things that are harder to determine are the gray-area expenses, the variables, which, in addition to the repair and replacement factors, also include the vacancy and collection factors. In dealing with these variables, compare the information you get from the owner's records to the industrywide standards to be sure that they are parallel. If they're not, keep asking questions of the owner until you're clear about the discrepancy.

When you're in the market to buy an apartment building, you'll invariably run across some owners who won't want to give you the information you need because they want to hide something. Ironically, they're primarily afraid you'll discover something that you wouldn't care about. For example, most people who own an apartment house have at one time or another thrown out a tenant, or they have had to replace some plumbing, and they think that such things will dissuade a prospective buyer. So they'll say, "I can't give you the records because I have a lot of expenses in my personal life, and I write them off as a business expense through the apartment building. They'll only confuse you." When people say that, just tell them, "That's okay—just show me the records and explain them to me."

Every seller wants to paint the picture that his building is perfect and that nothing bad ever happens; by checking various sources you can uncover the truth.

THE BOTTOM LINE WITH APARTMENT BUILDINGS

When you are considering apartment house expenses, the main thing to know in advance is that a double standard exists. On the one hand, there is an industrywide set of expenses, which is considered average, and you want any building you buy to fit into that; on the other hand, few buildings ever exactly fit into it.

Once you have some idea of what the owner's repair and replacement costs are, you will be able to make an estimate of what these expenses should cost you. Remember: regardless of how reliable the owner's figures are, for you they are only an *estimate*. You'll discover over time that the industrywide standards you find through your investigation probably will apply in the long run; on a one-year basis, however, it's impossible to predict repair and replacement costs. You'll learn that although the industrywide standards for expenses and your own researched estimate of expenses for a particular building may not apply immediately, you still have to use them as measuring sticks to evaluate the expenses on any building you're considering; otherwise you could never make any estimate of the cash flow, and you'd never buy any building.

The real trick, then, is to clarify what the expenses of a building are *in fact,* as opposed to what someone tells you the expenses are when he's trying to sell you the building. If the expenses of a particular building don't fall within the standards that you have researched and believe in, either discount its price or forget the building!

I want to state very clearly that it's not just difficult to quantify the expenses for an apartment building in a book, it's impossible. And this isn't just because specific expenses vary from location to location. Rarely does an apartment house exactly live up to its projected expenses. But in the end, given a couple of years of inflation and a building's *seasoning out*—the term I use to describe the process of bringing the building up to par—the building generally compensates for whatever the expenses might have cost by appreciating so much that it makes it worthwhile, or by otherwise giving you additional income that you never expected.

General rule: Apartment houses don't immediately work. They are sardines for buying and selling, not for eating. Once you know this, you buy them anyway—and own them happily for years. Once they season out, the cash flow will come! Then they will also be sardines for eating.

WHAT THE LEASES AND RENTAL APPLICATIONS TELL YOU

Your evaluation of any apartment building must include an examination of all the paperwork relating to the tenants. This paperwork consists of leases or month-to-month rental agreements, any house rules for the building, and rental applications.

Leases are very straightforward. They state the rules the tenants must follow to live in the building, including what rent they have to pay and when the rent is due, and what services you as landlord will be providing for them. It's easy to determine whether these agreements are acceptable to you or not.

Watch for clauses that promise services that you don't want to provide (for example, does the lease state that the landlord has to keep the swimming pool heated all year, or is it up to you the landlord to decide whether or not to do this?). It's important to know how many people may live in each apartment; if you may charge extra for additional occupants; what the rules state about subletting an apartment; who pays for utilities? You'll also want to see how many apartments have leases and how many have month-to-month agreements. In some smaller buildings, you may find that there are no leases at all or that there is a different kind of lease for each apartment.

The lease is always fine as long as people play by the rules, but if they stop playing fairly and no longer pay their rent then you have to play detective in order to solve the problem. Many prospective owners don't realize the enormous value of reading the tenants' original rental applications. If they show the tenants' bank accounts, automobile license plates, places of employment, employers' phone numbers, and relatives' phone numbers to call in emergencies, then you have all the clues you need.

We run a complete credit check on every prospective tenant as a matter of standard practice. People are generally willing to provide a prospective landlord with basic credit information. If they're not, don't rent to them; as soon as you give a tenant the key to an apartment he is going to be much more reluctant to answer anything. (And if you don't like what you find out about him, he can hold out until you win eviction proceedings against him.) If the landlord of a building you're considering doesn't have this information on his tenants' rental applications, it may be a clue that he's been managing the building in a slipshod way or even that he's been so hungry for tenants he would take anyone.

RAISE HIGH THE RENT, LANDLORD

As you've now seen, the value of a building is to a great degree determined by its rent roll. Therefore, the amount a landlord can raise the rent is a major factor in determining how much the building is worth. As a consequence of this, you have to look not only at the current leases, but at local village, town, or city laws that govern rental agreements to find out how much free rein you have to raise the rents with regularity. This consideration is crucial.

This information is relatively easy to obtain. In addition to getting it from the city or town offices governing rental matters and from your Free Board of Directors, you can get it from an apartment house association, generally run by fellow landlords who are supportive of unsophisticated owners. Their staff will be thrilled to talk to you on an informal basis, and you can attend their meetings from which, for a dollar or two, you can get a wondrous amount of information. Familiarizing yourself with the rules governing rental agreements will give you the knowledge to detect whether there's anything in the leases you read that's out of step with current provisions.

RENT CONTROL AND HOW TO HANDLE IT

Where rent control and rent stabilization are in effect, you have to write out a projection of the future rent roll under best-case and worst-case situations. The best case would be if every tenant moved out when his lease was up and you raised the rent to the maximum the law allowed; the worst case would be if every tenant remained, and you raised the rent the relatively low maximum allowed under those circumstances. In some areas, even in a worst-case scenario with rent control, a building will have a substantially greater income stream after two or three years than at the time of purchase because the rent control standard may be about as high as a minimal rate of inflation. Some regions, such as New York City, maintain rent control that is disastrous to building owners, while other areas have relatively mild rent control. One hidden benefit of rent control is that apartment turnover will be minimal, creating savings on expenses, on lost rent, and on replacements. The most important factor to consider is whether an apartment's rent can be raised to market value when a tenant vacates. If that's allowable, things will probably work out; if not, you can't expect great rises in the income.

WHAT MAKES AN APARTMENT BUILDING ESPECIALLY VALUABLE?

Another way of asking the above question is "How do you get the most points in the game?" Since an apartment building becomes more valuable primarily by increasing its income stream, you get the most points by buying a building in which you will be able to increase the income quickly. With apartment buildings, the main question is "How can I turn cheap rents into expensive rents?"

When I look at apartment buildings in Los Angeles, one of the things I look for is the number of long-term tenants whose rents have minimally increased from their original rates. In analyzing the rent list, I see how many of the apartments in the building are renting at the current market level (which I determine by making a rent survey of the area), and how many are renting for less.

I would say that an average building in Los Angeles has about 10 to 15 percent of its tenants at rents substantially below the market rate. In many buildings, as much as 30 percent of the tenants pay below-market rates. Once in a while I come across a building in which all the rents are very, very low.

Keeping in mind that buildings generally sell at a multiple of their income, the rent list is an important factor. Let's take an apartment that is currently renting for $300 per month but which would rent for $400 if the tenant moved out. If you took that $100-a-month difference and multiplied it by twelve months, you would get $1,200 a year more income. If you multiply that $1,200 a year by 8 (which, for this example, we'll say is the gross multiplier of the deal), it comes to $9,600—meaning that raising one tenant's rent $100 per month is worth almost $10,000 in increasing the building's value!

A building with longtime tenants in it isn't the only type of building with cheap rents. For one reason or another, landlords may neglect to raise the rents when they should. That's why stories about building owners who, because of laziness or personal problems, haven't bothered to raise the rents to market value and stories about owners who live out of town and haven't raised the rents because they don't know the true market value of the building, actually may be a tip-off that a building is an especially good value. The only way to know is to check out the facts.

APARTMENT BUILDINGS WITH IMPOSSIBLE PRICES

What if apartment building prices in your area are so high that it seems impossible to buy a building you like with a positive cash flow —or even a break-even cash flow—even in a non-blue-chip location? How can you determine if a building is still worth buying under these conditions? If you live in a currently hot (high demand/short supply) marketplace, you may very well find yourself in this dilemma. That's why I promised I would come back to the subject of negative cash-flow apartment houses: so that if you find a preponderance of such deals being offered in your marketplace, you'll see what might make one such deal an acceptable investment while another is unacceptable.

The first step in evaluating a marketplace that seems to have a multitude of negative cash-flow apartment house deals is to go to your Free Board of Directors, which by this time should include real estate brokers and other professionals in real estate. The reason your Board will include brokers and other professionals is that as you make yourself an expert in an area, you'll also be making some lasting business relationships. Smart brokers and lenders will realize that even if you're not going to consummate a deal today, you'll probably be a buyer, seller, or borrower in the future, so they will want to keep in touch. What better way to do this than to be on your Free Board of Directors? Now it's time to turn to these people and ask, "Do investors in this location really buy apartment buildings with negative cash flows? If they do, why? If they don't, why not? If they do, does that mean it's okay to buy a building that loses $10,000 a year? Is it okay to buy a building that loses $100,000 a year?"

As your Board members provide you with answers to these questions, test their answers by going out into the marketplace and getting hard facts about the apartment house transactions that are taking place now and have taken place in the previous twelve months.

It's very easy to unearth the selling prices of buildings. Just check comparable sales, and see when properties were last sold and at what price. You can find computerized lists that will describe the selling prices on those properties. Often this information is available through title insurance companies, and they are glad to do you favors because they want your business when you buy.

The title insurance companies—which are listed in your yellow pages—develop these facts by various means, including monitoring deed transfer taxes. These taxes occur when a property changes hands. In California, for example, there is a charge of $1.10 per thousand dollars. All this information is on the public records, and title insurance companies make it available to customers and potential customers as a public service. (You'll find a full discussion of title insurance companies, and why they have this information, in Chapter 11.) Most good brokers also are fully aware of what properties have sold in their area and what prices the properties have sold for. Frequently they can provide you with comps (comparable sales).

By talking with anywhere from five to twenty brokers, your Free Board of Directors, and whomever else you know, you will learn exactly how the game is played in terms of cash flow in your area. You will find out whether the game being played is generally a positive, negative, or break-even cash-flow game—or a more or less equal mixture of all three. Once you know, you can check out the hard figures on buildings being sold to make sure that what you've heard is true. At the end of this process you will have learned what the rules truly are, if the negative cash-flow game is really being played by many people in your area, and if you want to play that game, too.

A key question to ask in evaluating such propositions is: "Is a negative cash-flow deal better than the other potential investments around?" You have to be certain there are no positive cash-flow or break-even deals to be made on properties in the location you've chosen—or in an equally acceptable nearby location. If positive cash-flow or break-even deals are available, then you would consider a negative cash-flow deal only if the others don't offer the same quality or the same opportunity for appreciation.

One key issue in determining whether or not to buy a negative cash-flow building is what is creating the negative cash flow. It is helpful to analyze the building based on its income and expenses assuming the building was bought for all cash without any debt service. If the building without debt service has a positive cash flow and it's being sold as a negative cash-flow deal, then, clearly, it is the debt service that is causing the negative cash flow. It may still be a good investment if you can afford to handle the negative cash flow or if you can restructure the financing to change it to a positive cash flow.

If you believe rent raises will be substantial enough in the near future to justify current losses as a trade-off for large profits down the road, and you can afford the negative cash flow, this negative cash-flow deal may make sense.

Another question that is particularly relevant to negative cash-flow deals is whether the building's "trophy" value is sufficient to justify paying the price of the negative cash flow even if the cash flow won't turn positive in the near future. Historically, people have done very well using these deals as "sardines for trading."

However, this may be more difficult to digest today because the losses generated by these negative cash-flow "trophies" are not as useful to everyone's financial picture as they were before the tax changes effective in 1987. Some investors will be able to use these losses to shelter other income while the majority of others will not. Primarily, these losses will benefit owners of other real estate who can use them to offset profits from their other real estate.

Other questions that will help your decision about negative cash-flow deals are: What prices have similar buildings sold for in the same location during the last two years, compared with the three years before that? Based on that information, what is the average annual appreciation rate of properties in that location? Is it likely that this rate of appreciation will continue? Since many negative cash-flow apartment buildings are now being converted into cooperative apartments or condominiums, often giving building owners a tremendous profit as a result of the conversion, do you see many co-op or condominium conversions taking place near the negative cash-flow building you're considering? If so, how much is each apartment selling for? How many are already sold? How do those buildings compare in space and structure to the building you're considering? Could the same kind of renovation be done to the building you're considering? How much would it cost?

If you conclude that the negative cash-flow apartment building game makes sense to play in your location, and you determine that you want to play it, then the next step is to begin playing it exactly the same way you play the positive cash-flow game.

This means that once you see what the game's parameters are in your area, you want the figures on your building to be right. If they're not, you know that you don't want the deal, because even if negative cash-flow deals are commonly being made where you're looking—in fact, even if negative cash-flow deals are the *only* deals being made in the area—if the cost per unit, the gross rent multiplier and the negative cash flow of the building you're looking at are higher than those of similar buildings in that location, then you know there are better values available to you.

Once you've discovered that the negative cash-flow game is being played in your marketplace and you've learned how it's being played, you have to ask one final question before you commit yourself to playing it: "Does the game look like a fad, or does it look as if it's going to be around for a long time?"

On a marketplace-by-marketplace level I really don't know the answer. I can tell you from my own personal experience that the negative cash-flow apartment building game has existed as long as I've been in the real estate business. Often it's played with no-headache buildings—those that are clean, well maintained, have solid tenants, and are in prime locations. A building that meets these criteria frequently sells for a premium price, which gives the new owner a negative cash flow. Some buyers are willing to pay this premium in exchange for no-headache ownership. Whether or not you want to play the negative cash-flow game depends on who you are and what you want, as well as what your financial resources and needs are.

Apartment buildings offer opportunities for whatever cash-flow situation meets your needs and resources.

CHAPTER 8

PROPERTY MANAGEMENT: WHY I ALWAYS DO IT MYSELF

Every building is bought to make an operating profit based on very tight allowances for income and expense. As we've noted, expenses are often estimated by using industrywide standards that tend to be based on everything going well. If a potential buyer projected much more than this standard, he would probably never buy a building.

This being the case, the best manager you're possibly going to have for your building is yourself. You're the only one who really *must* have a building that runs perfectly. That's why, in the beginning, it helps to buy an apartment house (or any investment property) that is at most an hour or two from where you live: you have to be able to get there on an everyday basis if necessary, either to manage it yourself or to supervise whoever is managing it.

The only real qualification for property management is common sense. To manage a property well is a matter of discovering what's going to work for everyone: you, your investors, the tenants, and the people who provide goods and services for the property. It needs to work for all four groups, and to have it work you have to set up a management system that serves everyone. This means you must set up a management system that works impeccably.

If the rent is due on the first of the month, it's due on the first —not on the nineteenth. As a landlord, you cannot tolerate rent being late. If your tenants aren't paying on time, you can't pay on time—and the whole system begins to fall apart. When you manage a building, you have to make a 110 percent commitment to honor your agreements and see to it that all the other parties honor theirs.

This is why the quality of the tenants in the building is so important. And by quality, I am talking not about the size of their bank accounts or income; I am talking about their sense of responsibility in keeping their agreements with you. One of the primary jobs in managing a property is making sure that the tenants are quality tenants and keeping them happy.

A BLAST FROM THE PAST

When I was about twenty-four years old, I bought a fourteen-unit apartment building in Los Angeles. The deal was good: I bought it at a very low gross-multiplier and per-unit cost for its location. The seller also agreed to let me buy it with very little money down. The building, which had mostly singles and one-bedroom apartments in it, was in terrible shape—which was part of the reason I got a bargain—but I saw its potential. I saw that in owning the building, I could turn it around and raise the rents. To do this, I knew I had to manage the building myself.

My first problem came when I discovered that one of my tenants was a prostitute who plied her trade on the premises. If she wasn't standing in front of the building drumming up business, she was stealing the other tenants' laundry. I realized that I had to get her to move if I wanted to upgrade the general quality of the tenants and save myself from future headaches. One day I knocked on her door and offered her $200 to find another place to live. It was 1966, and $200 was a lot of money, so she was tempted. The major obstacle that stood between her and moving was that all the calls from her procurer came in on her phone, she explained, gesturing toward it as she made her case. Then I did something I had seen done in the movies: I yanked the phone out of the wall. That ended the discussion. I gave her $200 and she moved out.

The point is that there's nothing I wouldn't have done as manager of that building to make it work as an investment. When apartments became vacant, I would stay at the building all weekend and talk with potential renters. I functioned as a salesman, convincing them to rent my apartments. You don't normally see owners standing in front of little apartment houses with an "open house" sign, taking prospective tenants in by the hand and telling them what they want to hear—and meaning it.

If somebody said to me, "I'll take the apartment if the living room is green," I'd say, "What the hell? I'll paint it green." If someone said, "I'd take it if it had a refrigerator," I'd say, "I'll put in a refrigerator." If the kind of tenant I wanted said, "I'd take it if the rent were ten dollars less," I agreed to lower the rent. People will rent apartments from you if you're out there renting them yourself, while they might not if you were just sitting at home waiting for them to call. If you're doing it yourself you can make any on-the-spot agreement you want with a prospective tenant.

There's nothing wrong with retaining a management company. You just have to be clear about what you're getting and what you're giving up if you make that choice. If you're starting your career in real estate as a do-it-yourself project and you have little or no money to invest, then it's a real benefit to save the fee that a property management company will charge you. Furthermore, you will learn your craft from managing your own properties. If you're on location, you learn at the most human level what makes some investments better than others.

Most property management firms charge a fixed percentage of the rents they collect as their fee. When buildings are full, there is very little for them to do, and they get that fixed percentage of a full house; when buildings are half empty, they have an enormous amount of work and their fixed percentage provides them with hardly any compensation for doing it. In many ways this arrangement is topsy-turvy: how can a property management firm be expected to drop everything and turn your building around when their fee for doing it will be so little? And why pay them a premium price when it's full and you don't need them?

I'm totally self-taught; everything I know about real estate investments and management I've learned from my own experience.

Today, I'm the chief executive officer in a major real estate holding firm. Although I don't do any of the frontline management myself anymore, my years of managing my own buildings were an essential foundation in building the company. Without going through the steps, I never would have learned what I needed to know.

THE RESPONSIBILITIES OF PROPERTY MANAGEMENT

The following is a list of the basic responsibilities of property management. You can, as I will explain to you in the course of this chapter, fulfill these responsibilities on your own or with one or more full-time or part-time employees. In managing property you must:

1. Collect the rent;
2. fill vacancies with quality tenants;
3. refurbish apartments in order to fill vacancies;
4. make sure the building is maintained well, which includes:
   a. ordering and paying for all building services;
   b. ordering and paying for insurance;
   c. ordering and paying for fuel and/or utilities;
   d. paying property taxes;
   e. daily cleanup and maintenance;
5. maintain good tenant relations;
6. take care of problems as they arise;
7. keep accurate books and records. (It is important to keep a separate bank account for each property when using investors' money. It becomes a sacred trust not to commingle funds.)

The reason I put collecting the rent and filling vacancies at the top of the list is that vacant property is a perishable product just like fruit. If you're a produce seller and you have ten pounds of very ripe tomatoes, you have to sell them quickly or they'll go bad and you'll have to throw them away. If you own any rental property, you lose money every day you don't have a rent-paying tenant. To discourage such losses, I keep a running tabulation. Once a week I review the status of every building we own: I look at the vacancies and count on our management team to tell me the number of days the space has been vacant and which tenants are delinquent in their rent.

Our rents are all due on the first of the month. This standardized procedure makes it easy to control the business. Regardless of the property, if the rent isn't in by the first of the month, it's late. I start getting involved about the fifth of the month, on the premise that 90 percent of all the good tenants have paid by that time and only people trying to take advantage wait longer. So we start calling each delinquent tenant until we get paid or know why we're not, and we act accordingly.

WHAT ABOUT PHONE CALLS IN THE MIDDLE OF THE NIGHT?

Almost everyone who contemplates owning an income property, even a tiny one, and managing it himself worries about getting phone calls in the middle of the night. This is just one variation of the classic question "What do you do about the dirty part of the business?" (Another variation is "What do you do about difficult tenants?") The answer to all variations of this question is that you get a buffer to receive the middle-of-the-night phone call. There is no reason for tenants to have your home phone number.

The buffer can be an answering machine or an answering service. Another inexpensive buffer, for smaller units, is a person who lives in the building. The person with whom you make an agreement to serve in this capacity does not have to be a professional—not a manager or a superintendent. He or she is just a regular tenant who will receive all tenant calls, take note of any emergencies, and pass the information on to you so you can make a choice of how and when you want to solve a problem. The buffer tenant can also communicate on your behalf to the other tenants.

The simple fact of having someone between you and your tenants relieves much of the potential tension and pressure of owning and managing. And if you don't want your buffer to call you in the middle of the night, all you have to do is tell him that unless there is a dangerous condition, you don't want to be called before eight in the morning.

If you have a four-unit apartment house, just make the following offer to one of the tenants: "If you don't mind looking after some things [spell out what they are], I'll give you X dollars a month off your rent." I'm continually gratified to learn how much a responsible person will do in his spare time in exchange for this kind of rent discount.

Here's how a middle-of-the-night emergency in your building would actually work. Let's say the hot-water heater breaks down. When tenants call to tell your buffer about it at 3:00 A.M., the buffer will use good common sense and tell them the truth: a broken hot-water heater is a fact of life, and that it will get fixed the following day. He will not give out your home number because he knows it will serve no purpose, and because the tenants are accustomed to being respectfully treated, they will not insist on having it. Then the buffer will call you, either then or in the morning, depending on what instructions you've given him.

With most emergencies, the "what if"s really don't produce a building full of irate tenants. As long as you and your representatives act with integrity, your tenants will respect what you tell them.

HIRING AN ON-SITE MANAGER OR SUPERINTENDENT

Different municipalities have different laws about whether or not a building needs an on-site manager or superintendent (both words mean the same thing; the term "manager" is used in the West, and "superintendent" in the East). If you buy a building of a size that is not required to have a resident manager or superintendent, use your discretion about whether you personally would like one anyway or whether you would be comfortable directing all the work yourself with a tenant acting as your buffer in exchange for a small discount on his rent.

The maintenance practices of the previous owner will help you decide what arrangements you want to make. If you're satisfied with the way the building is being run, then you can simply continue with the same arrangements. But you should remember what a manager must do. Managing a building requires more than just hanging out and making sure that people pay the rent at the beginning of the month. The building must always be kept immaculately clean, which demands a lot of physical work, especially in making a vacant apartment attractive for a new tenant. Before the old tenant leaves, the manager must have all necessary work scheduled—painting, carpeting, cleaning, repairing, whatever is necessary so that work can begin immediately after the tenant has moved out. The manager has to have a good relationship with the tenants. He has to decide when to consult you and when not to consult you when problems arise. Anyone you hire as an on-site building manager must be capable of carrying out these responsibilities, because the on-site manager is representing you.

Our standard salary for an on-site apartment manager in 1986 was $15 to $20 per unit per month. Thus, for being resident manager of a fourteen-unit building, for example, a person would earn $210 to $280 per month, an amount that would be offset from his apartment rent. The size of the building determines whether or not we're going to give him an apartment and cash on top of it.

It is very important to have a written contract with resident managers, specifying their salary, their responsibilities, and how many hours a week the job requires. The market standards in your area will help determine the salaries and benefits of your superintendents or resident managers. Ask various professional groups, such as the Apartment House Association, for sample contracts.

Obviously, you have to check out any potential resident manager thoroughly before hiring him. We do credit checks and get references for all applicants. Keep evaluating your resident manager's performance. If the place looks horrible, you need a new resident manager. If you hire a person who is part of a couple, be clear about who's doing the work. You must know who is responsible; the mate is not your employee, even if he or she sometimes fills in for the spouse.

I have a rule of thumb in employing anybody: "Would I invite this person to my home for dinner?" A person I hire has to be someone who has integrity, someone who does not physically intimidate me, someone who has good manners and a pleasing personality. That doesn't mean the person has to have education or money, only that he or she is someone I'm going to like and be comfortable with on a day-to-day basis.

Communication is the key to creating good relationships with your managers. Demand that they do the best job they are capable of doing, and that they have a positive attitude: "This is my building; I take pride in running it well."

If a resident manager is doing a good job, tell him right away. If his work isn't up to your standards, tell him right away. If you are contemplating firing him for sloppy work, give a warning first —in writing. If he doesn't show sufficient improvement and you decide to fire him, then notify him in writing that you're terminating him. The clearer you are, the more smoothly the building will operate.

WHEN SHOULD YOU USE A LAWYER TO DEAL WITH TENANTS?

The general rule in property management is: Handle all tenant problems yourself until you need a lawyer.

When you have a tenant problem, facing the tenant yourself and showing him that you are a good human being even though you are his landlord will encourage the tenant, no matter what his situation, to respond by being a decent, regular person, too. Within that context, problems generally can be solved.

Just as generally, the problem you're going to be dealing with is nonpayment of rent. The tenant won't be paying, either because he doesn't have the money or because something is wrong in the building. If something is wrong in the building, you're going to have to fix it.

If it turns out that the tenant just doesn't have the money, you have to decide on the best way to handle the situation. ("Best" in this circumstance means least costly and troublesome to you and most responsive to the actual facts at hand.) If the tenant's inability to pay is temporary—and you trust him—you can agree on a time limit in which he has to pay his back rent and his current rent. If he simply will not be able to pay, then you have to consider your alternatives in getting him to vacate. Many times I've even handled a tenant by telling him that if he was out in five days, I wouldn't prosecute; I've sometimes offered to help pay moving expenses and given him some cash on top of that. Don't let the tenant stall or lead you on for more than a few days.

Once you've exhausted the commonsense approach, don't try

any further remedies yourself for getting the tenant out or forcing him to pay. To accomplish either of these objectives, you need legal advice, because:

1. legal intervention may be more effective;
2. you want to avoid exposing yourself unnecessarily.

WORRIES, WORRIES, WORRIES

As you begin to fantasize managing your own building, your head may start filling with worries: What if the vacancy rate is higher than I thought? What if the roof suddenly needs repairing? What if the plumbing goes bad?

Without doubt, sooner or later apartments are going to become vacant. When an apartment is vacated, it has to be raised to 100 percent perfection, because a perfect apartment always rents. Many landlords make a place 80 percent or 90 percent perfect, but when there's a slow time in the rental market, what rents apartments is doing the other 10 to 20 percent. This consists not only of sprucing up the carpets and the drapes and painting and vacuuming the apartment, but making sure there isn't a speck of dirt or grease in the oven, making sure the cupboards are clean and fresh, seeing that the caulking around the bathtub doesn't have cracks, replastering where the wall has been marred, and sanding down the place that's been replastered and wasn't finished properly the first time around. These repairs will never take care of themselves and they have to be done; they are part of the building's integrity.

Where is the money going to come from to pay for this work and for any other problem that may arise, like repairing or replacing the roof? Either from your pocket, from your investors' pockets, or from your rainy-day fund.

WHAT IS A RAINY-DAY FUND AND HOW SHOULD YOU PLAN IT IN TERMS OF YOUR TOTAL INVESTMENT?

A rainy-day fund, or reserve fund as it's often called, is money that you set aside at the time you purchase a building to handle any emergency that might arise in connection with it. The good news is that it gives you the money to cover these emergencies; the bad news is that it means that you need to figure on having more money to buy an apartment building than just the down payment. The problems a rainy-day fund will see you through all fall into the category of property management.

You have to return to the worrisome question of what can go wrong to determine how much money should be in the rainy-day fund for a particular building. This concern can be divided into two broad segments: the income from the building could fall short, or the expenses could be higher than anticipated.

If you're buying a building in an area where there has always been a solid demand for rentals, what's the worst that could happen in terms of income? Perhaps an apartment would be vacant for a couple of months and you wouldn't collect rent. So your initial step in calculating your rainy-day fund is to figure out how much income could be lost based on your estimate of how many apartments could possibly go vacant in a year.

Now ask yourself what potential catastrophes the future could hold for your building in terms of expenses, and for which of these potential catastrophes you are insured. If someone runs into the building with a car, the insurance company pays you; if the building catches fire, the insurance company pays you, and so on. By going down the list of "what if"'s you'll find that you are insured for most big crises.

I never worry about having unexpected problems with the plumbing, the electricity, the roof, or with termites when I calculate the rainy-day fund because I feel that the building inspector would have told me if something was really risky before I bought the property. If there had been a problem, I would have worked out a compromise with the owner so that he would compensate me for the estimated cost of repair, and I would add this to my rainy-day fund. If the owner doesn't agree to this, I wouldn't go through with the deal. I reason that the worst crisis for which I'm insured is if all the tenants moved out, and I had to make the vacant apartments 100 percent perfect to get new tenants to move in. So I say to myself, "If worse comes to worst, maybe I'll have to get every apartment ready for a new tenant." My next step is to figure out what this will cost, and that amount of money is what I put aside for my rainy-day fund.

I use a standard amount that I calculate can pay for new carpets, drapes, a total cleanup, and one month's lost rent for every apartment in a building. And if unexpected repairs are necessary for the plumbing, electricity, the roof, or anything else—or if, after a few years, the roof needs replacement—then these expenses come out of the rainy-day fund. That's what it's there for, even if you don't calculate it on the basis of these costs.

In deciding whether or not you want to have a rainy-day fund when you buy a building, you must ask, "If I don't have some kind of reserve at the time of the purchase, will it be easy for me to get it when I need it?" If you know that it will be easy, then it's not so important to have it now. Whenever I buy a building with partners I raise the rainy-day fund at the time of purchase because I don't want to have to go back to investors and ask for more money later. The rainy-day fund account that is raised in advance also has the advantage of increasing, because you put it where it will earn the maximum interest.

When you put your deal together, tell your investors that you need the rainy-day fund on top of the down payment. I also suggest that in presenting your deal to potential partners, you set it up for the worst possible set of circumstances, rather than assuming that everything will go right. Make the assumption that the expenses will be higher than they look on paper: if you think your building is going to have an 8 percent cash flow, tell your investors it will be 6 percent. If you buy a building that needs repairs, and from the inspector's and contractor's estimates you think they're going to cost $50,000, tell your investors it will cost $75,000. If the building does better, you're a hero.

I'm not using the word "hero" facetiously: whether you own a building yourself or with partners, you deserve to be called a hero when the building does better than you said because the victory will be due largely to your skills as a property manager.

CHAPTER 9

COMMERCIAL AND INDUSTRIAL PROPERTIES: EVALUATING DEALS IN FACTORIES, OFFICE BUILDINGS, AND SHOPPING CENTERS

Probably no other area of potential investment in real estate sounds more intimidating to a new investor than commercial and industrial properties. Even the words "commercial" and "industrial" are scary: they make you feel as if you have to be an expert just to know what they mean.

The truth is that you don't have to know much about either commerce or industry to be able to learn about investing in commercial and industrial properties. Owning and managing these properties is frequently no more complicated—and is sometimes even less complicated—than owning and managing apartment buildings.

The purpose of this chapter is to give you a clear picture of how investments in these kinds of properties are made and how to evaluate the opportunities for such investments.

UNDERSTANDING THE LANGUAGE

Now that you've learned the jargon for apartment building deals —gross rental multiplier, cost per unit price, etc.—I'm going to introduce you to a new set of jargon that's used in commercial, industrial, and office building deals.

Commercial properties house tenants that buy and sell goods and services. These tenants include any type of store from a dry cleaner or a pizza stand to a supermarket or a fancy restaurant. Industrial properties are those which house tenants that manufacture goods or store the raw materials or end products of the manufacturing process. They fall into three categories: factories, warehouses, and research and development facilities.

Office buildings house tenants that provide services either for their own companies (for instance, the executives of a manufacturing firm have offices in which they do the administrative work for the firm) or for outside consumers (for instance, all professionals, from accountants to doctors, have offices in which to serve their clients).

Office building tenants generally sign what's called a "gross lease," an agreement whereby the tenant pays a monthly rental fee and the landlord takes care of all expenses involved in the building's running and maintenance.

Tenants of commercial and industrial properties can sign one of two basic types of leases. The first is a gross lease, where the tenant simply pays his rent and the landlord assumes all financial responsibility for the building. Or the tenant can sign one of a variety of *net leases:* a net lease, a *double-net lease,* or a *triple-net lease.* Whenever a tenant signs any category of net lease, he is taking on some degree of financial responsibility for the building in addition to paying his rent. (Note that the terms "net," "net net," and "net net net" are local in nature and not standardized legal terminology. Since their precise definition varies from market to market, I'm giving you only a general explanation.)

With a "net net net" lease (or triple-net lease), the tenant, besides paying rent, has responsibility for all repairs on the building during his tenancy as well as all property taxes and insurance. With a net lease or a double-net lease, the tenant pays his rent and shares the financial responsibility of building maintenance, taxes, and insurance with the landlord. A net lease requires the tenant to assume only minimal financial responsibility for maintenance on top of his rent. Every net and double-net lease varies as to its specific terms. Typically, a net lease means that the tenant pays for nonstructural repairs—such as a broken toilet—in the space he rents while the landlord pays for structural repairs—such as the roof's needing repairs. With a net lease, the tenant may or may not be required to pay for tax and insurance increases on the building. A double-net lease usually means the tenant pays part of the cost for all repairs on the building, as well as for part of the cost of tax and insurance increases, and the landlord pays the balance.

Thus, the two extremes in leasing arrangements for these types of properties are the gross lease, where the tenant pays only his rent, and the triple-net lease, where the tenant pays his rent and all other expenses as well.

As I mentioned, tenants in office buildings generally have gross leases, while most industrial buildings and commercial buildings are on some form of net leases. The trend in shopping centers is for tenants to sign triple-net leases.

A LEASE IS LIFE

For any type of rental property, a lease with a solid tenant is life-blood for that property. That's what provides the property owner with income. The *type* of lease signed by a tenant determines what can be expected of him—and therefore what can be expected in income from the building.

The advantage of triple-net leases to the landlord is obvious. It specifies the rent he'll be collecting on the property and requires the tenant to pay for *all* of the expenses. Therefore, the landlord knows exactly what he's getting in income and exactly what he'll be paying in expenses. There could be only one unexpected surprise: the tenant's not economically surviving.

The disadvantage of a triple-net lease to the tenant is the mirror image of that: he only knows what rent he'll be paying; beyond that, he could incur any number of expenses. If a pipe breaks, he has to pay for it; if the roof goes bad, he has to pay for it; if any kind of structural change in the building is needed, he has to pay for it, and if he goes out of business for some reason, it's still his problem (unless he goes broke and declares bankruptcy—then it's the owner's problem as well).

Which lease a building owner gets is a function of his cleverness and of local supply and demand. All of this swings with the rhythm of the marketplace. To be successful requires the ability to observe what the rhythm is and to see value.

With leases on industrial and commercial properties, you're dealing with businesspeople. This is very different from dealing with the tenants of an apartment building. If someone doesn't like his arrangement with the landlord of his apartment building, he'll find a way to work it out or he'll move. In a business, where the tenant has an investment in the facility itself as well as in the goodwill he's built up in that location with his customers, if he doesn't like his arrangement with his landlord he's not going to make a quick and easy exit.

Thus, the provisions in leases for business properties carry special weight. Both tenant and landlord know this going in and both know they are in for the long haul, so most leases will be a minimum of five to ten years. Unlike apartment house leases, which landlord and tenant can negotiate face-to-face, leases on commercial, industrial, and office space tend to be negotiated by buffers—brokers or attorneys. As a potential buyer, it's very important that you have an attorney look at any existing leases *before* completing a deal on a commercial, industrial, or office property.

There's another consideration, too, in regard to leases. The lease means nothing unless the tenant has the strength to live up to his end of the bargain. In essence, a tenant becomes your marriage partner in the building, and if your marriage goes bad, it can become very ugly.

EVALUATING A DEAL: THE TENANTS

Overall, an office building is much more like an apartment house than a factory. One terrific thing about apartments is that they are unspecialized; if an apartment is average or better, you can be sure that where there is demand for rentals the apartment will rent.

Office space is similar in that innumerable businesses can use the same kind of space, with only minor adjustments to the floor plan. Although you may be called upon to move walls or build cubicles for a new tenant, clerical office space does not require specialized plumbing or unusual ceiling heights or heavy-duty electrical wiring. The space that is usable by one accountant is, by and large, usable by another accountant.

Now think about a medical office building. The situation is markedly different from the one you encounter with an office building that caters to law firms, accounting firms, and other general businesses. The interchangeability of space in these buildings contrasts sharply with the specialized space requirements of tenants in a medical office building. An eye doctor needs several small rooms with no windows; the only special plumbing he may require is a sink to wash his hands. But an orthopedic surgeon is going to need slightly larger rooms and a lot of plumbing to make plaster casts. So every time an orthopedic surgeon moves, you're going to incur a large expense for changing the plumbing if you can't find another orthopedic surgeon to replace her. Thus, the costs of owning a medical office building are very different from the costs of owning a professional office building.

An industrial facility may require extensive customization: the entire space might need to be specialized for the needs of the individual tenant. The manufacture of greeting cards, for example, requires a totally different facility and totally different equipment than the manufacture of machinery. Though the same factory with a given amount of square footage could be used by both companies, a greeting card manufacturer may need large open bays and very few tenant improvements; a machinery manufacturer needs floors of reinforced strength and areas where people can be segregated to protect them from noise and danger. Thus, the cost of customizing an industrial property to the needs of a tenant are potentially very high.

All these factors in regard to tenants' needs and the expenses involved in accommodating these needs have significant consequences for the way that rental arrangements are made between tenants and landlords in these types of properties. The needs/expenses factors make it impossible for owners of office and industrial properties—and, as you'll see, of commercial properties as well—to have the same kind of leases with their tenants that owners of apartment buildings have. Therefore, as a potential investor, these factors provide an important new basis from which you will evaluate any deal. They will affect what you look for in the properties themselves and what you look for in the current tenants and the current leases.

With an apartment house a one-year or even a month-to-month lease might be fine. Not so with office, commercial, or industrial buildings, which may require a wide variety of costly alterations to accommodate a new tenant. To make certain that this expense is going to be worthwhile, you want any lease to be for a long enough period to earn back the expenses; you also want a lease with escalations.

With office buildings the questions you want to ask are:

1. Do you have a positive feeling about the building?
2. How do you feel about the tenants? Are they quality tenants?
3. What is the gross multiplier of the income stream from the building, and how does it compare to the gross multipliers of other office buildings in that location being offered for sale right now? This is one factor you can use to tell you if the price is right.

   (Instead of double-checking this with cost per unit, as I do with apartment buildings, I use *price per square foot.* This is determined by dividing the number of square feet of rentable space into the selling price. For example, a building with 10,000 square feet of rentable space selling for $1 million would be $100 per square foot of rentable space. Compare this price per square foot to price per square foot of similar office buildings in the neighborhood.)
4. What is the projected positive return for the property, and is it better than other deals being offered in your marketplace right now?
5. Is the actual space average or better than average for the marketplace? Is each office of at least average space and overall dimensions, including ceiling height? Are the walls easily mov-

able, or are they load-bearing walls that can't be moved or adjusted?

6. Is the basic layout of the space (including lobby, elevator, halls, bathrooms, and parking, if applicable) average or better for the marketplace?

7. How much of the space is vacant?

8. If space is vacant, how long has it been vacant and why is it vacant? How does this compare with the vacancy factor in the whole area? (And does your research indicate that there is a constant or growing demand for this type of space in this area?)

9. How long are the current tenants' leases for?

10. What kind of rent increases, or "ups," do the leases call for, and how does this compare to the market standard in that area?

11. Are these ups sufficient to increase the positive return and therefore the future value?

12. What kind of improvements have been made for current tenants, and will these improvements serve a broad range of new tenants in the future? Or will the office space need to be altered to suit other tenants?

13. How much of an investment would it take to alter the space if the type of occupancy changes?

14. Is the type of tenant suitable for the neighborhood? For example, the local major hospital may have constructed its own office building, making previously existing medical buildings obsolete. Doctors may no longer want to rent premises in the medical building you are looking at, and it may be inappropriate for general business since it is not a business neighborhood.

15. Are there many new buildings being developed in the same location? If so, is there likely to be too much of a supply in relation to the demand in the immediate future?

16. How does the existing rent per square foot of the building you're considering compare to the competition's?

With industrial facilities, the same factors are important, but the tenant's line of business becomes much more important to your thinking as a potential owner. You have to begin with the knowledge that most small businesses are very undercapitalized. That's why, if you own an industrial facility, you must check out your prospective tenant's financial status thoroughly. If you don't, you may be stuck with an empty building customized for a tenant whose business failed. If the previous owner didn't evaluate his tenants' financial stability thoroughly, you may end up buying a property that has been customized for a tenant with a long-term lease, only to have his business dissolve, leaving you with a vacant space that needs costly work to prepare for a new tenant.

With industrial facilities, the creditworthiness of the tenant is of utmost importance, because what you're really buying is an income stream, and the income stream depends entirely on the success of the tenant's business. It's crucial to investigate the prospects of the tenant's industry, because in renting him the space you're becoming one of his heaviest investors.

In evaluating commercial properties, another primary factor is the size of the space: what you are looking for is space that is easily rented out to a variety of tenants.

For example, the little mini-malls that are springing up all over the country offer great flexibility in the range of potential tenants they attract. A typical mini-mall was formerly a corner gas station of 15,000 to 25,000 square feet that was torn down and replaced by a group of 1,000- to 1,500-square-foot stores. These can house fast-food restaurants, laundromats, or any one of a number of other vendors of goods and services. The only thing the landlord has to provide for each of these businesses is four walls and a bathroom. For this reason, spaces in mini-malls are suitable for almost any tenant who moves in, and at little or no renovation cost to the landlord. If the commercial space is huge, however, the opposite applies. One-thousand-square-foot tenants are plentiful, but 50,000-square-foot tenants are comparatively few.

LOCATION, LOCATION, LOCATION

As with any other type of property, the location, location, location principle is of paramount importance when considering any type of business property. Examining the neighborhood and determining the need for a particular kind of space in that neighborhood is crucial.

Location has a different impact on industrial and manufacturing properties than it does on commercial properties. For a commercial property, where people are selling goods and services, population density, traffic, and accessibility at a particular spot are the most important aspects of location. These factors mean customers for the businesses that rent the space; customers mean a higher demand for the space on the part of tenants who need customers; a higher demand for the space—and a bigger volume of business for the tenants—means higher rent.

Retail space that requires customers to drive in and park needs easy entry, exit, and parking. Most of all, look for visibility: if customers can't see a store, they won't shop in it, and you'll never keep a tenant. It will be difficult to rent. If a property has a driveway that people can't drive into from both sides of the street because an island or median blocks it, that will be bad for business. Is the stream of traffic constant, or is it present only at certain times of day? Is the amount of traffic enough to support business? Does something about the location—such as its proximity to a densely populated residential area or an office complex—make it especially likely to draw customers?

If you're looking in a large city such as New York or Chicago, where most people walk or travel by public transportation or taxis, you have to translate these questions into urban terms: "Are people walking by this location and is it accessible? Is it plainly noticeable from the street? Is the area itself easy to get to from other neighborhoods by public transportation? Is there a reason that people from other neighborhoods are drawn to this location?"

Your answers to these questions will be the tip-off to whether or not a particular commercial space is going to be profitable. The most attractive mini-mall in the world isn't going to have any customers if it's in the middle of the desert, while even a poorly planned center can't go wrong if it's on the busiest corner in town.

When you look at the impact of location on an industrial property, consider the manufacturer's needs. One of his primary needs is to be located so that his raw materials can be transported in and out easily. At the same time, he wants a location that's centrally located for his employees, one that offers ample parking if they drive to work, or one that's accessible to public transportation if they don't.

In considering any industrial property (or office or commercial property), be sure to find out if the government that has jurisdiction over that location has regulations favorable or detrimental to the type of business that would be conducted there—if, for example, there are special taxes, zoning restrictions, or pollution ordinances.

Remember, too, that our country is manufacturing less than it used to. Many of the best "smokestack industry" facilities are vacant because the economy doesn't have need for them or the industries themselves no longer exist. Therefore, a terrific deal on a smokestack property may not really turn out to be much of a terrific deal if there's no one to rent it, or if there's no other immediate and profitable use for which it can be appropriately converted.

Warehouses are unique. Here, location is vital, as is the structural configuration of the property: How high are the ceilings? How high can it be loaded? Is it served by railroad? Will you as the owner have to run your own warehousing business? Will you have to provide forklifts or security for multiple tenants? Today there are also mini-warehouses in which hundreds of small garage-sized storage spaces are rented, an enterprise that amounts to an industry itself. A mini-warehouse has to be convenient for the people to whom it offers storage space, and it has to be in an area that's not already saturated with other mini-warehouses.

UNEXPECTED OPPORTUNITIES

One type of industrial property that is found in many marketplaces and often provides a good opportunity for investment is a light manufacturing facility. Let me take you through an example of a shoe factory we bought in the late 1970s.

When we bought the factory the tenant had a ten-year triple-net lease, which meant that our only responsibility as owners was to make our mortgage payments and collect our rent. The rest of the expenses were the responsibility of the shoe company. According to the terms of the lease, every two and a half years the rent would go up by the cost of living, with a maximum cap of 8 percent per year.

One of the interesting things that happened with that particular lease is that through a series of circumstances the shoe company ended up being acquired by a Fortune 500 company. All of a sudden we ended up having a property with a lease guaranteed by one of the richest companies in the United States. An 8 percent or 9 percent return from a company of this stature is worth substantially more than it was from the small shoe company. This is because investors grade tenants in the same way Wall Street grades bonds. Investors will pay a premium for space leased by General Motors and discount the value of a lease from a small undercapitalized firm. The factory had thus become a premium property. If the new company's name had been on the lease originally, I could never have bought it for the price I did. But just by having a major company as the tenant, the value of the property went up about one third.

The shoe factory deal confirms an observation I've made over the years: no matter what a long-term lease says, no matter how binding it is, something will probably happen that turns it into an opportunity for you as the property's owner. Over the long period of the lease, the tenant will probably need to expand or sell his business. At that point he will need something from his landlord, and whatever he wants, the landlord may well have the opportunity to renegotiate the lease. A new buyer, for example, will want a new and probably a longer lease, which means the landlord would have the opening to charge a higher rent.

In commercial properties, too, a long-term lease often means an unexpected opportunity for the landlord. One of the primary reasons for this is that existing tenants frequently decide to sell their businesses during the course of their lease, and the consequences of this decision almost always place the landlord in a highly advantageous position.

Let's say that a store owner's lease is ten years, and he puts up his business for sale after the first five. At that point, the potential new owner, who will be paying a substantial amount of money for that business, will undoubtedly say, "I'm not going to buy this business if I don't have more than five years on the lease."

At that point, the present owner of the business will go back to the landlord and ask to renegotiate the lease. This is very often a windfall for the landlord because it gives him the opportunity to insist on raising the rent. And even though the new owner of the business has to pay a higher rent, he gets a longer period of time over which he can amortize the cost of buying the business. Aside from the substantially higher rent he gets for the next five years, the landlord may also have the opportunity five years down the road to renegotiate the lease if the business is sold again.

Another thing that often happens when you have a long-term lease with a substantial tenant is that the tenant's business changes, and he wants to make a major tenant improvement. After getting the landlord's permission, the tenant pays for the tenant improvement. Not only does this increase the value of the facility, but the landlord often gets some extra revenue from it as well. For example, if a company decides to build a second floor on the facility to expand their business, they would pay for the cost of construction (all according to plans you, as landlord, would approve) and they may pay additional rent, too—all at no cost to you.

In shopping center properties, an unexpected opportunity may arise from an external event causing a dramatic improvement of the business at that location. It could be the construction of more housing or an office complex, or both, bringing new customers into the neighborhood. It could be a new tenant who rents the space from you and does fantastically well. In either case, if the lease specifies that you as landlord get a percentage of the business on top of the rent (this is called an *overage* or *percentage rent*), your income rises drastically.

On a hilltop near my house is a small shopping center in an otherwise totally residential neighborhood. It has a pizza shop, three restaurants, a convenience market, and about eight other shops. Nobody expected that it would be anything out of the ordinary when it was built. As it turns out, however, it is the only commercial property in the area, and the restaurants are now considered chic. Because of this, and because additional houses have been built near the center, business has been so good that the owner of the center is receiving substantial overages and premium rental —more than anyone could have imagined.

EVALUATING WHETHER A LONG-TERM LEASE IS GOOD FOR YOU

The benefit of industrial properties is that they should be very little trouble to own. Nevertheless, they are more suitable for people who are in for the long haul than for those who want to build a big estate quickly. The reason is related to the length and terms of the leases.

It's easy to see that the value of residential property goes up in direct proportion to the rent and, because the leases are comparatively short-term and rents rise with inflation and increased demand, the rent can often go up quite rapidly. Leases are generally somewhat long-term with office buildings. Rents on office space will go up purely by supply and demand, and the conditions specified in a lease will reflect the demand at the time the tenant signs it. If office space is in short supply, not only will you be able to obtain a higher rent, but tenants will generally agree to escalation clauses; if the office space market is "soft," the tenant is likely to drive a hard bargain, which will pull down rents and escalation clauses. The rhythm of the marketplace can create drastic shifts in the owner's position.

If a tenant in a shopping center is investing heavily in customizing and improving the space, he's probably going to want a long lease. In fact, since his major asset is the spot where his business is located, a long lease is going to be very important to him. If he is at all clever, a tenant in this category is going to allow his rent to escalate only in a manner that parallels his income as a storekeeper. Thus a landlord dealing with such a tenant would be able to negotiate only a lease that will get a flat rent on the store, with a clause stating that if the tenant's business jumps by specified amounts, the landlord will receive a percentage of the increased revenue as well. Perhaps there will be rent escalations based on increases in the cost of living.

In evaluating whether a particular lease is right or not for a particular property, look at the conditions of the lease within the context of the needs of the tenant's business and your needs as a landlord. A lease is right if it meets the needs of both.

What attracted me to the shoe factory deal from the beginning was the idea that over the ten years of the lease the income would rise from an 8 percent return on the money we invested to purchase the building to about a 32 percent return. I saw this opportunity by using what I refer to as "the collander approach." In filtering all the calls that come to my office about shopping centers and industrial properties, the questions I always ask are: What is the income? How long are the leases? Are there ups (do the leases have escalation clauses)? If a lease does have ups, exactly what are the terms? If a property has tenants with just a flat lease, I generally don't get involved.

In evaluating shopping centers and industrial properties I look for good tenants, strong landlord-favoring leases, and good potential increases or fixed increases built into the lease. If you do this, you will find that after ten years the exact same facility with no improvements generally gets far more valuable as a result of supply and demand. You've also had a good return on it all along due to the increase in rent based on the CPI (cost price index) or fixed increases built into your lease.

If you have picked out a good, creditworthy tenant, over the ten years you've gotten what you've bargained for: a return on your investment with the escalations, and no trouble in managing the property. Your tenant has also gotten what he bargained for: a space that meets his needs. Now, at the end of ten years, since you have a place that's much more valuable, you renegotiate with your tenant and charge him a substantially higher rent. If that doesn't work, then you get a new tenant who is willing to pay the current market value rent.

One of the primary disadvantages of a long-term lease to the landlord comes about if the lease starts off in a down market.

Historically, rents rise substantially when the economy is going up; when the economy is going down, residential rents stay about the same, but they rarely go down. Business properties react differently. The reason is that fewer businesses open in a down economy than in an up economy. This is very different from the apartment market, where people need homes in bad times as well as good. If your business property is vacant in a down economy, you're likely to be anxious to rent, and you'll rent it out cheaply. If it is a residential property, you offer only one-year leases, and a year later you renegotiate. But a business property has a long-term lease so you may be stuck with a low rent for a long time; you can't change it. In that sense, a long-term lease would be a disadvantage.

It goes back to our old rule: you have to know the marketplace. It's the only way you can judge a deal. Even an industrial space with a long-term lease started in a down economy can be a good deal, as long as all the other components make it worthwhile. A long-term lease with a cheap rent can be a good deal as long as you buy the property from an owner who is selling it for a price far enough below market level to make the rate of return on your money competitive.

WHAT DOES A PROPERTY DO STANDING ON ITS OWN FEET?

Many times, as an inducement to buyers, sellers of office, commercial, or industrial properties will guarantee the rental income of a vacant property or even subsidize extra income for a property rented at a low rate in order to make the property appear to be a more attractive investment. Whenever a seller says that he will guarantee or subsidize the income, ask why he will do this and evaluate his response. He may say he wants to guarantee or subsidize the income because his property is a newly developed shopping center and all the space isn't rented; his guarantee or subsidy will end when all the space is rented, and he'll specify a time limit for how long that should be.

One key question that must be asked about commercial, office, or industrial property is "What does it get standing on its own feet, without any guarantees from the seller?"—that is, how much income will it bring in right this minute without a guarantee or subsidy? If the prospects with no guarantees are negative, I suggest not buying the property, because this guarantee figure may very well be all the income you're going to get.

One further caution: once the deal closes, it may be hard to get the seller to honor his subsidy commitment. His guarantee is worth something only if he fulfills it. What is his reputation in the area? What are his assets?

In the course of our purchasing of properties, we buy many new shopping centers in which the spaces are not yet filled. In such cases, we get the developer of the center to guarantee that he will pay the projected income on the vacant spaces to us and pick up all the expenses, including leasing commissions and tenant improvements, until the spaces are filled. We then ask his banker if he has the money and examine his financial statement to determine his ability to meet these obligations.

The next step is to check out if his assets are real. Talking with people who have done or are still doing business with the seller will give you an idea of whether he will honor his commitments. Here is where your own personal experience with the seller comes into play: What do you think of him? What clues has he given you regarding his integrity? Has he told you any stories that would indicate that he shouldn't be trusted?

In approaching this type of transaction I always take the attitude that even if the seller has the wherewithal and integrity to pay now, that still doesn't mean he will be so willing to pay if things go sour. So I like to build in a guarantee of his guarantee. To do this, I make sure that he carries a substantial amount of equity in the sale price of the property in the form of a second or third mortgage (which means, in essence, he is lending us part of the money with which we are buying the property). Then I write into that mortgage that if he doesn't pay us what he is obligated to pay us, or if he doesn't fulfill his obligations in any other way, I can deduct whatever he owes us straight from the mortgage payment. That way there's no possibility that we can't collect. If he doesn't pay us altogether, in effect it cancels out the money we owe him, which means that we bought the property for that much less. Having reduced our mortgage payments, we can afford to lower the rent because our expenses are substantially less, and the property can still yield a positive cash flow from lower rents.

One more thing to watch out for in looking at commercial and office properties is sellers salting the mine. This refers to the sellers' practice of inducing tenants to move into a property so that it appears full when you buy it. Even legitimate people whose businesses are only semi-stable can be attracted by an offer of free rent that may not be specified in the lease you are shown. If you don't check to see if the businesses are stable, you may mistakenly think you're buying a building with quality tenants. Remember: a five-year lease signed by a tenant who goes out of business means nothing. Salting the mine doesn't just produce a fake cash flow, it can also hide the fact that the property isn't in high demand by renters; once these unstable businesses move out or go bankrupt, there may be no takers for the space.

ENVELOPE DEALS

True triple-net leases on single-tenant buildings are sometimes called "envelope deals" because the landlord's only work is getting an envelope with the rent in it and sending out another envelope to pay the mortgage. These triple-net lease deals are advertised in the paper all the time. They come in large sizes and small sizes.

Let's say a major company owns an office building in New York City that's worth $100 million. The thinking goes, "Okay, my office building is worth $100 million. If I sell it to the local real estate syndicator or the insurance company, they'll give me $100 million, and I'll stay in the building as a tenant." Many firms find that they can get greater yields on their capital by using it actively in their business rather than by using it to own their building and be their own landlord, or they may simply need to invest their capital in their own company to survive or expand. This is called a *sale lease back*. It is simply a big envelope deal. At a smaller scale, envelope deals include freestanding buildings, like stores, occupied by credit-worthy tenants who bear all responsibility for the property.

Besides requiring no work, an envelope deal has very little risk if the tenant is reliable. Generally it is not a maximum profit deal, for good envelope-deal tenants know what they are doing. They drive very tough bargains and get very favorable rental rates. What makes one deal better or worse than another is the rate of return it brings in on the cash required for purchase, the creditworthiness of the tenant, the property value if you didn't have a tenant in it, and its appreciation potential.

Let's say there is a building in the middle of Atlanta, and it's got a small bank branch in it. "Bank of the U.S.A." built it in 1950 and sold it using a sale lease back in 1960 with the idea that they would pay a flat rent of $100,000 a year to stay there. Since at the time of the sale an 8 percent return on money was considered a good value, it was bought by an investor for $1.25 million cash, and the bank guaranteed that for twenty years they would pay $100,000, giving that investor an 8 percent return (8 percent of $1,250,000 = $100,000). Typically, the bank insisted on an option to continue renting at a predetermined rate for another ten years after that. So they have the building tied up for thirty years.

This is very typical of what has happened with banks and similar tenants who have built their own buildings in prime areas and then sold them on a sale lease back arrangement. These situations present another type of opportunity for you as a buyer. This same "Bank of the U.S.A." property, for example, may be up for sale several years into the lease, long before the lease expires. Although the property still pays only $100,000 per year, it may pay to buy it now for $2 million even though the cash flow would be only 5 percent (5 percent of $2,000,000 = $100,000), knowing that in a few years, when the lease does expire, because the location has become such a prime rental location, you could get $400,000 per year from a new tenant—which would be 20 percent (20 percent of $2,000,000 = $400,000).

Sometimes you may be able to develop a property like this in other ways. You can pay the tenant to vacate the property so that it can be redeveloped. Or you can increase the property in size by utilizing the space above the current structure. But that depends on the degree of control that the lease gives to the current tenant, the zoning, and what the future will bring.

The main reason to get into a triple-net lease investment is the security and simplicity in running it. You know you're not going to get any headaches unless the tenant goes bankrupt. And even then your building has a value—with the passage of time and with appreciation, you may even receive a higher rent than the current tenant is paying.

CHAPTER 10

MANAGING OFFICE, COMMERCIAL, AND BUSINESS PROPERTIES

The basic points I made about the management of apartment buildings also apply to the management of office, commercial, and industrial properties. Of course there are differences too, some of which I discussed in Chapter 9.

Of the three types of business properties, only office building owners generally give the tenants a gross lease, meaning the tenant pays only his rent, no expenses. Like apartment buildings, the office building's expenses (insurance, property taxes, utilities, maintenance, trash collection, repairs, and replacements) are in general the total responsibility of the landlord, as are all property management tasks. But office buildings also present the landlord with the additional expense of adapting present space for new tenants—after *finding* new tenants. Potential tenants for offices want space planners and hand holders. Renting office space requires lots of negotiation, specialized leases, and big leasing commissions. Tenants and landlords must work out possible problems in advance: what happens, for example, when one out of thirty tenants keeps late working hours and needs air-conditioning, and the central air-conditioning system serves all or none? Clearly, such problems can be expensive to solve.

Your use of on-site managers in office buildings depends on the size of the building and how much work you want to do yourself. Even a small building requires a part-time cleaning and mainte- nance staff. Just about all office buildings must provide complete janitorial service for all tenants. This is a constant source of annoy- ance for the landlord. Tenants expect the janitorial staff to do a perfect job and often the janitors don't perform up to this expecta- tion. In large buildings the janitorial service has a supervisor on site each night. On smaller jobs there will not be a supervisor. Tenants complain to the landlord—not the janitor. Most office buildings also provide security twenty-four hours a day: since they are empty at night, who else will keep the offices and office equipment safe? The previous owner's arrangements will help you decide what to do, but it's important to know that the way an office building is cleaned and maintained has a great deal to do with keeping it rented.

Leases for commercial space are usually long-term net, double- net, or triple-net leases, with tenants taking varying amounts of responsibility for the expenses. Leases for industrial space are usu- ally long-term triple-net leases. With any kind of net lease, of course, the tenant is assuming financial responsibility for maintain- ing his interior space, so your economic responsibilities in property management are decreased. With a single-tenant triple-net lease, your responsibilities as property manager may even be reduced to the envelope deal we described in Chapter 9: collecting one enve- lope with the rent and sending out another envelope with your mortgage payment.

Your primary responsibility with any type of net lease is to make sure the lease stipulates who is responsible for what and to make sure that you choose a tenant who will live up to his end of the agreement. The complicated part is the "common area." Every shopping center, big or small, has areas such as parking lots and hallways that need cleaning and maintaining. You may be responsible for allocating the tasks of maintenance and then billing the tenants for them. This is referred to as common area maintenance, and it's often an annoyance. Each tenant lease may specify a different type of payment—from nothing to full pro rata (paying a percentage of this bill that is the same rate as the percentage of square feet the tenant occupies in the center.

If he leased 1,000 square feet in a center of 10,000 square feet he would occupy 10 percent and pay 10 percent of the bills). And each tenant has to be billed and fees have to be collected. Unfortunately, many leases even at the same shopping center are drawn up at different times and with different terms.

Tenants in commercial space get into problems among themselves. At one of our shopping centers we spent many hours and lots of money on the "tuna wars"—two tenants were fighting over who should have the exclusive right to sell tuna salad sandwiches. Even from this one example, it's easy to see that managing commercial properties frequently means encountering sophisticated problems. Your Free Board of Directors can be an especially important resource in dealing with these challenges successfully. Again, all the answers are out there: one just has to put the question into the world, listen to the answers, and choose the advice that investigation shows you is the best.

RESPONSIBILITIES OF MANAGING BUSINESS PROPERTIES

To help you envision yourself managing business properties, I'm going to run through the fundamentals of managing a commercial property. Many of these are the same as those involved in office and industrial management. As is the case with any type of property management, your first two responsibilities in managing commercial properties are:

1. collecting the rent;
2. filling the vacancies with quality tenants.

While the next grouping of property management responsibilities would be exclusively yours if you owned an office building and signed a gross lease with your tenant, these responsibilities for a commercial or industrial property would be undertaken either by you, by the tenant, or by a combination of both, depending on the stipulation of the lease. These responsibilities are:

3. refurbishing vacant space to accommodate the new tenant;
4. making sure the building is well-maintained:
   a. ordering and paying for garbage collection;

b. ordering and paying for insurance;

c. ordering and paying for fuel;

d. enforcing daily cleanup of property, which includes handling the maintenance of all common areas.

Regardless of what kind of property you own and the amount of responsibility the lease requires the tenant to assume for its improvement and maintenance, the last two basic responsibilities of property management fall at least partially into your lap. They are:

5. getting along with the tenants,
6. taking care of problems as they arise.

Although a tenant in a commercial or industrial property may be responsible for any structural or nonstructural problem in the building, you are responsible for any problems that arise with the tenant.

STARTING A HAPPY RELATIONSHIP WITH A COMMERCIAL TENANT

Your general rental application for any commercial space (from a small liquor store to a supermarket to a restaurant) should request the addresses and phone numbers of your prospective tenant's present residence and business; his previous business and work history —with references; a bank reference; three or four trade references; a personal reference, and the name, address, and phone number of his nearest relative in case of an emergency. Ask for a financial statement and the prior year's tax return, or the previous two or three years' tax returns. (This is exactly the same as the general application you would use for office or industrial space.) It is very important to call and verify every fact and reference personally. Most landlords don't do this and they often get burned. I repeat: *Check out every fact and reference yourself.* It's a good idea to have a credit check done as well. If lawsuits or any other type of negative information show up on the prospective tenant's record, it's best not to rent to him.

Familiarize yourself with all variations of leases on commercial space in your area. Make yourself an expert by asking property management firms and other owners of similar properties. Ask an attorney who works with commercial properties for his advice.

Most areas have standardized industrial and office lease forms prepared by trade organizations and real estate boards. These generally raise all the broad issues to be confronted in creating a lease. Your attorney will adapt the standardized leases taking into account any unique facts about your property or your personal requirements. Retail leases are not as easy to standardize. Researching other people's retail leases is a good way to see the kinds of issues that can be part of such leases. Discussing with an attorney your own particular retail space, prior leases on that space, and what your considerations are as a landlord for that space is essential.

The same process applies with leases for industrial or office properties. Once you have this knowledge of leases you must determine whether your particular space is in demand or not. This can be done by calling real estate brokers, running ads, and making calls to prospective tenants. The response of local tenants who may move to your site will tell you immediately if your site is "hot." Once you know this, it will be easy to decide whether to negotiate tough or not. If the type of space you are leasing is in heavy demand, or if the demand is just heavier than it was at the time a tenant's lease originated, you may be able to get much better terms. (Don't be afraid to ask; it may be your only opportunity for years to come.)

Be sure to include an escalation clause that gives you a fixed annual increase or an annual cost-of-living increase in any lease with a commercial tenant. You can make arrangements to receive a percentage of the business's income if the income increases over a base amount, though it's very difficult to collect with small tenants who may not report accurate sales. Your attorney should specify in the lease that the tenant must make periodic reports of sales, which you have the right to audit. (While escalations are also typically stipulated in leases on office space and industrial space, leases that call for the landlord to receive a percentage on the customer's business are customary only on commercial food and retail space.)

Any type of net lease must spell out who is responsible for which expenses. Who will take care of structural repairs? Nonstructural repairs? Maintenance, including trash collection? The cost of property taxes and/or insurance? Recently, many leases have provided that tenants pay for professional management fees. Also, specify which of the tenants is actually responsible for taking care of the tasks involved: there may be many tenants on the property, each with his own ideas and style. The arrangement won't work unless the *lease provides the landlord with the right to be sole judge of who does what for how much.* The lease should also provide for extra management fees to handle these tasks.

Make certain that an attorney experienced with leases on these types of properties helps you formulate your lease. You can be certain the tenant will have an attorney on his end. The expense of your legal fees will be worth it: it can save you thousands of dollars.

If a tenant wants to assign his lease on commercial space to another party, require all the same information from the assignee as you would require from a new tenant—which, of course, the assignee is. In many areas a properly drawn lease may give the landlord the ability to raise the rent upon assignment of the space to a new tenant.

As owner you want the rent paid on time. Therefore, state in the lease how much money your tenant will be charged as a late fee if he is slow to pay his rent. To make all of this clear, spell out how many days after notifying him in writing you will wait before you will begin legal action in case of nonpayment of rent, abandonment of premises, or any other violation of the lease.

Your commercial lease should state that the tenant is responsible for your legal bills if you have to bring action against him. You'll find that when a tenant knows he's going to be paying your legal fees, it discourages him from causing you any problems!

HOW MUCH SHOULD YOU COMPROMISE TO RENT VACANT SPACE?

If you have a lot of vacancies and are desperate to rent your property, you will obviously compromise.

In compromising to fill a vacancy in commercial space you may accept a tenant who is not quite as strong financially as your ideal tenant; you may have to give him a better deal and a lower rent. But if possible, you will include some kind of "up" clauses in the lease (perhaps pegged to the success of the business).

Thus, although you will compromise, you will still protect yourself.

WHAT DO YOU DO WITH SLOW-PAYING COMMERCIAL TENANTS?

Let's say I have a fast-food restaurant tenant who is delinquent with the rent. The tenant has said nothing to me about his situation. The first thing I do is go to the restaurant and ask, "Why aren't you paying me?" People will tell you many things in a letter or over the phone that they won't tell you in person. It's much more difficult to lie when there's a human body in front of you. I also check to see if the restaurant has many customers at busy hours. If it's empty, it's obvious that it's just not making enough money to stay in business.

If it looks as if the tenant is doing all right, but he says that he doesn't have the money, I'll say one of several things. I may say, "Look, if you don't pay immediately, we're going to have our attorney handle it; you may end up having a lot of legal costs, so it's foolish for you not to come up with the rent right now." If it's obvious that his business is bad, we just start to find the best way to get him out and get a better tenant in. The goal in regard to rent is always the same: to attract tenants who pay in a timely fashion. You can deal with an occasional problem from a good tenant; if you're always having to deal with problems from a difficult tenant, you should replace him with a better one.

The major way to prevent problems in owning and managing commercial, industrial, or office properties is to make sure when you buy that:

1. the property is well suited to the area;
2. the building is structurally sound and appropriately improved;
3. the leases, as written, assure you a good return on the property;
4. the property is filled with quality tenants who pay on time.

Now that you know the basics of evaluating the different types of investment property, we can get down to the actual nuts and bolts of how real estate is bought.

Part
Three

TYING UP PROPERTIES WITH NO LIABILITY AND LITTLE OR NO CASH: OR, CHINESE CHECKING ACCOUNTS, REAL ESTATE-STYLE

Let's say that I'm a buyer, you're the seller. We agree on the price I will pay for your property and on the terms. In order to make our agreement binding, we each sign a *deposit receipt* (some states simply call it a *contract*). In essence, this legal document states that I buy and you sell at the specified price with the specified terms. Before I close the transaction, I want to assure myself that I can do a number of things—one, that I can get the proper loan; two, that I can inspect the property to make sure it's structurally sound; three, that I can inspect the leases and financial history to make sure that they are what I expect; four, that the title documents (the papers that state who the owner of the property is and what rights others may have regarding the property) are satisfactory.

The document may state other rights that the buyer has before completing the purchase. If someone were building on the property, for example, he would want to check soil and geological conditions to make certain that the building he plans to construct could be erected safely. Whatever the buyer thinks he needs confirmed and the seller agrees to allow him to verify is detailed in the deposit receipt or contract. These conditions of purchase are called *contingencies.*

At the time the document containing the price, terms, and contingencies is written, both parties also agree on how to handle the logistics of the sale.

The person who holds the money and handles the logistics of the sale is the *stakeholder.* In many states this stakeholder is an *escrow officer.* The escrow officer receives the contract (the deposit receipt) and agrees to hold the money and documents of the transfer impartially. When an escrow officer serves as stakeholder, this process is called *escrow.* Escrows can be handled by a private escrow company, a bank, a title company, or an attorney. The process of escrow solves the problem of who will trust whom. Otherwise the seller might say, "I want the cash proceeds in my hand before I hand over the deed" and the buyer would say, "No, after the deed is recorded I'll give you the money." The escrow holder will also send out the requests to existing lenders who will be paid off as a result of the sale. The lenders will trust the escrow with their documents (trust deeds, which ultimately must be taken off the title), and allow the escrow to hold them until the transaction is completed.

The escrow also works with the title insurance company to assure all parties that insurance of their position will be in effect when the transaction is legally closed. Title insurance is very important, and during the period prior to closing it is arranged for by the escrow officer or attorney. Title insurance is a form of insurance that says specifically what rights you have in buying a property. In America, many rights go along with real estate, and these rights can be separated and owned by various parties. Lenders have rights to protect their loans, for example. Also, a property can be leased so that the tenant (lessee) has rights. Other rights exist for underground minerals, oil, etc. So, for instance, the owner of the land can lease it to a convenience center company who builds and owns the building, paying the landowner rent, while an oil drilling firm may own subsurface rights to extract the oil.

Many times I have sold buildings and withheld the oil and mineral rights from the new buyer. In such cases, I no longer own the real estate and I still get paid for the oil that the driller takes. In some major cities, like New York, people sell off or lease the air space over their properties and second structures are built on top of existing structures. These are just some of the rights that are part of the bundle of rights that goes along with any piece of property. In the vast majority of properties, they haven't been separated and are all intact.

Prior to the closing of escrow (in many parts of the country it's simply called a *closing*), the title insurance company researches what rights have been taken by others and what rights will be conveyed when you own the property. Once you've closed on a property, your title insurance policy insures you against economic loss in the event that another party makes claims on any of the rights associated with the property. If the title insurance company doesn't uncover the proper information about any of the rights before you own the property, it is their responsibility, not yours, and you are protected.

The community record keeper for each area, often known as the county recorder, records who owns various rights. When a property is sold (or transferred), the deed (or title) is *recorded* in the public record. This is why when a deal closes, it is said to be "recorded." In this way, it becomes part of the public record, which will inform all interested parties of who has rights and what those rights are. The order of who records first lets us know whose position must be considered first in the event of a dispute. This is particularly important when loans are secured by the property. If I own a house and pay all cash, I own it free and clear. When I borrow on it, the lender will record its *trust deed* or *mortgage.* In this way, when I sell property, the new buyer will know that unless the lender is paid off, his purchase will be subject to the loan. The lender feels safe because his rights are protected. The first lender is said to have the first position (hence, a *first trust deed* or *first mortgage*); the second lender, second position (a *second trust deed* or *second mortgage*); and so on. All of these processes take place by the time the transaction is closed, and most of them take place without the buyer's ever being aware of them.

Banks and title companies often have escrow departments as a service for their clients. A private escrow company specializes in escrow services. The fees among the independent escrow companies in any one town or city are fairly standard and are also subject to negotiation. Banks' fees are usually comparable to those charged by private escrow companies. At title companies, the fees are often less, since the title companies want to attract business for title insurance, and are willing to handle escrows at a discounted rate as a customer service.

In some states the person who performs the stakeholder's function is generally a lawyer, and the process of drawing up the written document that specifies all the conditions of purchase is called *going to contract*. The process that parallels escrow in these states begins with going to contract and ends at the closing, when the former owner of the property gets the money and the new owner gets the property. In these states, the entire process is handled by attorneys, who may charge a flat fee (very often based on a percentage of the overall purchase price) or an hourly fee.

I'm going to discuss what takes place during the time after which you have gone to contract or are in escrow on a property as if it's a rational matter. But it's very important to remember that buying and selling real estate is an emotional experience, and when people are doing it, they rarely behave rationally. Consequently, the atmosphere during this period is often volatile, and the discussions are not necessarily businesslike.

A friend of mine who is an escrow officer in Beverly Hills tells the story of a multimillion-dollar deal that was postponed and revised because a cockroach walked across the desk just as the buyer and seller—and two lawyers—were about to conclude the transaction. And the cockroach in question was not even on the property being negotiated! The buyer had "buyer's remorse" (cold feet) and viewed the cockroach as an omen bad enough to cancel the transaction.

Horror stories abound about people's emotional reactions to selling property: stories about sellers' ripping up contracts just before the close of escrow (even though they are legally bound to go through with the deal), tales of sellers' having fist fights with buyers, about sellers' specifying in contracts what color the buyers must paint the kitchen in the homes they are buying, and at what height the chrysanthemum bushes must be kept.

There is no end to the melodrama that can take place in the process of a property's changing hands. A seller is selling something he is proud of and cares about, something in which he's invested life and emotion; the buyer is buying a future dream. Sometimes those views don't gel, and each side takes it very personally. And the escrow officer or attorney as well as the various brokers are in the middle—fighting for their income and their sanity. Indeed, the brokers may already have spent the commissions that they hope to earn.

STEPS IN OPENING AN ESCROW OR GOING TO CONTRACT ON A PROPERTY

By law, all contracts to purchase real estate must be in writing. Once the initial written deposit receipt or contract has been signed, a series of new documents will eventually be needed that either complete or dissolve it. The contract or deposit receipt contains the price and terms of purchase along with the contingencies on which that purchase depends; it also serves as a receipt acknowledging the "good-faith" deposit made on the deal.

A good-faith deposit is a sum of money that the buyer gives when making the offer. It can be any amount that is mutually agreeable to both the buyer and seller. It is posted as an expression of sincerity and financial ability on the part of the buyer. It is generally held in the broker's client trust account or by some other third party, such as the escrow officer or attorney. It should always be made with the clear written understanding that it is not at risk (refundable) until all contingencies have been removed.

Once the contract or deposit receipt comes into existence, it becomes the "Magna Carta" of the transaction. The contingencies go into the contract immediately, at the time the deposit is made and the initial contract or deposit receipt is signed. As a buyer, this is your escape clause; it states that your action of acquiring a property is dependent on certain conditions that you've specified must be met. *If properly written, the buyer has sole approval of whether or not the contingencies have been met.* If, for example, in the deposit receipt or contract you require a building inspection and you clearly state that only you have the right to analyze the information produced by it, then only you have the right to decide if you want to go ahead with the deal. Building inspections are always very subjective, and generally you can find a reason in the inspection report to cancel the purchase if you want to do so.

You can press for anything you want going into the original document and anything you want will become a contingency as long as the other party to the transaction agrees to it. The major premise to keep in mind is that whatever is essential to your completing the deal must be in this original document.

The basic contingencies in contracts on real estate generally refer to loans, physical conditions, financial information, and title matters. In addition to these, you can even specify that your uncle and aunt and next-door neighbor—your entire Free Board of Directors, in fact—have to examine the property and approve it. As long as the seller agrees to it, there is *no limit* to the number or type of contingencies.

There isn't a seller in the world who wouldn't want every contingency to be over in ten minutes and not a buyer in the world who wouldn't want as long as possible to complete the contingencies. Somewhere between the seller's preference and the buyer's preference is a time limit they will agree on in order to complete the contingency phase of the transaction.

One important thing to remember is that as long as a contingency is contained in the contract or deposit receipt, you have the right to act on it—even if it is inconvenient for the other party.

The next step is to communicate to the escrow agent or attorney the instruction "Please carry this forward." If you are dealing with an escrow officer, you or your broker deliver this instruction. If the seller's attorney is acting as stakeholder, then your attorney handles all the communication with the seller's attorney for you.

In theory, the person functioning as stakeholder will carry forward the original deposit receipt or contract. In practice, however, many buyers and sellers try to better the transaction for themselves, especially with investment properties. Due to the nature of real estate—because everyone puts such emotional pressure on the transaction—the original agreement is often viewed as simply a starting point. Even though the buyer of a commercial property has already made an agreement with the seller, he talks to his Free Board of Directors and comes up with new concessions he believes he needs or he finds conditions he feels he shouldn't have accepted.

So he starts trying to renegotiate—to convince the seller to give him concessions based on information he's discovered in checking out the contingencies he put in the original agreement.

At the time this process of changing the agreement begins, you (or your broker or attorney) go to the person functioning as stakeholder to communicate the changes you'd like to make; often, this person then becomes forced to function more like a referee than a stakeholder. (If the stakeholder is the attorney for the seller, he clearly isn't an impartial referee. With an escrow officer, this is less likely to happen; in theory, the latter is a "robot" carrying out preprogrammed instructions. In practice, however, he frequently gets forced into acting as an arbitrator.)

The escrow period on a property (or the time it takes from going to contract on a property to the closing) can be any length of time the buyer and seller agree on. The process can be as short as a day; at the other extreme, I've known instances where it's taken a year and a half.

WHAT IF YOU CAN'T AFFORD A GOOD-FAITH DEPOSIT AT THE TIME YOU WRITE THE ORIGINAL DOCUMENT?

Let's say that you see a property that excites you, and you and the seller agree to a deal you believe is a good value. You want the agreement in writing right away so you can take the property off the market, but you don't have the money at the moment for a good-faith deposit. Does that mean you should postpone signing the offering agreement? No! There are many solutions to this problem. I generally make my offer (including contingencies) and have the good-faith check made payable to the escrow company on the condition that the check cannot be cashed until the escrow is opened and signed by both parties. The offer also states that the escrow doesn't have to be opened until five days after the inspections have been completed. This is a common practice. This usually means the check won't be cashed for days or weeks.

You may use a number of instruments (*instrument* is legal parlance for a formal document) to tie up a property without money. One such instrument is a demand note, a written document that the buyer executes to the order of the seller or, in some cases, in favor of the escrow holder. In essence, the demand note says, "I promise to pay a certain amount of money when this deal is consummated." The stakeholder holds the note for this particular transaction until all the money comes in and the transaction is completed.

Again, all of these items—deposits, contingencies, and price and terms—depend on the agreement between the buyer and the seller. Making deals is very much like courtship and dating. When we are dating, we all dress nicely, apply our makeup perfectly, and have beautiful manners. But God knows, as soon as you are bound to one another, things change. While you are dating your seller, he's going to be gracious about everything if he really wants to sell; your stakeholder is going to be equally gracious. Be aware of this and take full advantage of the courtship—ask for what you need to complete the deal. Be polite and firm, not apologetic; there is no reason why you shouldn't use a check with the instruction that it shouldn't be cashed until the contingencies are removed.

WHAT OTHER MONEY SHOULD YOU BE PREPARED TO PAY?

If you live in a state in which escrow companies, banks, or title companies typically handle the selling of a property, be aware that they may expect to get their fees even if the transaction doesn't go through. Read through any agreement with an escrow company, bank, or title company *before* opening escrow so that you know what expenses you will be incurring if you complete the deal and what expenses, if any, you will be incurring if you decide to forgo it. This information often appears in a voluminous preprinted form, generally referred to as boiler plate.

In those states in which title companies do title searches, you may also be expected to pay a fee even if the deal dissolves. The fee may be waived if the company regards you as a customer whom it would like to encourage with future transactions. The decision is theirs, however. If you decide against a deal *after* the title company has done its work or any part of its work and you are requested to pay a fee, your commitment to paying it, even if your funds are very limited, is another step toward presenting yourself as a professional real estate investor.

If you live in a state in which the seller's attorney serves as your stakeholder, you too will need an attorney to represent you and you should discuss her fees in advance. Review what her fees will be if the transaction is completed and if it dissolves. Since she may be basing her fee on a percentage of the purchase price of the property, you have to find out if she plans to charge you an hourly rate if the deal falls apart. If she does, you will want to know exactly what work will be involved and her estimate of how many hours this work will take. You may also want to make certain she doesn't go over a specified budget. Again, it's all subject to negotiation.

CAN THE SELLER EVER KEEP YOUR MONEY IF YOU DECIDE AGAINST THE DEAL?

The answer to this question is "Yes, but not often, and then only if you as the buyer agree to it—twice—in writing."

It's common in certain transactions, especially those involving large sums of money, for a seller to specify in the original written agreement that if a deal falls through, he is entitled to a certain amount of money as liquidated damages for holding his property off the market.

Although both buyer and seller may sign a contract guaranteeing these liquidated damages, the seller, trying to collect his liquidated damages the day the deal falls apart, often finds that the stakeholder will not release the funds at the request of the seller. Generally the stakeholder requires another paper from the buyer, giving him permission to hand over the money to the seller. If the defaulting buyer refuses to sign, then the seller can do nothing except sue, which will probably cost far more in attorney's fees than he would collect in liquidated damages. There will be a lot of posturing for position before any lawsuit, with room for negotiation and forgiveness, and the seller may well decide against pursuing the liquidated damages because it may tie the property up in the lawsuit. Thus, collecting liquidated damages is a very tricky business. The rule of thumb is, "Don't count on it."

IF YOU HAVE A CHOICE ABOUT WHO SERVES AS THE STAKEHOLDER

If it's possible in your area, my advice is to choose an independent escrow company to handle escrow for you. The argument in support of this is much the same as the argument in favor of choosing and paying for your own family physician instead of randomly getting a physician through socialized medicine.

Let's suppose that the seller and the buyer don't know each other, and that for one reason or another they get an escrow officer at an escrow company to handle the transaction. In the eyes of the buyer and seller the third person, the escrow officer, may become something more than a service producer. The third person may become the holder of the scales of justice that judges the principals' thinking. The transaction may go easily if both buyer and seller believe that each of them has the escrow agent's approval. But the sale may move toward falling apart if they believe they don't, and it could be based on something as simple as the escrow officer always smiling at the seller and always giving the buyer the "evil eye."

If the transaction is handled by attorneys, obviously there is no neutral third party. In these circumstances you will often depend on your attorney's feedback: he can be your filter and your mirror. He can also act as soldier or referee.

When attorneys handle the selling of a property, it's customary to handle the closing in one day. They meet and execute all the documents and control the funds; you may or may not have to be present. If title insurance is not available, one of the attorneys performs the title search on the property by going to the courthouse and checking that the seller has clear title to the property, verifying that the new owner will not be encumbered with unexpected liens.

A CHECKLIST FOR YOUR OWN MAGNA CARTA

Before moving on to the crucial question of how to negotiate a deal, I want to give you a list of some of the basic contingencies you may want to include in your original written agreement. Remember that you can ask for any contingency you want. As long as the seller agrees to it, it becomes part of the deal. Also remember that if the seller doesn't agree to include in the original document a contingency you need to make the deal, you're not going to get the contingency later; you may have to forget about this property and move on to another one.

The basic contingencies are:

1. the right for you and whatever experts you choose to inspect *every* physical aspect of the building, the entire structure of the building and all equipment, including all apartments and/or offices;
2. the right to obtain the kind of financing that would make the deal attractive to you;
3. the right to approve all title documents, contracts, and other loan documents;
4. the right to inspect and approve all leases or rental agreements (where applicable);
5. the right to inspect and approve all books and records (where applicable).

CHAPTER 12

NEGOTIATION: GETTING THE BEST DEAL POSSIBLE WHILE BEING THE BEST PERSON POSSIBLE

I'm indebted to my mother for the following observation: "When you go to buy, it's dirt. When you go to sell, it's gold." That's the basis on which most buyers negotiate. They feel if they demean the deal—by making the property dirt—the seller will lower the price. The seller, however, likes to feel that his property is gold. Obviously, these classic positions don't blend. Throwing them back and forth at each other isn't negotiating.

Negotiating is a game unto itself. The really important negotiation takes place in your own mind: you come up with a price for the potential purchase or sale, you negotiate with yourself until there is clarity, until your fear is gone, and until you know the deal works for you. That combination of fearlessness and clarity creates power—in this case the power of knowing the value.

While you're negotiating with yourself, you may bring in your Free Board of Directors, get their input, and test all possible hypotheses on the value of the property until you sense you know the value. At this point, you have "ball-parked" the price. You make your offer and get a yes, no, or maybe, under certain circumstances.

Here is where the other negotiating comes in. If you tell the seller that his property is dirt and he says it's gold, you're just arguing. *Good negotiation is trading.* The trick is to find something you don't mind giving up in return for something you want that the other party doesn't think is as valuable to him as the concession you're willing to give in exchange. In other words, each party to the transaction has to feel he's getting something that justifies what he's giving up.

The chips that we play for are real—money (a better price or better terms), or emotional satisfaction (simply making ourselves or the other party feel good about our actions).

A SAMPLE NEGOTIATION

For simplicity's sake, let's start with the example of a private house that's listed for $125,000.

Say I've looked at all the houses in my price range in the neighborhood I'm interested in and I've found a particular house I like. At this point, the real estate broker says to me, "Steve, do you like Mark's house?" I answer, "Yes, I do." She says, "How much do you want to offer?"

In coming up with the figure I'm going to offer, my reasoning goes like this: I've made myself an expert and determined that the house is worth, at the most, $125,000; I know I'm only interested in buying it for at least 20 percent under that—which means I would get the house for approximately $100,000. Now, even though $100,000 would be a terrific price, I feel I'm entitled to get it for $10,000 under that, because I want to make an incredible deal (why not try?). That would make the purchase price $90,000. But my sense of the seller is that he's a real haggler; he's not about to agree to any reduction right away. Therefore, if I expect to end up at $90,000, I'd better offer him $80,000. So I tell the broker that's the offer I want to make.

Establishing the right kind of relationship with your broker is your first major step in negotiating the deal. This relationship has to be both friendly and businesslike. Remember, your goal in having a broker is for him or her to help you get the property you want at the price you want. Therefore, it's very important to establish the same tone between yourself and the broker that you want the broker to communicate to the seller. Telling the broker, "Try to get it for $85,000 and if you can't, I'll go up to $90,000" is the same as telling the broker to offer $90,000. (Good brokers get the buyer to go up and the seller to go down as much as they can.) If you were playing poker, you would not show your cards to the opponent, so don't show them all to the broker. Hold back a few.

As the broker writes up the offer for $80,000, she says, "Steve, I really don't think this is enough, but I'm going to take it to the seller." She brings the offer to Mark, and Mark tells her, "Well, Ms. Broker, the house next door sold for $135,000. But I'm a realistic man. My kid's going to college, and I've already bought a condominium. That's why I priced it low at $125,000, and I'm not taking a penny less."

The broker then says to Mark, "Look, the house next door sold for $135,000, but it was on the market for nine months. It also has many things yours doesn't, and the owner was very lucky to get that price. You'd really like to move immediately, not wait nine months, and who knows what you'd get then? Let's see now, how much would you lose if your house stayed unsold for nine months? If you invested the money at 10 percent interest, that's about $11,000. Wouldn't you rather sell your house now for $11,000 less and be done with it? And besides, if your neighbor's house was worth $135,000, yours doesn't have the same amenities, so it's worth much less. So you should be realistic and come down in price to save time, which is also money." After she's said this, she might add: "And don't you think that with the volatile state of the economy, you should act right now?" A broker will list reason after reason about why the seller should lower the price. She'll keep assuring the seller she worked very hard to get your offer up—and that if the seller bends, she can persuade you to bend.

This conversation will continue for as long as it takes to arrive at the end point of any successful negotiation: the point at which everybody involved has been able to rationalize how far he will bend. It can take anywhere from a moment to a lifetime.

If the seller is really committed to selling, not just being a perpetual seller who never sells, then he knows in his heart that he's going to have to compromise to consummate a deal with someone. He doesn't know exactly what price he's going to get for his property, he doesn't know who will buy it, but he does know he wants out!

Ultimately he must agree to a price for which a buyer is willing to buy his house. The broker knows she has to make a living by mediating between people buying and selling houses; she knows it doesn't make a difference whether she sells that house to Joe or anyone else because she'll get a commission either way. She is committed to making deals. The trick is to keep the process of refining going until it meshes in such a way that an agreement can be reached. Tenacity and inventiveness are the main ingredients.

In negotiating for the house Mark has listed for $125,000, I convince the broker to present a low-ball offer; the broker convinces the seller it's appropriate to lower his price; the seller convinces himself that the broker's telling him the truth about why he should lower it, and he lowers it—but not enough to suit me. The broker then convinces me that I should come up in my offer, because I'm being unrealistic; she says that Mark will eventually take an offer of $105,000 because he's so anxious to move out; I then convince myself this is the best I'm going to do with Mark because the broker's convinced me that he's adamant. It's also near the price I figured on paying for the house to begin with.

However, still feeling that it's legitimate to get the best deal I possibly can, I want to negotiate further, and ask myself, "How can I reduce the price even more?" I figure that if the broker is to receive a 6 percent commission on $105,000, she would get $6,-300. Maybe in the spirit of making the deal, she'll give up some of it; maybe she'll take $3,000. So I say, "Why don't you halve your commission so I can afford this deal?" Let's say she answers, "I can't do that." Then I convince her why she should, and the seller convinces her why she should, and we're all convinced we've made a deal. It has nothing to do with what the house is worth; it has only to do with our having convinced each other.

There are some situations where it's not necessary to negotiate. The property is offered at the right price and the right terms, and your only response is to say, "Fine." There are other situations where you know exactly what you want, and you're firm: you'll take the property if you get what you want and you won't take it if you don't. Your method of negotiating in that circumstance may be not to negotiate at all, but to state exactly what you want and then stick to it. There are other situations, like the one I just described, where you involve yourself in a prolonged negotiation to get to the point you want to reach—because you sense that without this process you don't stand a chance of getting there.

Most sellers feel that one needs to negotiate before committing for the same reason we usually want foreplay before sex. Therefore, your first step is usually to ball-park the deal. This involves seeing the value of the property and, through the give-and-take of offer and counteroffer, getting the seller to agree to a price that makes the property a good value to you. With the hypothetical house listed for $125,000 I saw the exceptional value at $100,000, so I wanted to get it for about that. The process I went through to get it for as close to $100,000 as possible was ball-parking the deal. With another seller who wouldn't require the drama of haggling, I could have just offered $100,000, and we could have agreed, or perhaps we would have compromised at $105,000.

I believe that negotiating is a talent and comes with experience. It is self-taught through trial and error. Techniques can also be learned from others, and this can speed up your own self-teaching. Ask your Free Board of Directors to share their suggestions and experiences. Tell them the situation and ask them how they would handle it. Have a practice negotiation using the facts of your deal and asking one of your Board members to act out the seller's part. It will work.

Another helpful approach is to sit with pen and paper and write down all the pros and cons of the deal for the buyer and the seller. What are the buyer's arguments to justify his price and terms? What are your arguments to justify the price and terms you are offering? Ask your Board members to assist you in this process. It will crystallize your position, showing where your strengths and weaknesses are. Go through them with the broker. It will be beneficial.

Before we move on to the next step of negotiating—what I call "fine-tuning the deal"—I want to show you another aspect of what you have to know so you can ball-park the best deal possible.

PRICE AND TERMS: AN INSEPARABLE PACKAGE

It's vital to understand that in constructing a deal you can't separate the purchase price of the property from the terms of the financing; price and terms are both integral parts of the transaction. A well-constructed deal is one that uses both elements to come up with the most profitable package.

Take two houses that are identical in every respect except price, and make different arrangements for financing; the more expensive house with better financing may be cheaper than the less expensive house. *When you're negotiating, you don't necessarily want to get the least expensive price; you want the combination of terms and price that give you the best overall deal.*

Let's say that you are in a 12 percent interest-rate market and you find a particular property that is worth about $1 million, based on 25 percent down and 75 percent financing at 12 percent. If the seller says, "I will sell for only $900,000, but I want all cash," you know it's a bargain to pay all cash. After you own it, you can refinance it with the same 12 percent loan. If the owner of the same $1 million property were to say, "Instead of $1 million with 25 percent down and a 12 percent loan, give me 25 percent down, I'll carry the balance myself for 20 years at 9 percent, but you'll have to give me $1.1 million for the property," you would have an even better deal because you will have saved 3 percent annually in interest payments on $750,000, which equals $22,500 per year (.03 × $750,000 = $22,500). So even though you've paid $100,-000 extra in the purchase price, you will benefit for twenty years in savings. Therefore, once you've owned the building for a little more than four years, you will have recouped the $100,000 (4 × $22,500 = $90,000), and the benefit of the lower interest rate will continue for the life of the loan. Given the choice, you would make that deal for the purchase. You have to know which of the many possible transactions is a better one.

Once you understand which is the best deal, then the question is "Okay, now how can I improve it?" That's where fine-tuning comes in.

MAKING BETTER INTO BEST: I TRY IT WHEN I'VE GOT NOTHING TO LOSE

A deal is tied up when both sides agree in writing. When this agreement is written up with contingencies, you have the right to walk away from the deal if those contingencies aren't met. The seller, however, with no contingencies to cancel the deal, is bound to sell to you for the agreed-upon price and terms if you choose to consummate it. Once you are in the contingency period you, as the buyer, are in the driver's seat, and a great deal of potentially valuable negotiation can take place.

Now that you have it in writing, it's time to fine-tune the deal. To do this you go to the seller and bring out all the information you've been collecting in your inspections that supports your belief that something about the property has been revealed which makes it less attractive and that therefore the price or terms should be improved.

You might say, for example, "You know, I noticed that the roof doesn't look too good, and the rugs are in bad shape, and some of the tenants, who I thought would be wonderful people, are from a tough motorcycle gang. It's going to cost a lot more money to fix it up than I thought. I'd still like to buy it, but only if you take $50,000 off the price."

The seller, probably having already mentally spent the sale proceeds, may think over what you've said and figure, "Well, it's a million-dollar deal and a bird in the hand is worth two in the bush. His points are well taken. I don't think they're worth $50,000 off the price we agreed on, but I'll give him $25,000."

With this scenario, you've definitely carved out a better deal for yourself.

Let's say it goes the other way. Suppose that the owner says, "I won't reduce the price one dime." If you really want to be hard-nosed, you might respond, "I want $50,000 off, and if I don't get it, I'm not going to buy it." The owner then would answer, "Well, if you don't want to do the deal, forget it." Your next response might be "Well, all right, maybe it shouldn't be $50,000 less, but I need at least $15,000 or $20,000. You misrepresented some of these facts."

Let's say the owner gets hostile. You again point out all the things that from your perspective make the property worth less than the initial agreed-upon price, but he still says no. You keep repeating your observations until the last day of the contingency period, and you still don't get a single concession. Meanwhile, the property has been inspected, and the inspector has told you it's generally in good shape; you've also found out that the interest the bank is going to charge you on the loan is something you can accept. You have determined exactly how much it will cost to take care of the roof and the carpets and gradually get better tenants, and you know you can live with these costs. On the last day, you say, "I'll take the deal anyway." It is still a good deal!

Trying to better your position or fine-tuning can go on until the deal closes. I've been a seller in more than one transaction where the buyer had the gall to say he was backing out even though all his contingencies had been removed. In these cases, the buyer was generally attempting a last-minute maneuver to hammer down the price, hoping that it was so late in the game and I was so anxious to complete the deal that I'd renegotiate to make a better deal with him rather than to let go and find another buyer. When you are buying a property—or selling one—you could use the same tactics. The main cost is your integrity and reputation, and the risk of a lawsuit and losing the deal.

Another approach to fine-tuning the deal, instead of asking for a lower price, is to ask the seller to give you a mortgage with a lower interest rate or to accrue some of the payments or lengthen the number of years over which the mortgage will be paid off, all of which lessen the present payments on debt service.

HOW BROKERS WORK FOR YOU IN NEGOTIATIONS

Brokers are wonderful because they serve as buffers in this process. A broker acts as a trial balloon: have him ask questions and see what happens. Use brokers as your eyes and ears to test the possibilities. It's easier to have them be noncommittal than to be noncommittal yourself.

With a broker you can do whatever you want in any manner you want, and the broker will translate whatever you do and say into terms that are palatable to the person on the other side of the deal. It's safer. Without the broker's serving as buffer, this process may be harder. I do it by first getting a feeling of what the other person in the transaction is like, and then my instincts tell me whether to sidestep the broker and handle the negotiation personally, or to use the broker. The other person's personality will also tell me what manner to adopt in the negotiation. My primary rule is to be as straightforward as possible.

Whenever I'm negotiating a deal, whether as buyer or seller, I try to get a personality profile of the other person. It's a very easy process: just start a conversation with him. Find out what he does for a living. Right away you begin getting a flavor of what he's like by the way he responds, and then you act accordingly.

For example, if it seems as if he has the macho point of view, he may feel he has to get his way. You know you have to negotiate with him—or her—in such a way that you never cause a confrontation, because if there is a confrontation, your deal may fall apart. The other party might dig in his or her heels and aggressively say, "No, I won't do it." The opposite extreme is the kind of person who doesn't like confrontations; people in this category are willing to negotiate any little point rather than to risk a fight.

HOW TO NEGOTIATE FROM THE TRUTH

Most people don't realize that the truth is simply the truth. They think they have to come up with a surreptitious point of view in order to get what they want; they're back to calling the property dirt when they want to buy it and calling it gold when they want to sell. But the truth *is* just the truth: when you're negotiating, if you know exactly what you want, say exactly what you want and intend to get exactly what you want, it becomes very, very difficult for anyone to argue if you're clear and firm.

For example, if you can afford only a certain down payment, it would be best to say, "I have this amount of money. I could live with a deal with these terms. If you meet these terms, we have a deal." This is not only the easiest way of negotiating, more often than not, it works. And if it doesn't work, you have saved yourself a lot of time and aggravation.

Many times people will give you what you want if they like you. People always like an honest person. So when a buyer brings truthfulness to a potential seller, the seller often will get on his bandwagon simply because the person is sincere; the seller will probably not like him at all if he is insincere. Sincerity in and of itself may help to create the deal. The sincerity is grounded in truth, and it grounds the deal in truth.

Truth gets you exactly what you want and what you deserve. You become a better person when you can be honest and not manipulative. The person you're negotiating with becomes a better person because it's contagious.

All Deals Are Just a Broker's Commission Away

In general, the last element of the deal that gets handled is the broker's commission. In the example of the $125,000 house that I wanted to buy for $100,000, I mentioned that the broker agreed to cut her commission in half to make the deal work. In almost every real estate deal I've ever worked on, when the buyer and seller are really close to an agreement, the deal always seems to be a broker's commission away from happening.

As an example, if a property is listed at $1 million and the original offer to the seller is $900,000, the deal will often end up with the seller's saying he wants $1 million for the property and the buyer saying he's willing to pay $940,000. They're $60,000 apart and they both get stuck there. They're stuck because they each know they're satisfied with the deal as it stands and they are each secretly conscious that that $60,000 is exactly the 6 percent broker's commission on $1 million.

So buyer and seller put the broker in the position of pulling the rubber band so tight that he knows it may break. Even if the buyer or the seller or both do not have the gumption to ask the broker directly to reduce his commission, once the broker has gotten the message that the deal may not go through without his help, he will often suggest that his commission would probably work at less than 6 percent. This breaks the ice, and everyone makes the deal.

When I feel that both the seller and the broker have been

stretched as far as they're going to be stretched, I again state my reasons for why I should be able to buy the building at my price. Then I suggest, "Why don't we split the $60,000 in thirds, and that way it won't be painful to anybody. Since we're just $60,000 apart, why don't we each absorb $20,000?" In general, when I present this proposition to the broker, he says, "Well, that isn't going to be as painful to me as it might have been. I'm not committing myself to doing it, but I will communicate your offer to the seller."

At that juncture, the ball has started to roll, and it gives each side the opportunity to save face. Often it works out that we each do contribute a third. If the seller doesn't agree to contributing a third, then, without my even saying another word, the broker may still throw in his third to save the deal, or he may offer more than a third. Other times I might say, "I understand that the seller is adamant, and I'm willing to compromise a little, but the least I'll take off the price is $25,000. I don't care where the rest comes from, so if you can figure out a way to do it, that's fine with me." That gives the broker the perfect opening for suggesting that he'll reduce his commission. I've completed deals with the largest brokerage firms where brokers have done just that.

FINDING YOUR OWN WAY TO DO IT

Now that I've given you an idea of some of the different steps involved in negotiating, I want to make it very clear that every person has to find his or her own personal style of negotiating. This includes both the type of negotiating and the timetable for completing each step. All the events of negotiating that I've described must take place, but the sequence changes depending on the players and the situation. I'll show you what I mean.

A few years ago I ran into an acquaintance in the park. In his early forties, he was teaching himself to ride a bicycle. He was doing it the same way that kids do it; he obviously had never ridden a bike before, and he kept falling down and persevering. After I had been in the park for about an hour I noticed he was actually riding his bike all the way around the park. I was amazed by the realization that most people in the world learn to ride a bicycle, but not necessarily before they reach adulthood. Most of us learn when we're five or six years old, and when we're forty we learn to do something else. This man was the kind of person who at four years old had a lemonade stand on the corner. When he was a child he learned to make money. Now he was learning to ride a bicycle.

In most of the deals I do myself, I operate from common sense and within the framework of a hypothesis. Once I've tied up a property at a good price, I investigate it to double-check my thinking. If I see that the deal doesn't meet my expectations, I rework it and figure out how to make it viable. I usually learn to ride the bicycle after I've bought and owned the bicycle; a lot of other people will work out all these details beforehand. I like to check out my hypothesis about a deal by tying up the property first because then the seller can't change his mind, and no one can beat me to the winners' circle.

There's also a mystical element to this sequence that often comes into play: as soon as one person wants something, it seems as if everybody wants it. As soon as a property comes to your attention, you can be sure somebody else out there is attracted to it, too. So the question is, who ties it up first?

I figure that by the time I find out a deal is good, someone else in the marketplace will notice it, too; if I tie it up then nobody else can. And in ball-parking the deal *before* I tie it up, I am generally sure that the price and terms the seller and I agree to in the contract are figures I can live with if I decide to go through with the deal.

That's the order in which I sequence the events of negotiation; you may choose to sequence them differently—and that may work for you.

We're really talking about more than negotiating here; we're talking about *actualizing* what we're doing. I've said it before and I'll say it again because it's true: most people don't take a stand; they simply keep looking for more history and more information. They keep looking without taking a stand because when they take a stand things actually happen. They become powerful! I like to take a stand very early in the game because I know that deals will happen as a result. It is easy to cast off the deal using the contingencies. If you overresearch the property first, it's too easy to avoid getting to the buying stage and end up a person whose stories are always about the one that got away.

Remember: the object of negotiation in real estate is to buy a property at the right price and terms, not to find reasons not to buy it.

CHAPTER 13

How to Start, and Where Do You Get the Chutzpah?

Now you have an overall picture of how to buy and manage real estate. So obviously you're ready to just go out and do it, right? Maybe.

You might be thinking, "That sounds great, but how do I really go about doing it?" Even though you've learned the fundamentals of what makes a good deal, you may still see yourself as unqualified to approach a broker and say, "Serve me, find for me, provide me with, and work for me, all for free," because you feel you're not a real estate entrepreneur. But you'd probably think it would be totally acceptable for a property-owning big shot in a limousine to approach the same broker.

At an *est* course, I was introduced to a concept called "be, do, have" that framed this whole issue clearly for me. We think we have to "have" real estate and money in order to "do" real estate trans-actions in order to "be" a real estate entrepreneur, instead of "being" the real estate entrepreneur, which consists of "doing" real estate transactions and "having" real estate. We don't see that first you have to "be"—you can't "have" or "do" (real estate transactions or anything else) without already "being."

So let's say that you've decided what kind and size of property you want. Let's also say that you're going to buy the property with money you're going to raise through investors. You've searched your soul and decided that you want to buy an apartment house with an overall purchase price of approximately $750,000 and a down payment of $250,000. You know that real estate brokers work on a commission of about 6 percent—even though it often gets negotiated down from there—so you know you're presenting the broker with a potential commission of about $40,000. You're scared, since you've never done anything like this before; you may be feeling that you don't have the nerve to approach a broker.

Since, in this example, you lack the bank account you think you need to support the "I belong" attitude, you have to make yourself "be" a real estate entrepreneur anyway. All you need to make yourself "be" a real estate entrepreneur is *chutzpah,* a Yiddish word that's come to mean "nerve." Chutzpah doesn't come from arrogance, just from realizing that nobody "has" it before they "are" it; you have to "be" a real estate entrepreneur before you can complete real estate transactions.

You'll soon discover that the broker does not necessarily recognize outstanding deals; if he did, chances are he would stop being a broker and grab them himself.

The broker's job is to help you find the deal; he finds it by exposing you to different properties.

It doesn't take much chutzpah to approach a broker if you realize that in a very important sense the broker isn't much more sophisticated than you are. He may know where the potential sellers are, and he may even know what prices they've told him they want for their properties, but he has not yet fully tested what they *really* want to make the deal. That's done only when the deal is made. So when you're looking at a property with a broker you're teaching him about the deal. If you view him as a "have," because you believe that he has experience and therefore he must have all the answers, then you're making a false assumption. The broker is at the "be" stage, too, because at the starting point he just "is" a broker with the ingredients; now he must "do" the transaction; only when it's completed will he "have" a deal.

So while your process as the buyer is looking, making an offer, negotiating, and then deciding whether or not to go through with the transaction, the broker's process is showing, presenting the offer, negotiating, and then supporting you in whatever decision you make.

Remember the advice that's frequently offered to people who are afraid of public speaking or performing: whenever you feel frightened, picture the audience naked. The psychology behind this advice is that, since we are dressed, we will feel less vulnerable than they are in their nakedness. Similarly, it's very easy to have the chutzpah to approach brokers once you see that all brokers are naked. Their nakedness is that they don't know what the seller is going to take for a property: They're in the dark, just like you. Even when a seller has refused an offer, he may change his mind and accept a similar one. It happens all the time, and nobody ever knows *when* it will happen.

Remember that brokers make their living by putting deals together; by working with them, you are helping them make their living. The broker can't do his job in real estate without you—and that's true whether you have the money at the moment or not.

I've been in transactions where the broker was so supportive that he helped make the deal in lots of ways. I've participated in deals where brokers put up the money to help me buy the property; in other deals brokers have asked if they can use their commission to buy into the deal. Even the sellers have often supported me in making deals, and this is not at all uncommon. The point is that by putting yourself out there and telling the truth, you get support from unexpected places.

If you are willing to "be" the real estate entrepreneur and tell the broker, "I have $10,000 of my own to use as a down payment, and I am convinced my family and some of my friends are going to put up the rest of the money I'm going to need for this transaction, I want a property that meets these specifications, and I would like you to help me find it," that broker is going to work for you. He's going to do his best to participate in your success. He has every reason to do it.

THE BROKER MAKES A GOOD STARTING PLACE

All you really need to begin your career as a real estate entrepreneur is a willingness to share your expectations with a broker. And once you have your starting place, then things unfold by themselves.

Let's say that you walk into a broker's office and tell him your expectation of finding a property that can be purchased for $300,-000 with $100,000 down. While you're sitting there the broker takes a phone call, and you overhear a story about a $600,000 apartment building that was inherited by an elderly widow. If it could be sold very quickly it could be bought for $500,000 with only $100,000 down because she needs the money to pay inheritance tax. Across the room, you hear another broker in conversation with a potential buyer who is looking for a $600,000 apartment building that matches this one perfectly. As soon as your broker gets off the phone, you say, "I'd like to see that building." And the broker immediately arranges for you to see it.

So without even having intended to look at that property, without having planned to buy it in order to sell it off to the other broker's client, you suddenly find that buying it is a possibility! My point is that the opportunities magically appear—if you see them—and the path magically appears—as long as you are alert for it.

HOW DO YOU FIND A BROKER?

As we've noted, your first step is to determine the area in which you're going to look for property. Some possibilities will come to mind, one will seem more appealing than the rest, and that will be the one you'll investigate first. See which of the brokers' ads appeal to you and call them. If you're looking at properties in person, simply walk or drive around and look at the brokers' signs; call the broker whose sign is on the property that you like.

Just by putting yourself out in the marketplace, brokers will appear. You'll either find them by seeing their names in the paper or seeing their signs on properties and you'll call them, or you'll go to an open house and they'll find you. Then comes the chemistry. You'll discover that with some brokers, the chemistry clearly says, "We'll work together," while with the others the chemistry just as plainly says, "Stay away."

From your first contact with a broker, you should be completely frank and enthusiastic. Your enthusiasm will be contagious. He's going to catch it and say to himself, "My goodness, this person is really going to do something!" And he will support you. If he can't help personally, he may introduce you to someone looking for clients at a different level of brokerage who would be thrilled to work with you. If a person is honest, sincere, and enthusiastic, it's almost impossible for him to walk out of any bona fide broker's office without a lead.

HOW MANY BROKERS SHOULD YOU SEE AT ONE TIME?

I would compare using different brokers to juggling. Some jugglers can keep two balls in the air at a time, some juggle five, and others juggle every number in between. The question is, how many can you juggle? I work with a hundred brokers at a time. After years of doing it, it's easy for me to remember all the various deals I'm working on. There are other people in real estate who prefer to work with only one broker. It's just like dating: some people feel comfortable dating one person at a time, others like to date many.

Because I know how to see value I like to look—and I'll work with any broker who can find me what I want. If you feel comfortable juggling relationships with different brokers and keeping track of the variety of potential deals they present, utilizing the services of many brokers may be the best way to familiarize yourself with the marketplace quickly and to present yourself with the fullest range of opportunities for finding the property you want.

WHAT QUESTIONS CAN YOU APPROPRIATELY ASK A BROKER?

In dealing with a broker, it's appropriate to ask any kind of question you think of. Never worry about looking foolish; if you avoid asking questions, you won't look foolish, you will actually be foolish.

Once you assess the broker, you'll have a perspective for evaluating his answers. Looking back at my own interaction with the hundreds of brokers I've worked with, I can see that it's easy to ask a few questions and determine whether a broker is knowledgeable or not. If he's not knowledgeable, you may find that it's the blind leading the blind.

Interview the broker while working with him. The interview is a way of scanning the information he provides and finding out who and what he is professionally.

When a broker starts telling me about deals he's done, or how this or that is true in this neighborhood, I always ask specific questions to pin him down so I can find out exactly what he has and hasn't done. When you do this, you discover the level of sophistication on which the broker is basing his observation, and that helps you determine whether what he is saying comes from fact or wishful thinking.

By asking a broker what he has accomplished, you are giving him a chance to show his trophies. Everybody loves to show his trophies, so your specific questions are giving him a golden opportunity. If the answers you get are attempts to put you off, then you're being told that you're dealing with someone who can't be honest and straightforward. Then you have to wonder, "Why work with someone like this? I'm going someplace where I can work with someone who will find what I want." The same is true if you find yourself dealing with a person who thinks he or she is too important to answer your questions. A person in this category really doesn't want to serve you—and that certainly isn't going to work for you. The key test to determine if you're working with the right broker is to ask him every single question that occurs to you and see how he answers.

The more that you prove what the broker tells you is true, the more you know that the broker is a reliable source of information. But you still never depend just on the broker.

Remember that at the same time the broker is educating you, you're educating the broker. You're each serving the other. If you don't ask him all the questions that occur to you, you don't serve him and he doesn't serve you.

One additional point I want to make about this give-and-take with a broker is that even an incompetent one can serve you: By enthusiasm alone he can lead you to a fabulous deal. So if you have the time and the patience, follow all the leads he provides.

SHOULD YOU EVER BUY A BUILDING WITHOUT A BROKER?

In order to answer this question, we have to define the broker's functions. One function is to locate property. Another is to negotiate. Another is to ask questions. Still another is to bring more people into the transaction; for example, he can help you find lenders, appraisers, and others who can provide you with goods and services you might need for the property. The question to ask in deciding whether you're going to work with or without a broker is whether you can perform these functions yourself.

It becomes very easy to see whether or not you need a broker when you break down his role. For example, some people have a knack for negotiating and are willing to do it, while other people have enormous barriers to negotiating. So whether or not you need a broker to do your negotiating depends on how you feel about your own skills as a negotiator. Even if you would like to negotiate for yourself, once you think it over you may realize that you would be better off having a broker to rephrase what you would say in a negotiation and to work out compromises that you would be incapable of devising yourself.

If you wanted to locate properties yourself, your first step would be to discover where they are and who owns them. You could do this by going to the city records or to a title company. Another way of locating property is to look at what's being advertised for sale. Once you find out who owns the property you're interested in, you can call the owners on the phone. This is a very difficult project for a beginner.

One by one, go over each of the broker's functions to see if you can perform them without him. I think there are many more advantages than disadvantages to using a broker.

On the negative side of using a broker is the idea that his services will cost money, and it's tempting to think that we can cut him out and make his money ourselves. Another possible negative is that he may come between us and the seller. Perhaps we might have a better rapport with the seller directly and therefore make a better deal.

But if you look on the positive side—and I'm talking strictly from the buyer's perspective now—you're not going to be paying the broker's commission anyway because you're not going to pay more than the value of the property no matter what. Thus, the commission comes from the seller. (And if that commission is driving the price up too high, you can always negotiate with the broker for him to cut it down, as I pointed out earlier.)

It's important to realize that the broker works at his job full-time; he sells properties all day long. So if you make it your business to look at a hundred properties, he's probably going to be looking at a thousand properties. Another point in favor of using a broker is that if he's been in the business for a while, he's probably very familiar with the available properties and knows their history: Even if he hasn't been in the business very long, if he's a go-getter he has access to the information on these properties from his colleagues in the office who have been around longer.

Still another reason to use a broker is that he's more familiar with the protocol of how the game is played. There is a great deal of paperwork and running around in real estate transactions, and your broker can do all this for you.

Remember too that brokers are wonderful buffers. With a broker, no matter what you say or do, you have a way of changing it around if it doesn't work and saving face, using him to re-create the deal. As we think of our real estate as trophies, our properties become extensions of our egos. So when someone comes along and says, "I'll offer to pay you so much for your property," the seller may get insulted. It's easy for him to take things personally, and if he doesn't like your offer, the whole communication may begin to sour.

When the buyer and seller square off in the negotiation, it's like two fighters starting a match. But they may not be well matched; they may not be using the same style of fighting; they may not even agree on the same rules. In the ring, there is a winner and a loser.

But in a good real estate deal, there must be *two* winners and no losers! The broker separates the parties and orchestrates their moves so that they avoid destructive confrontations.

If the broker serves no other function for you than being a buffer, he has been worth including as a player in the game.

CHAPTER 14

RAISING A DOWN PAYMENT EVEN IF YOU HAVE NO MONEY

I gave you a thumbnail sketch of how to raise money for a property when I described the example of Joe and his first house. Regardless of whether you decide to buy a single house, apartments, or any other property, the same fundamental principles apply. In this chapter and the next, I'm going to describe the processes for raising money and structuring your deal with investors.

As a real estate entrepreneur, you have to do really only one thing to raise money: You have to bring an investor a good opportunity.

It's interesting to note that investors in real estate projects view their investments with far less emotional charge when they are investing with a group than when they are investing on their own. Group investors don't pressure themselves with the attitude that their own egos are on the line.

People also generally accept that there is simply no such thing as the "best deal." There are "better deals," "okay deals," and "bad deals." The fundamental criterion for any good investment in real estate is that it's "solid"—not overly risky—with the strong probability that it will appreciate. The investor will be judging from this perspective when he decides if a particular package is appetizing or not.

As a real estate entrepreneur you have to come up with an appetizing package that will be comprised of two major components:

1. the property itself with the deal you have made on it (What kind of property is it? At what price and terms have you bought it? What are the projections for appreciation and return on cash invested? Does it shelter its income? Is there excess shelter?);
2. the terms being offered to investors for making their investment (How much money is required of an investor and how much of a percentage of the overall investment will go to him? What are you taking for putting the package together? How will the profit be split?).

To raise money from investors you have to show them that:

1. the deal being offered on the property makes the investment worthwhile;
2. the terms you are offering them for their investment make the investment worthwhile.

In Chapter 16 we'll describe how you're going to structure the deal with them to make it a wonderful opportunity. This chapter examines the first aspect, showing investors that the real estate being purchased stands on its own as a solid investment. It's this solid investment that will provide the foundation on which you will be able to raise the money, and the way you present this information to investors is a major factor in attracting them.

PUT ON YOUR SHERLOCK HOLMES HAT

In order to make your package appetizing to potential investors, you have to know the financial facts of other property being offered to investors in your area. Once you do this, you'll be able to state exactly how the deal you are offering is better.

In most marketplaces, a quick look in the newspaper will help you start your fact-finding investigation. In many areas, the Sunday paper contains a dozen advertisements or solicitations aimed at potential investors. You can go to the free seminars these sellers sometimes offer and ask questions about what kinds of deals they've put together. Make yourself an expert on the deals people are offering investors. In general, you'll find that the kinds of purchases you make on properties are superior to most offerings that are advertised. Some of the reasons for this are:

- Although there is a great demand for small transactions, large real estate groups can't work economically on them.
- Many professionals are forced to add such heavy commissions and miscellaneous costs that their deals become only marginally attractive once it's clear how the investment money is being allocated.
- These large groups are very often pressed to buy simply in order to support their large overheads. They have to make deals whether the deals are superior, good, or just the best they can find that week!

To do this comparison effectively, make a study of offerings by investment professionals. Today most major stock brokerage firms are in the real estate syndication business, as are many accountants and attorneys. Ask your Free Board of Directors for leads. Scan the offering brochures very carefully, reading between the lines, and you will become expert in understanding them. The brochures teach you what the competition has to offer and the way they merchandise it. Visit the properties they describe. If there is any-thing that isn't thoroughly understandable, ask questions of the firm doing the offering until you do understand all aspects of the offer. This is a wonderful way for you to learn how to put your own offering into writing. You'll see that these professionals have no magic wand; everything they do to structure their offerings can apply to the transaction you are planning. No matter how large or small, all real estate deals are fundamentally the same.

One rule to remember: every professional is very aware of what type of return the marketplace is bringing. So when they find that one truly extraordinary deal, do you think they're going to pass it on to investors, or keep it for their own account? If they do bring in investors, they will probably find some way to dilute it. They have exactly the same market conditions to work in as every one of their competitors—and now *you* are one of their competitors. And for the reasons I've outlined, you stand a good chance of being able to offer a better deal for investors than they can!

PREPARING YOUR DEAL FOR THE INVESTORS

After having found exactly what other people are offering investors and having tied up a deal of your own, the next thing is to make sure that yours is well thought out. By going to your Free Board of Directors, telling each of them all the details of the deal and listening to what they have to say about it, you'll hear very quickly what they consider the pitfalls, and then you will be able to decide whether or not they are true pitfalls and whether or not they can be avoided. You must test your plan with your Free Board of Directors and then test their responses before approaching potential investors. (Remember, lots of times members of your Free Board of Directors will ask if they can be investors. This may come out of their "team player" spirit as well as their instinct about how good the deal is and how good you are.)

All the research that you did prior to tying up the property with a deposit receipt or contract with contingencies begins paying off when you present your deal to your Free Board of Directors. Because you've done your research, you know what the industry-wide standards and terms are, and your deal is going to look outstanding in comparison.

If you're talking about an apartment house, for example, you talk about the building in terms of cost per unit compared to others on the market. Say to your Free Board of Directors, "Look, all these other people are paying $40,000; I've got this building for $35,000 per apartment unit. There's no reason why we can't sell it right now for $40,000 per unit if we wanted to. Don't you agree?" If they don't agree, listen very carefully and test their answers.

Another way of presenting the deal to your Free Board of Directors is to compare the average rent per apartment in your building with the average rent per apartment in similar buildings on the block. If the average rent in your building comes to $350 per month, and all the other rents on the street are about $450, it's easy for your Board members to see that your building is a good deal, simply because raising the rents to current market value would make the building far more valuable.

Another way of presenting the deal to Board members is to describe it in terms of the gross income multiplier. If all the other buildings are selling for 8½ times the rent roll, and you're buying one for 7½ times the rent roll, you have a very clear statement of why it's a good deal.

Before presenting the deal to your Free Board of Directors you have to get a handle on the various aspects of the transactions. You want to find four or five different ways of comparing deals, all of which show why your deal is good. Explain the advantages of your project. You are essentially preparing the presentation for the investor. If you've done your homework, talked to your Free Board of Directors, evaluated what they've said, and refined your plan to take care of any potential pitfalls, then the investor will probably come to the same conclusion you did: "Hey, this is a good deal!"

It's vital for you to show the investor what advantages the investment offers him. Once you've done this, you're ready for what is perhaps the most important step you have to take with your investor, to tell him quite clearly, "I really want you go to into this deal. You'd be helping me out and I'll be helping you out, and I believe it will work perfectly." This statement, along with all the information you've presented to him, expresses your total confidence in the deal and your total confidence that it's appropriate for him or her to be part of the deal.

What About the Responsibility of Investing Other People's Money?

Of course, raising money to buy a property involves more than simply knowing what deal to create and how to present it to investors. To present your deal with confidence you first have to feel confident about taking responsibility for investing their money.

I've found that the anxiety that people experience when they invest other people's money is proportional to how risky the investment is and how truthful they have been in communicating the facts. The riskier the investment, by definition, the less probability that it will work out, and the more likely it is to lose some or all of the investment. The knowledge of this is bound to create anxiety for most people. My solution to this problem is *never* to go into deals that have the potential of a major loss, and always to state very clearly every negative aspect of the situation as well as the positive ones. The more truth, the less worry.

This whole subject is related to the important fact that there are different kinds of real estate investment games for different people. The transactions I personally like are what I would classify as non-risk transactions; they contain very few variables and are very predictable with little downside. This is the kind of game I'm most comfortable playing. If there's a lot of downside potential, it's not a deal for me.

One doesn't generally get rich on these low-risk transactions overnight, but one does get rich on them in just a few years. It's a very personal matter for both you and the investors. Are you (and they) willing to bet on a two-to-one shot? A five-to-one shot? Or a ten-to-one shot? The risk and the rewards are directly proportional. For some investors, a ten-to-one shot—high risk and comparatively huge potential profit—would be a viable gamble. Such investors are high-risk takers at heart. Other investors would be more attracted to a property that, though it offers a relatively modest return, doesn't depend for its profitability on a sequence of variables falling into place.

HOW TO PRESENT THE FACTS

As important as it is to know what kind of investment a particular investor is likely to be attracted to and to bring him only that kind of investment, it's equally important to know how to present the investment to him with integrity.

Let's say that you've checked out all the facts of your investment. Let's also say that the rest of the investment world is telling you they're going to get you a 10 percent return on cash invested, but you know, from using the real figures that you've found through your investigation, that you're going to get only a 2 to 3 percent return. Then you have to tell the investors that you're going to get a 2 to 3 percent return on the property. Tell your investors up front that you're going to need a rainy-day fund in addition to the down payment, and tell them how much money you need for this rainy-day fund.

The first requirement of presenting a deal to your investors with integrity is discovering the truth about the deal. The second requirement is getting over the fear of telling the truth.

If, as in this example, you're faced with figures that tell you the return is going to be 2 to 3 percent, not 10 percent, you have to get over the fear of stating that there is likely to be little or no cash return on the investment for the first year or two.

The way I would state the truth in this case is, "If you would talk to my friend, he would plug in his figures showing the expenses and the income of the same building, and would come out with a 10 percent return. So you as an investor have to look at it on two tiers. The way the industrywide standard works, it comes to 10 percent; the way I'm showing you, you get 2 to 3 percent. My feeling is we should hope to get the 10 percent but plan on getting 2 to 3 percent."

When you realize how simple this is, you automatically get over the fear of telling your investors what the facts are. You also get the bonus that comes with dealing from integrity: You get power because all of the investors you are talking to about putting money into the deal are going to support you for your truthfulness. People are smart; they know what's going on. People know when you're coming to them from your integrity.

TAKING THE STEPS TO GET INVESTORS

Let's go back to Joe. I want to remind you that I'm using him as an example because I want to show how even a person of the most limited means and experience can put together a solid deal and attract the investors he needs. If Joe can do this at age twenty-four with few assets of his own, so can you, even if your resources are equally limited. If you have more assets, ready cash, business sophistication, or even just a more extensive Free Board of Directors already in place, then it will be that much easier for you to put together a deal. In any case, as I mentioned before, if you are planning to raise the money for the deal from investors, the process you will go through will be exactly the same as the process used by Joe.

Joe's first step is to make a list of people he can approach for money. He's going to write down the names of family members, friends, and perhaps a few business acquaintances who he senses might be potential investors. He's going to have his goals and his expectations on that list, too. His goal will be to get them all to invest. His expectation is that the ones who care for him and trust him are going to invest with him no matter what; the others are possibilities who may or may not invest with him. He will also write down his goal and expectation for the amount of money that each person will invest. He will base his goal and his expectation of the amount on what he knows or senses each person can afford. He will also synchronize his budget for the purchase and for the rainy-day fund with his expectation of how much money he can raise. He is making his expectation his goal.

Once Joe has tied up a solid deal that meets his budgetary requirements, he is going to present the deal to everyone on his list. If he has done his homework, and if he's coming from his integrity, it's going to be a well thought out presentation of a well thought out deal. Before he presents it he will put it in writing. If he can't reduce his deal to writing, then he hasn't done enough research. If he can communicate it clearly on the written page (instructions for writing a brochure are in the next chapter), then he is ready to present it to his investors. In his presentation, Joe is going to compare the deal he's offering to other deals on properties that are being offered to investors. If his is well thought out and well presented, why shouldn't his family members invest in it? Who else are they going to invest in?

Part of the reason that some of his family members will invest in the deal is that Joe isn't asking for $300,000 from each of them; he's asking for $5,000 to $10,000, depending on his expectation of what each person can afford to invest. Let's say he has an uncle who is financially successful; Joe doesn't know his net worth, he just knows he is affluent. If he goes to that uncle and says, "Would you put $10,000 in this deal with me?," the uncle may say to himself that other people are asking him for a couple hundred thousand for other types of deals, so why shouldn't he support Joe by investing

$10,000—especially since Joe's deal is so sound? One of two things will happen: either Joe's request will be granted, or it won't, and then Joe will go on to other potential investors. And when Joe's first deal makes a profit, in all probability Joe's uncle will come to him!

How to Get Over Your Resistance to Approaching Investors

If you sense that you would be uncomfortable presenting your transaction to investors, it's probably because you have accepted a mental position that says it's impolite or improper to ask for money —especially for something that your mind tells you is self-serving. But by proving to yourself what a good investment you have put together you know that you will be able to benefit your investors as much as you are benefiting yourself. Knowing this, you realize that you are not only asking for something to support your own goals, you are offering something to your investors to support their goals. If you've made yourself an expert and done your homework properly, then:

1. you're not telling the investor to invest with you, you're presenting him or her with an opportunity to invest;
2. your investor stands to gain as much as you do from the investment opportunity—perhaps more, depending on how you structure the deal—and if there is a loss, it's your loss, too;
3. if you're willing to do the work to support the success of the transaction for everybody concerned, you have a right to ask investors to support your desire to become rich from it;
4. your potential investor can always say no.

It is important to inquire what laws apply to raising money from investors. In addition to very stringent federal laws, most states also have laws governing this area. Consult an experienced attorney before approaching your investors.

CHAPTER 15

STRUCTURING DEALS WITH PARTNERS, OR WHO GIVES WHAT AND WHO GETS WHAT BACK?

When you present your deal to your potential investors and they tell you they're interested in investing in it, naturally they're going to want to know the kind of terms you're offering them for their investment: What are they going to get and what are you going to get? Before they can even ask you the question you're going to show them on paper exactly how you will apportion the return and the profits. You'll also show them how you plan to structure the partnership.

I'm going to offer you several possibilities for the terms you can offer your investors. As with every other aspect of becoming a real estate entrepreneur, you have to see what terms the marketplace is offering investors for their money, and then make your terms on par with those or better; you also have to make terms that you are comfortable with.

SOME SUGGESTIONS FOR CUTTING THE PIE

One formula you might use in structuring a deal with partners is to specify that after the purchase the investors will get back the first money received by the partnership until they get back 100 percent of the money they've invested, and the rest will be split: 75 percent of the profit will go to them and 25 percent will go to you for putting the deal together.

Another formula you might use is to specify that when the building is sold the investors will get back 100 percent of the money they've invested, plus a fixed percentage per year for every year you've held the building; whatever profit is left after that, you will split 50-50 with them, and they'll get all the tax benefits.

When I first started putting together real estate investments I used the second formula I've suggested, giving my investors 100 percent of their original money back plus a reasonable fixed interest rate per year on their money prior to our splitting profits. My logic then, which I still think is sound, was that by giving my investors 100 percent of their money plus a reasonable annual return, I was telling them that they would benefit substantially before I took any profit. With these deals, I also charged a management fee for managing the property while we held it.

When I started working with my partner, Howard, we came up with a formula that we still use. When we acquire a building for investors, we always make a commission on the purchase of the property. We also charge the industrywide standard property management fee. From the time the investment is formed, whenever money is generated from that investment—whether the money is profits from rentals, equity buildup, appreciation, proceeds from *refinancing* the building (getting a new loan after the building has appreciated or after you've paid off some of the original mortgage), or profits from selling it—the investors get back 100 percent of the money they put in, we take up to 25 percent of the profit, and the investors get the rest.

THE HEART OF BEING AN ENTREPRENEUR

In my opinion, the formula that's fair for the promoter of the deal and for the investors of the deal has a lot to do with the positions of both parties. Our friend Joe, who has no track record and for whom this deal is a very important opportunity, would probably be wise to offer the investors extremely generous terms. If I were Joe —and I was Joe earlier in my business career—I would say, "The investor is going to put up all the money. Therefore he should get a good rate of return on his money before I get anything. He will get 100 percent of his investment back, then I'll give him 8 percent per year, and then I'll get 25 percent of the rest of the profit and he can have 75 percent." Joe feels he has to bend over backward to let the investors know that he's going to take the position that traditionally sea captains have taken—to be the last man to leave the ship.

Part of what you're saying when you structure a deal is that if anybody isn't going to make money on this deal, it's going to be you. That's why the investors get back all of their original money plus the interest they would have gotten on that money every year for as long as the property is being held, before the rest of the profits are divided. That's also why the rest of the profits are divided with the investors' getting at least 50 percent, maybe even 75 percent. When you set up a deal in this way you're making it clear that you're going to do everything you possibly can to make the transaction work so that there will be some profit for you.[1]

Joe knows that the only way he'll get something out of a deal structured in this manner is if he's willing to do whatever work the property requires so that it will realize his goal. He knows that he has to be 100 percent committed to his investors to do the best he can so that they can do the best they can with their investment. This means putting aside any false pride he has and devoting himself to the project without reservation. If he has to spend hours trying to find the best and most economical ways to solve problems in the building, he will, even if solving them might strike others as beneath his professional level. Remember when I stood outside my first apartment building and looked for prospective tenants? That is the entrepreneur's commitment: to do everything he can to find the best and the most economical solutions to the problems, regardless of the amount of time and energy it takes, and to *want* to do it. Joe has to be clear about this commitment, and he has to make it clear to his investors that he has this commitment. When they see this quality in Joe, they know why they're investing with him. Their

[1]When Joe is more experienced and has a proven record of success he can change the profit structure for future deals.

investment is as much an investment in Joe as it is in the property itself.

WHAT KIND OF A PARTNERSHIP SHOULD YOU MAKE?

Traditionally, the type of partnership that you would form if, like Joe, you were putting a deal together with investors, is a *limited partnership.* In a limited partnership, the *general partner*—Joe, in our example—has some exposure (meaning financial and legal responsibility), and the *limited partners*—the investors—have no exposure other than possibly losing the amount of money they've put into the investment (the down payment and the rainy-day fund).

The main concept involved in structuring any partnership for such a venture is that the person putting the deal together will take all the risks, while the investors risk only their initial investment.

The risks include not only the time and stress involved in handling the day-to-day problems of building management (which the limited partners never hear about), but also the legal risks. In the kind of partnership I'm suggesting, Joe becomes what is referred to as the *general*, or *managing partner:* if the tenants sue the landlord, Joe is the landlord. Joe will handle the forming of the partnership with the maximum tax advantages for his investors, by getting a capable tax adviser, an attorney experienced in this area (see chapters 18 and 19 on accountants and lawyers), who will instruct him on exactly what form it should be.

One important point in executing a partnership agreement is to make very specific arrangements for what will happen if more money is needed for the project. Will a vote be taken among the investors with the outcome to be decided by majority rule? In the event that the majority votes to put up more money and some partners don't want to, will investors have the right to buy each other out? At that point, will those who want out be able to sell their shares to anyone who wants to invest or just to those who are already investors? Who controls the decision making? What advantage will a partner who puts up more money have over one that won't put up his share in such a situation? Can the partnership sell off the interest of a defaulting partner?

The partnership agreement should consider all the possibilities of a deal. For example, if the transaction is the buying of an apartment building and the plan is to convert the apartments into cooperatives or condominiums and sell them, the agreement has to consider the possibility of what will happen if, because of a complication, the building isn't converted. Will Joe have the decision-making power in this case? Obviously, the more complex the plan for a property, the more possibilities the partnership agreement has to consider. With straight rental properties, there are fewer variables.

HOW MANY PARTNERS SHOULD YOU HAVE?

My personal view is that for someone like Joe, who is just starting out as a real estate entrepreneur, the fewer investors involved in the purchase of each property, the better. A good number would be five or six, and certainly no more than ten.

In order to determine how many investors you want, you have to start from your expectation and figure out what's realistic. For example, if Joe intends to raise $100,000, then five people would need to put up an average of $20,000 each; six would have to put up an average of about $16,650. Joe has to determine if it's realistic for him to expect that five or six of the people he is going to approach will have—and choose to invest with him—between $16,-500 and $20,000. He may decide he needs ten people who will invest $10,000 each.

The basic rule is to have the fewest number of investors who will provide you with the amount of money you need for your down payment and your rainy-day fund. In order to make certain that you comply with the regulations that may affect partnerships, be sure to consult with an attorney experienced in these matters.

GET IT IN WRITING

Before you approach investors you have to put the entire proposal in writing. This means, of course, that you have to become clear enough about how you see the deal to be able to put it in writing. We all have thoughts, fantasies, and hypotheses that may make terrific sense in our heads, but when you commit them to paper and read them back, it's a very different experience. The mere fact that you outline your deal and spell it out in detail in writing means that you're going to have to become clear about all the various factors involved, refine your thinking about these factors, and, if you find you haven't thought them out properly, restructure your thinking.

Once you've put your deal in writing, your next step is to distribute it to your Free Board of Directors. When you give the written figures to someone who has a nine-dollar calculator and a willingness to prove you wrong, you're going to see very quickly if you've made any errors. Distributing your plan to your Free Board of Directors becomes a tremendous double check. More often than not, you'll find that the investment turns out to look even better on paper than you had expected.

How to Write Up a Deal for Investors

Create a brochure or "offering memorandum." The first page gives the physical description of the property. The second page tells how much you are paying for it, how much you need for a down payment, what is going to be allocated for a rainy-day fund, and what is going to be allocated for legal expenses and miscellaneous fees. The third page shows a projection of income and expenses for the first year. The fourth page shows a projection for the next five years. The fifth page talks clearly about the tax ramifications for an investor (this should be drawn up by a CPA). The sixth page talks about the specifics of the financing, including pitfalls. The last page talks about the potential risks.

There should be a discussion of the risks in the investment. What can go wrong? Make sure you discuss this section with your attorney. Also have your accountant list all the tax considerations that he thinks appropriate.

The figures for the income and expense for five years must, of course, be a projection. If we're dealing with an apartment building in Los Angeles, say, we would project an increase per year in rents equal to what rent control laws allow, and then we would assume an increase for the expenses equal to the current cost-of-living rise. We carry out those figures for five years to show that because the income and expenses rise while the debt service remains fairly constant (assuming a fixed-rate loan), the profit of the building gets bigger every year. You have to devise your formula according to a conservative estimate of the rise of income in your area. In making your projections, remember that *it's better to underestimate income than to overestimate it.* Have your accountant go over these projections. If the scenario turns out better than expected, you're a hero.

In the section on the pitfalls of financing, tell what you know about the way the property is or will be financed and what adjustment you know will have to be made in the future. For example, let's assume that in eight years the first mortgage is due on the property Joe is buying. Joe will have to explain that the mortgage is due in eight years so that investors will know that if they still own the property at that point they'll have to refinance the mortgage or raise additional funds. Another pitfall of financing may be that the mortgage is a variable-interest loan. (See Chapter 16 for a complete discussion of loans.) In that case, you must tell the investors the terms of the loan and explain that the debt service could conceivably rise to a point that would make a significant difference in the investors' evaluation of the investment.

It's very important that your attorney and accountant inspect your brochure and give their opinions. Your offering may benefit from some prudent editing and legal and accounting advice. Your brochures should not be freely passed out. They should be numbered and a record must be kept for securities law purposes, so you know how many "offers" of this investment opportunity have been presented. Get legal advice about this procedure.

THE QUESTION OF A MANAGEMENT FEE

When Joe buys his first property he has to decide whether or not to take a management fee. My own feeling is that even as a beginning real estate entrepreneur, Joe should take a management fee. While he certainly wants to bend over backward to present investors with a generous opportunity, depriving himself of a management fee to sweeten the deal may ultimately make the deal sour for him. The management fee pays Joe for his time. It also makes him that much more committed to the building. Since the building may demand considerable attention, especially at first, Joe will put in his time more happily if he's getting paid for it.

The management fee of a building is always projected into the income and expense estimate of the building, so it's part of the budget anyway.

If you and your investors buy an apartment building, you should take the industrywide standard fee to manage it. The fee for commercial and industrial properties depends on how much real work is involved. If it's just bookkeeping, phone conversations, and opening an envelope with the rent check every month, the fee should be minimal. You may be entitled to a leasing commission on a commercial or industrial property, but you may decide to handle the leasing without charge as a function of your being a general partner.

The decision to take a fee may depend on how profitable the building will be. If this fee is not in your projections, it may seem inappropriate to take it. This should be discussed with your investors before the partnership is formed and mentioned in your partnership agreement.

It is important to note that in some areas it may be necessary to have a real estate license if you manage properties for others, including your own partnership. Consult your attorney.

REPORTS FROM THE FRONT: WHY THEY ARE ESSENTIAL

I strongly recommend making a complete quarterly report to your investors. We give our investors a copy of all the books and records of the property, and we give them a letter saying exactly what has transpired during that quarter; we also tell them what has transpired in the marketplace.

Generally, real trouble erupts only when general partners try to hide the truth from limited partners. Many times the general partners are not engaged in anything dishonest; they are just embarrassed about the financial condition of the investment so they try to cover it up in the hope that it will improve later. When that later never comes and the truth emerges, investors always see the missing information as the product of the general partner's lack of integrity and attempt to defraud them. The investors, angry at not having been informed, want to punish, rather than console, the general partner. Again, the truth is just the truth, and if you make total disclosure honestly and take complete responsibility for every fact, your investors will support you. Certain states have adopted limited partnership acts that specify a minimum standard and frequency of operating reports. Ask your attorney or accountant to advise you on this.

The key word in all this is communication: it keeps partnerships on the right foot.

CHAPTER 16

FINANCING: TODAY'S MENU OF MORTGAGES

A loan for your first real estate investment—whether it is a house, an apartment building, or a commercial or industrial property—will probably come from a savings and loan institution or a bank. They are the most aggressive lenders for loans of between $100,000 and $400,000. Larger lending institutions such as insurance companies generally make substantially larger loans.

EAST COAST/WEST COAST

Depending on where you live, the primary loan you take out to buy the property will be called the first mortgage or the first trust deed.

In some states, such as California, lenders use what are called notes and deeds of trust. If you are a lender, and I borrow from you to buy a house, we write up a note in order to recognize that you have lent me money, which is secured by the house. Then, to make sure that you have the right to take the house if I don't pay you, we agree that a third party will hold the deed to the house, and we each instruct him that if I don't pay, he'll hand you the deed. We both "trust" him to hold the deed for the length of the loan—that's why it's called a *trust deed.*

The owner of the property is called the *trustor;* the person who holds the trust deed is called the *trustee,* and the lender is called the *beneficiary.*

In other states, particularly in the East, buyers traditionally take their loans in the form of a *mortgage.* The borrower is called the *mortgagee;* the lender is the *mortgagor.*

FIXED RATE VERSUS ADJUSTABLE RATE: ADVANTAGES AND DISADVANTAGES

There are two basic types of real estate loans: *fixed-rate* loans and *variable-rate* loans.

A fixed-rate loan is paid back at a constant interest rate. At any given time in the market the interest rate on a fixed loan varies from one bank to another, as do the "points," or fees charged to initiate the loan, the *prepayment terms* (if any fees are charged for early payoff), and the length of the loan. A variable-rate loan (often called a "VIR") generally begins at a lower interest rate than a fixed-rate loan, and then rises or falls in direct proportion to a specified index.

Variable-rate loans are still in their infancy in the United States; as late as 1981 nobody had heard of them. Today, they're very common because lenders are reluctant to commit their funds for long periods at a fixed rate when interest rates may leap higher; if rates rise rapidly, lenders could be in the position of having to pay their savings account customers more interest than they collect from their borrowers. That's why most VIR loans "float" at a predetermined rate over an index that is theoretically based on the cost of funds from savers.

Fixed-rate loans have been popular because they have the enormous advantage of being predictable. But when interest rates began to rise, variable-rate loans became more attractive to some buyers, especially since lenders went out of their way to make the initial rates very low. Problems started setting in, however, when some buyers who could afford the initial lower rates found they could not afford the increases.

As these problems became evident, consumer groups began to pressure lenders to make a more realistic relationship between the lower initial rate offered and later rates. Lenders were also forced to spell out the rise more clearly to borrowers, and some put ceilings (called *caps*) on future interest. These changes are also new. For the moment, it is basically a "buyer beware" situation.

The entire process of applying for a loan is frustrating at best. Borrowers often make bad loans simply because they are convenient. Many borrowers lack the patience needed to go through the process of finding a good loan.

Most variable-interest loan rates have a beginning rate below the rates used for fixed-rate loans. But this low teaser rate generally applies for only between six months and a year, at which time the rate may change drastically. If you pinned down the lender and asked him what the loan would cost after the teaser period if all other variables remained constant, he may have to tell you that it would rise considerably. All indexes change constantly according to market conditions. Once you know this, you have to decide which kind of loan would be most advantageous. The primary advantage of variable-rate loans is that they are easy to find. Currently, they are a mainstay of the lenders' loan portfolio. Every major lender offers them; fixed-rate loans are harder to find, and because of this, lenders who offer them may also be more selective.

Another advantage of variable-rate loans for investment property is that since they start off at a lower-than-market interest rate, they initially give you a better cash flow by lowering your debt service during the teaser period. If you turn over your property before the interest rate rises, then your property has generated a better cash flow for the entire time you've held it than it would have with a fixed-rate loan. The more positive a cash flow you can present, the more attractive your setup on the building will look to your prospective buyer. This makes it very tempting to choose the VIR. That's why the most important fact to find out is what the rate of the VIR would be after the teaser period, and how much and how fast it can go up.

I will use my previous example of a good buy for a hypothetical apartment building in an average Los Angeles neighborhood (60 percent of income covers debt service, 40 percent covers expenses; it breaks even; the purchase price equals 7 times the gross rent roll; the per-unit price is $37,000 a unit) to illustrate the difference between fixed-rate and variable-rate loans. If you are playing by these rules and if you use a variable-rate loan on a $100,000 mortgage, then, if the variable-rate loan is 10 percent for the first year, the loan will cost you about $10,000 a year. Using a fixed-rate loan at 12 percent, the loan would cost you $12,000 a year. The difference would be $2,000 net income. Many investors buy property based on cash flow only. So if your buyer is willing to pay an amount that will yield 5 percent on that $2,000 income stream, then you divide 5 percent into the $2,000 and you get $40,000. On that basis, the apartment appears to be worth $40,000 more with the variable-rate loan.

Thus a variable-rate loan initially makes the property better sardines for eating, and, as a consequence, it may also make the property better sardines for trading, too. In fact, at least in theory, variable-rate loans have some advantages for the sardine game. The variable-rate loan is especially palatable because in theory it doesn't make a difference if the loan rate goes up or down; it will always stay in proportion to income and expense.

With a non-rent-controlled apartment house, for example, as long as tenants' leases are month-to-month or yearly, the worst that can happen is that as soon as the cost of money goes up—which means that the variable-rate loan goes up and therefore debt service on the building goes up—the cost of the apartments will go up correspondingly. In theory you are not economically hurt. As soon as the cost of money goes down, the cost of the apartments will go down. One can logically assume that variable interest rates will be judged by the same market factors that make money and rents go up and down, so your interest rate will go up and down in a parallel fashion. *In theory, then, the ratio between rental income and debt service always would be nearly the same.* As a result you can't get caught in the middle. And have you ever seen rents go down? Generally the law of supply and demand will favor the landlord's keeping rents up even in times when interest rates go down.

If, however, you're buying shopping centers or commercial properties where tenants have long-term leases, and rents can't be raised monthly or yearly to reflect the higher cost of money, then a variable-rate loan could easily produce a situation where the income would not produce an adequate cash flow to service the debt. Even with apartment buildings where tenants have longer than one-year leases, or where rents are controlled or stabilized, you can find yourself in trouble with a variable-rate loan. Variable interest rates are not appropriate for people who don't like to live with uncertainty.

In evaluating whether or not you want a variable-rate loan, you have to view all sides of the issue. I think that the trendline of any index used by a lender will be up over ten or twenty years. But over a five-year span, the trend could easily have a few ups and downs, which, on the whole, may not be too painful. It may even present you with a bargain.

The drawback to a variable-rate loan is that it may go up much higher than a fixed-rate loan. If you hold on to your property for longer than the teaser interest rate applies, you may find that your income doesn't meet your new expenses, and the property drains cash. In time, if the variable-rate loan continues to rise and if it's still not worth your while to sell the property, you may have a substantial negative cash flow.

On the other hand, you can calculate the expense of a fixed-rate loan for its entire length. Typically, this will be your major expense on the property, and knowing what it will be allows you to project the expense of the loan more realistically than you possibly could with a variable-rate loan. Aside from giving you more sureness in your financial planning, a fixed-rate loan also helps you to calculate a more realistic rainy-day fund—since none of it will be eaten up by increased mortgage payments—and gives you the flexibility of knowing that you can hold on to the property until the market tells you that you want to sell. You're not going to be forced to sell because you can no longer make the mortgage payments.

Although over time a fixed-rate loan may cost you far less than a variable-rate loan, its main disadvantage is that it will cost you more initially. It's also possible that after you buy a property interest rates on loans will fall, and you'll find yourself tied to a fixed rate with a higher monthly payment than you'd be paying if you could initiate a loan at the new market rate. If, however, when you originally approach the lender about the fixed-rate loan, you negotiate one which states that you can pay it off early without having to pay extra money—(a prepayment penalty)—then, if there are lower interest rate loans available, you may simply renegotiate or pay off your loan and take advantage of the lower rates. This is one form of "refinancing the mortgage."

Let's say that in order to get your first mortgage on a property you must agree to a prepayment penalty with your fixed-rate mortgage. If interest rates fall and you want to refinance the mortgage at the lower rates, you can figure out if a new loan at the lower interest rate would make it worth your while to pay the prepayment penalty plus the costs of the new loan. If the new interest rates are low enough, even paying a prepayment penalty and new loan costs might be insignificant compared to the amount of money you'll be saving on your future payments. Unfortunately, some lenders making fixed-rate loans want these loans "locked in," to protect them in case loan rates do go down, so they may build in very costly prepayment penalties or even not allow a prepayment for the first few years.

If I have to initiate a new loan on a property I'm buying, I prefer a fixed-rate loan because I would rather know what my expenses are going to be than gamble with a variable rate. At this point, I'm not as interested in the sardine game for trading as I am for eating. I want deals that don't have any major risks. I also don't expect rents to go down; I expect them to go up. The worst that can happen with a fixed-rate loan is that I'll get what I expected. Given the choice between the risk of a VIR and getting what I bargained for, I'll take getting what I expected and forget about variable-rate loans.

If future interest rates surprise me and fall significantly, then I know I can renegotiate the mortgage at the lower rate, and if I have to pay a prepayment penalty, I know exactly what it is and it's easy to figure out if it's worth paying.

Your decision on variable-interest versus fixed-rate loans should be determined on the following basis:

1. Will the deal work at the rate that the VIR would be at after the teaser period is over?
2. Would the fixed rate that's available be attractive compared to the after-teaser VIR, assuming rates stay constant?
3. What are the annual and lifetime cap rates on the VIR?
4. How long do you expect to own the property?

5. Is the fixed-rate loan transferable to the next owner? If it isn't, and you're planning to sell in a couple years, what do you gain with the fixed-rate loan? The new buyer may not benefit from it.

6. If you're planning to own the property for a long period and the fixed rate works today, why gamble? If rates go up, you win; if they go down, you can refinance; if you can't refinance because it isn't practical with the numbers involved, you still get what you bargained for.

7. If VIRs are available and no fixed rates are available, ride the horse in the direction it wants to go—get a VIR.

Remember that although smart guys like me who have been around a while may be saying, "My goodness, I don't want a variable-rate loan, it's too uncertain," many, many smart guys are making real estate deals today with variable-rate loans.

THE ADVANTAGES OF ASSUMING THE SELLER'S MORTGAGE

Frequently, the best loan you can get on a property is the one that the seller already has. The seller's mortgage may be beneficial because it may be at a lower interest rate than current market rates. In addition, often a seller has a huge equity in the property being sold. In a situation like this, ask the seller to lend back some of that equity himself. This can be done as a first loan, a second loan, or even a third. These loans can be negotiated much more attractively than institutional loans—no points, no penalties, and better rates.

If you are considering assuming the seller's loan and only a short time remains until it must be paid back—say one to three years—then you have to figure out what will happen when the loan is due. At that point, you would have to renegotiate the loan at prevailing interest rates, which might be far higher than those on the current loan. If this happens, your debt service would go up to the point where the cash flow of the property would change significantly.

This is one of the pitfalls of financing that you have to disclose to your investors when you approach them with the deal. If you are the sole investor in the deal, then you have to know exactly where you'll get the money to cover the higher debt service if the cash flow of the building doesn't provide it. You also have to determine if it's to your particular advantage to get involved in this situation. In general, you should not buy a property based on favorable financing if the time remaining isn't sufficiently long to merit paying a premium for it.

No such problems exist with buying a property on which there is a long-term low interest-rate loan that you can assume. Financing is a large part of the life or death of a property. It has a value in itself, and you have to be able to analyze the difference between good financing and poor financing.

Let me show you why this is so.

We will use the same model I've given you for figuring out the income/expense ratio for apartment buildings, which says that approximately 40 percent of the income goes to expenses (a category that covers everything except debt services) and the other 60 percent goes to the debt service; this model projects a break even. Using this model as a basis for analyzing a deal, *the interest rate on the debt service can drastically inflate or deflate the purchase price of the property.* Here's how.

Again, let's assume that the gross scheduled income on a property is $100,000. With 60 percent available for debt service, the debt service would be $60,000. Let's also assume that our down payment will be fixed at $175,000. Now, if $60,000 equates to the debt service on an *interest-only loan* (meaning there is no reduction of principal on the loan) and the interest rate is set at 10 percent, the total loan will be $600,000. Added to our down payment of $175,000, the total purchase price of the property will be $775,-000. If, however, the interest rate is set at 12 percent and the debt service equals the same $60,000, then the total loan is $500,000. Added to our down payment of $175,000, we have a total purchase price of $675,000. Therefore, the lower interest rate means we may pay more for the property.

I'm providing you with this example merely to show you how rates affect purchase prices. If you were given these alternatives, the choice of which is actually a better deal is very subjective. The factors that make one choice preferable to the other are:

1. the length of the loan;
2. the loan's transferability;
3. the tax consequences of one choice compared to another;
4. the interest rate of the loan vis-à-vis the purchase price. By paying a premium for the financing you may be overpaying for the property based on its reproduction cost; if a higher purchase price makes the cost per unit (or cost per square foot) skyrocket, the deal may not be worth making.

The general principle to keep in mind is that the value of the property theoretically goes up and down dramatically in proportion to the interest rate of the loan that you owe against it; the lower the interest rate on the loan, the higher the value of the property.

HOW DOES A BUYER OR A SELLER OR A LENDER LOOK AT A PROPERTY?

When an appraiser evaluates a piece of property, he looks at it from three different points of view:

1. what it would cost to reproduce (this is called the *replacement factor*);
2. its economics (how much net income it generates);
3. comparable market values (what other people have paid for a similar property).

When I want to buy a piece of property, I appraise it in much the same way. I determine:

1. how much I'm buying it for per square foot compared to the cost per square foot to reproduce it (this is the replacement factor); or, if it's an apartment building, what the CPU and GRM are compared to similar buildings that have sold recently;
2. what I'm going to get as the rate of return on the investment;
3. what other people are willing to pay me for the property if I sell it.

When you look at a property, you have to examine it from all these points of view, see what factors have the heaviest weight for you, and determine what you think about the property.

Everything I'm telling you about financing is a factor in terms of the cash flow of the building, which, of course, determines the yearly rate of return on the investment. If you're paying higher rates on a loan, the same building will not have as great a cash flow as if you were paying lower rates for the same loan.

Lenders, too, look at properties from the same three perspectives: replacement, income, and comparison. The information provided by appraising a property from these perspectives is one of the main factors that determine if lenders will grant you a loan and how much they will lend you on the property. But the same information can lead different lenders to different decisions. It can also lead different buyers to different conclusions about what price they will pay for the same property.

Go to lender A and say, "I want a loan equal to 80 percent of my purchase price at an interest rate that will take 80 percent of the building's annual income to make the payments," and lender A will feel there will not be enough income left after expenses to make your payments. If, at the same time, lender A knows that in the event he forecloses on the property he's going to get it at a very advantageous price, he may close his eyes to the fact that you won't be able to make your payments and grant the loan, because he doesn't see himself as having much "real" risk if it doesn't work out. Lender B, in the same situation, would refuse the loan because foreclosing to make a profit isn't his style, and he doesn't want the aggravation.

Just as there are people in the real estate marketplace who play all the angles they can think of and calculate how they're going to come out, there are people in the lending marketplace playing the whole gamut of angles from a straight line to a total circle. Many lenders have a rule of thumb that they will loan no more than the property can legitimately be expected to pay to cover debt service while safely maintaining all other expenses, and other lenders will lend far beyond this point, regardless of the ratio of debt service to income. Some lenders won't loan to anyone who has ever had a bankruptcy; other lenders don't care about previous bankruptcies. Some lenders look only to the property for security; others take into account the borrower's integrity and history. It really is a question of the personality of the lender.

SHOPPING AROUND FOR A LOAN

Shopping for a loan is nearly as important as picking out the property. You must comparison shop.

If you start talking to all of your friends and business associates (your Free Board of Directors) about the various components of loans and what is being offered in the loan marketplace, you'll find that there is almost as much information available about loans as there is about properties, and it is less subjective. Most people are unaware of how important it is to learn this information and how to make use of it.

It pays to familiarize yourself with the loan market when you look at properties. That way you have a head start on figuring out what your interest expense will be, which will help you calculate how much you can afford to pay for the property. Once you find the property, having this knowledge about loans at your fingertips will give you an edge on being able to write up the deal profitably.

As we've noted, each institutional lender has its own unique personality. Some of them are a lot more aggressive than others and will loan larger amounts of money. Some are more in touch with the times than others. Some have more liberal requirements for a borrower than others. If you don't make a commitment to investigate the personalities and practices of all the lenders in your area, you may not end up getting the best deal possible.

In choosing your lender you will have to take several factors into account. The first, of course, is the initial interest rate of the loan. The second is the length of the loan—the longer the loan, the smaller the monthly payments. If the loan is to finance an income-producing property, a fifteen-year loan will have a rapid equity buildup at the expense of a lower cash flow or spendable income that would occur using a thirty-year loan. If the loan is to finance an owner-occupied residence, the higher payment of a fifteen-year loan may not be painful when weighed against the alternative of thirty years of payments. The third factor is the prepayment penalty (will you be able to pay off the loan early if it's to your advantage to do so?). The fourth factor will be how many points the lender is currently charging to make loans, as well as any other charges or fees the lender will require. One lender will insist on the borrower's paying for an appraisal, while another lender will not. You must ask each individual lender what all its charges will be.

Points are what banks call "initiation fees." They will be charged and paid for at the time the loan is taken out. Each point is equal to 1 percent of the loan. So if the lender charges two points to make a $100,000 loan, he will be getting $2,000 in extra fees. I look at points as additional interest on the loan. In practice, they call for another judgment and decision on the part of the buyer (borrower). If you are talking about a twenty-year loan at 10 percent and you expect to own the particular property for twenty years, then you can rationalize that the rate is only slightly affected: $2,000 amortized over twenty years is only $100 per year—which is very little for a $100,000 loan. If it's a ten-year loan (and the interest rate and number of points remain the same), it's twice as much per year—$200—which is still not very painful. But what if the loan isn't transferable and your expectation is that you will own the building only for one year? Then, even though the loan may be a ten- or twenty-year loan, since it isn't transferable and it serves only the purpose of being the financing that you need to buy the property for that one year, then the 10 percent loan will really cost 12 percent. The points are tax deductible over the life of the loan.

In the end, the lender's charges (points) will be one more factor you must consider in making the major decision of whether or not to purchase a particular property, and a larger factor involved in the decision about which loan to choose. Remember that lenders vary widely as to how many points they charge on similar loans. Many times the points end up partially as commissions to outside *loan brokers* (independent agents who arrange loans for lenders and do not work directly for the lender). It's fair game to negotiate the loan costs when you're negotiating with a lender; again, the worst that can happen is that you don't get exactly what you want.

The next factor is whether the lender will give you the loan without an *acceleration clause* (an acceleration clause means that the loan is not transferable and has to be paid off if the property is sold); without it, you can transfer the loan to the next buyer if he wants to assume it.

If you got a transferable fixed-rate loan, and if the interest rate on that loan is lower than the market rate at the time you're ready to sell your building, you can transfer that lower-rate loan to your new buyer. This will make the property much more attractive at the time of sale if interest rates have risen, and you can therefore charge more for the building. So by having a transferable loan without a stiff prepayment penalty or lock-in position, you have a potentially great advantage.

By negotiating with various lenders in order to get these factors in your loan, you will know that you've asked for everything that could benefit your deal and that you left no homework undone that could have made the deal better.

For a variable-rate loan, there are two other factors you must consider in deciding where you will initiate your loan. First, you have to compare the initial rate being offered by the various lenders and the points; next, and equally important, you have to compare the terms by which each lender's loan will rise. Be sure to check what index the lender is using to calculate the percentage the interest rate will rise or fall per year. Each institution can choose from a variety of different indexes, and this choice has crucial repercussions for you. By checking the performance of the various indexes over the last ten years, you will see if the index used by each of the lenders has shown dramatic or gradual rises. Compare one index's performance to the performance of other indexes.

Learn the formula each lender uses to calculate the rise, and make comparisons among these formulas, too. Be sure to ask each lender what the interest rate would be today if there were no teaser period. See if there are hidden penalties. Also, see which lenders put a cap on their variable-rate loans, and if there is an annual cap—so that, for example, even if the cap for the entire length of the loan is 5 percent, the annual interest rate can be raised no more than 1 percent in any one year. Find which cap is the lowest. The cap is important, since it may assure you of modest raises in volatile periods. Some lenders may also have a low-end cap, a rate below which the interest will not fall. Variable-rate loans are made to float over an index that represents the cost of funds to a lender. The lender wants to make a profit over that amount, so he charges on top of it. Therefore, in the lender's language, the loan rate to a borrower may be "a sum equal to 200 basis points over the specific index used by the lender." Thus, in addition to comparing indexes used by different lenders, it's important to compare how many basis points over the index one lender charges to what the next lender charges and to translate this difference into dollar amounts that would apply to your property.

PAPER: SECOND AND THIRD MORTGAGES

When the word *paper* is used in real estate transactions, it often refers to second and third mortgages (or second and third trust deeds). When sellers help finance the property by making a second or third mortgage to a buyer it is called "carrying back paper." Second and third mortgages are fairly common. They are usually made by the seller to induce the new buyer to purchase the property.

By doing this, sellers generally find the property is easier to sell, because the buyer doesn't have to make as large a down payment. The buyer could conceivably find a professional lender to make this same loan so the seller would actually be *cashed out* (having his entire selling price in his pocket). But this inducement by the seller makes the transaction look "sexier"—as if the buyer gets something for nothing. For this reason, when a seller makes a second or a third mortgage, it is traditionally on very attractive terms.

When first loans are relatively easy to come by and have reasonable terms, many sellers feel it isn't necessary to carry back much financing. *Getting the seller to carry back paper is generally a plus for you in the financing.* There are three reasons for this:

1. The interest rate is often lower than the institutional rates and it doesn't involve any extra costs.
2. It creates greater leverage for you as the purchaser, since the more that is financed, the lower the down payment.
3. The seller may later give a discount for an earlier payoff.

I've taken advantage of this third benefit many times. Let me run through an example of how, after the purchase of a property is completed, you would buy up the paper at a discount. For the sake of this example, I'd like you to look at the transaction from the point of view of the seller, to see why as the seller you would give someone a second trust deed and why it would be acceptable to reduce it in return for a quick payoff later.

Let's say you're the owner of a building, and you list it for sale at $1 million. Someone who wants to buy it approaches you. He says he will put down 25 percent and get a first mortgage for 65 percent, if you will carry back 10 percent of the deal in paper in the form of a second loan. You negotiate back and forth during the contingency period and finally agree on a selling price of $975,000 —a penny more or less and the deal would break. Let's say that in reducing the price of your building $25,000, you decide you're going to take the $25,000 off the paper, so you're still carrying $75,000 in paper. Now everybody's in agreement; everybody's pushed as hard as he could.

The paper is to be carried ten years at 10 percent paid interest only. That means that for ten years the buyer will pay you $7,500 per year. If you assume that the mortgage goes out to the end, and you assume that the value of money that you could get in an alternate investment is 12 percent, then you're going to lose 2 percent a year on $75,000. Ten years means a loss of over 20 percent (10 years × 2 percent) or $15,000. So if some months later the buyer of the property comes back to you and says, "I'll give you $75,000 less 20 percent today [$15,000]," and if you have something better to put the money into, you will be thrilled to take it. But if at the time of the sale the buyer had said, "I want to take $1,000 off the purchase price," you would have said, "No," and it would have stopped the deal cold.

I often give seconds on the properties I sell, and I usually write them up at the lowest interest rates possible. Let's look at the same deal I outlined above, and I'll show you why I do this. Seeing why it's to my advantage as seller not only teaches you why you would do the same thing as seller; it also gives you information you can use to negotiate a low-interest second or third mortgage with a seller.

Let's assume that the buyer of the $1 million building expects a cash flow or return. If he pays 13 percent on a second mortgage of $100,000, that means he has to give me $13,000 a year to service that loan. But if I change the interest rate on the loan to 10 percent instead of 13 percent, that same $13,000 can pay me 10 percent on a $130,000 loan instead of 13 percent on a $100,000 loan. So I can ask $1.03 million for the property and the buyer gets the same cash flow. I always take the lowest interest rate because I would rather have a low-interest rate and a higher purchase price for the property.

Another reason I like to give people as low an interest rate as possible on second and third mortgages is because more often than not they sell the property in a few years anyway. So no matter what you give them in financing, provided you have put an acceleration clause in the loan, the entire loan gets paid off when the property changes hands anyway.

If the buyer says he won't buy the building if I insist on an acceleration clause, and if I want the deal to go through, I will take out the acceleration clause. It often doesn't even matter if I don't have an acceleration clause in the second mortgage I'm carrying. Here's why: in general, most first-trust deeds have acceleration clauses. So when the new buyer sells the property, he has to deal with the acceleration clause in the first-trust deed—which means that the holder of the first-trust deed will ask to be paid off or for a change in terms in the loan when the property is sold. As soon as the first-trust deed holder asks for a material change (the interest rate going up) of terms, the holder of the second-trust deed technically has to approve them. If you as the holder of the second-trust deed won't accept the change in terms—which you are not legally required to do—then you get paid off anyway, even if you don't have an acceleration clause.

Thus, as a buyer it's important to know that even if you negotiate with the seller so that you get a second- or third-trust deed without an acceleration clause, you still may not be able to transfer that loan to a new buyer when you sell the building.

The last reason to give a low-interest carryback loan is to make the deal look good in order to attract potential buyers.

A FINAL WORD

Borrowing money from a savings and loan institution or insurance company on real estate is different from borrowing for personal use, such as borrowing to pay for a vacation. With real estate, the loan is secured to the lender. If you don't pay, he takes the property. Since the property can't be picked up and moved (like a car or a boat), he is sure he will have something to collect, regardless of what happens to you. Therefore, lenders have an entirely different way of handling these loans from personal loans.

Generally, there are special loan agents to handle loans on properties, and their compensation is often tied to the number and dollar amount of loans they generate. Often, the potential borrower never even physically goes into the lending institution. The agents are much more interested in getting the loan made because it may mean more money in their pockets. The lender is primarily making his decision of whether and how much to loan based on what the property is worth rather than what your personal net worth is as the borrower. There is no reason to feel squeamish about applying for this kind of loan. A refusal from one lender doesn't mean that you'll be turned down by all lenders. Many lenders are also very greedy, and will make a loan that others won't if they get more points or a higher interest rate than their competitors are receiving. Getting mortgages and trust deeds is a laborious task, but in the long run it is simple. Don't be intimidated by the process.

CHAPTER 17

WHEN INTEREST RATES ARE HIGH: HOW TO MAKE THEM WORK FOR YOU

In conversations about real estate, the topic of interest rates invariably comes up. I'm going to begin this chapter with an extremely basic statement: *low interest-rate loans are definitely better than high interest-rate loans.* That said, I'm going to add to it what may strike you as a more controversial statement: *if high interest-rate loans are the only loans available in the marketplace, you can use high interest-rate loans to purchase properties and still do very well on them.*

High interest rates tend to frighten people and add to the resistance we all have to taking action. Since most people are afraid that if they put themselves on the line they might find out they've made a bad decision, they'd rather resist taking action and complain. And one of the perfect things to complain about as far as real estate goes is interest rates. They give the investor an excuse: "Why bother to look?" "Why bother to make a deal?" But the truth is that although interest rates are a major component of whether a real estate deal will pan out, they are not the only component that will make a deal work.

If you decide you want to be an active real estate entrepreneur in a high interest-rate climate, then you have to find out how higher interest rates modify the rules of the games: you have to discover what kinds of real estate games are played in high interest-rate markets. Then you can begin to see how you can use high interest rates to your advantage.

Let me start you on the road to observation by pointing out that in any economic climate, there are always people in the marketplace who want to buy and others who want to sell. People will compensate for high interest rates by giving some other benefit, and obviously, the biggest benefit they can offer is selling a property at a better price. Even if high interest rates drive the price of property down, there will still be people who will want to sell during that time.

The trick in a high interest-rate period is to find someone who is willing to sell a building based on a fair return after deducting the high interest rates. When you do this, you know that if interest rates come down again and everything else remains the same, you are going to make a large profit on the building because you can sell it to the next buyer at a significantly higher price than you paid for it—because he will be able to get a lower interest-rate loan.

HIGH INTEREST RATES/LOW INTEREST RATES: ONLY THE SHAPE OF THE DEAL CHANGES

Any business deal, especially a real estate deal, can be compared to a balloon. Let's say you have a round balloon, completely filled with air. If you put your hands around the middle and squeeze, the balloon conforms to your fingers: instead of being a round balloon, it is now an hourglass-shaped balloon. But the same amount of air is in it. The theory holds true when you apply pressure to the components of a business deal to make them accommodate one particular pressure imposed by the market, such as high interest rates. It will look a little different, but if it's a well-structured deal it will still be an equally solid deal.

The opposite occurs when interest rates are high and you get a deal on a property that shows a good return because you are able to assume the previous owner's low interest-rate loan, but the loan has only a few years to go; then you have to see how the deal will change in the future when that loan is due, and determine if it will still be a good deal. You have to ask yourself, "Is it smart for me to buy the property with this loan on it? Am I paying a premium for attractive financing?" It's fine to pay a premium for financing that is truly attractive—a low interest-rate loan for a long period with no acceleration provisions. If the loan is for a short period, you have to know how you'll compensate for the extra expense that will be incurred when the loan is due if interest rates are higher. Will this pressure make the balloon burst?

A deal that works with a high interest rate is generally much safer than one that works with a low interest rate. When rates come down it can be refinanced creating a larger yield. This is where we come back to one of our general rules of financing. If you get a high interest-rate loan, you want to make sure that there's no provision locking you in so that you can't pay off the loan. To get the most out of your investment, you must be able to pay off a high interest-rate loan in the event that the interest rate falls significantly.

How Commercial Tenants Are Responding to Fluctuating Interest Rates

Before 1980 interest rates climbed or fell at a modest rate. Today, with the lending marketplace offering shorter-term loans and with fluctuating interest rates, most tenants of business properties are forced to compensate for the situation in which property owners find themselves in regard to loans.

Many of our commercial properties are rented by convenience stores owned by major corporations. In the past, most of the leases were written for long periods (perhaps twenty years) at a fixed rate of income, and we would get a small percentage of the gross if the store's income exceeded a specified amount. For years that was the only kind of lease the tenants would accept; now most of the leases contain escalation clauses increasing the rent.

The reason for this change is that these companies have no choice. Most landlords, when given the opportunity of renting to a solid tenant but one with no upside potential, have to say they won't do it. Knowing that they are facing a big downside potential with a mortgage that will most likely go up or have to be refinanced, landlords can't afford to take even the best tenant without allowing for the eventuality that their mortgage payments may go up in a few years. Even the biggest companies can't dictate the rules that were made for a different marketplace. They have to play in the current marketplace or stop expanding. I think that all major businesses are accommodating for fluctuating interest rates; just as the balloon in our example allows for pressure, so does the business world.

ARE INTEREST RATES EVER TOO HIGH TO MAKE A DEAL?

No matter how high it is, the interest rate is only one factor among others in the deal. If the price is low enough, no interest rate is too high. The question really becomes: What is the income compared to the expenses and the debt service? When viewed as a whole, is it still a good deal?

There's another way to answer the question of whether or not interest rates are ever too high to make a deal.

Let's say that a piece of industrial property has a very low rate of return from the tenants, and a very high interest-rate loan, so there's going to be significant negative cash flow. Let's also say that the tenant has a lease for ten years at a fixed rent, so you know you're going to lose money on it for ten years. Deals like this are made all the time. Some investors like them because the replacement cost of the property might be so high that even with ten years of negative cash flow the property is still a bargain at the price for which it is being offered on the marketplace.

For example, the replacement cost of the industrial property might be $1 million if it were built today, but it's quite possible that it can be purchased now for only $500,000 on the basis that for the next ten years it would lose $10,000 a year. As the potential buyer of a property like this you would have to guess what the rental climate and demand for the property will be in ten years—since the property's future value is what this particular deal is all about. You might end up saying to yourself, "In ten years the location is going to be even better than it is now; so the fact that I'm able to buy it for half the price of its replacement cost today makes it a tremendous value! I'll make a killing on it when the present lease expires."

So even a deal with a high interest-rate loan and a long-term cash loss can be terrific for somebody. It wouldn't be terrific for Joe, because that would be a great deal of money for him to raise to carry the ten-year negative cash flow. Equally important, he isn't as interested in being a millionaire ten years from now as he is in creating a lot of money today. But this kind of deal is perfect for someone who has plenty of money to put away, and who is willing to set a long-range goal.

When interest rates are very high they tend to throw a wet blanket on the real estate market for most people who are earning their living in real estate. When interest rates rise you have to raise yourself up to the level of observation in order to look at the whole real estate deal being offered, to see if it's worth taking. Don't discount any deal simply because interest rates are high and they're discouraging the "biggies" in the business.

People who have been dealing in real estate professionally for some time generally find it hard to raise themselves to this level because they are old dogs unwilling to learn new tricks. If you're just coming into the market you have to start playing by the rules you see, but you also have to start in the marketplace exactly where it is at that moment.

No matter where you come into the game, the game has no beginning, and it has no end. Real estate investment is going to be here as long as we are a free democratic society. And as long as we are a free democratic society, you can always start playing the game. If interest rates were to rise to 15 percent, it would make it dreadful for many old dogs, but 15 percent interest rates will not make it anything other than "the way it is" for the new people coming in.

What makes the system work is the astonishingly simple truth that every property has an owner, and because every owner will eventually need to sell or die, it stands to reason that occasionally each piece of property comes onto the marketplace: perhaps at a time when loans are at 8 percent; or when loans are 10 percent; or when loans are 15 percent. There will always be a market or a "game." And there will always be players—the interest rates are just one of the factors that keep the game spicey!

CHAPTER 18

BRINGING IN THE PROFESSIONALS: WHY YOU NEED AN ACCOUNTANT AND HOW TO CHOOSE THE RIGHT ONE

Although in all probability an accountant and a lawyer will not be members of your Free Board of Directors—because, except in very unusual circumstances (such as your being married to one) they want to be paid for their advice—you will need their expertise in completing most real estate transactions and in owning and managing properties. They may be important in determining how good a deal is or they may simply help you execute documents and file tax returns in the proper manner. How much or how little you need an accountant and a lawyer depends on your degree of sophistication in the areas in which they are experts.

Before you go into the real estate marketplace, I'd like to give you an idea of the kinds of services these professionals can provide for you, and what you can do to create an optimum working relationship with them. This means creating a relationship based on clarity: the clearer you can be with accountants and lawyers about your needs and objectives, the better you will be served in getting your needs satisfied and accomplishing your objectives and the less expensive your bills will be.

BEFORE THE CLOSING

Once you've tied up a property, accountants can perform two basic services to help your decision on completing the deal. The first is to look over a deal and determine if you're really getting what you think you're getting; the second is to help you figure out how to make the deal fit you.

The right accountant will review your analysis of the deal and give you his opinion of whether any aspect of your financial analysis is incorrect. He may report to you, for example, that what you're expecting in tax ramifications will not be there, or that, based on your preliminary numbers for the property and the seller's fact sheet, he believes that you are being sold a pipe dream.

The accountant can also help you reconcile your projection about the future to the reality of the property. If you bring him the preliminary numbers—the current rents for the property, a projection of rents for five years, and a projection of the expenses over the same period—the accountant can prepare a projection with tax consequences that allocates the depreciation and estimates what the return on the investment will be. If you are going to bring in investors to complete the purchase of the property, you can use this information in your presentation to them.

PROTECTOR OF YOUR TAX BENEFITS

After you own a property, your accountant is the expert who ensures that you get all the tax benefits you are entitled to. As I mentioned earlier, it's un-American to lose money in real estate. Through its tax system, our government encourages us to buy and to own real estate through such benefits as depreciation, the deductibility of mortgage interest payments, and tax-free exchanges.

From year to year, the specifics of the tax laws change. Historically, even after the tax reform of 1986, the laws have always favored real estate investors. For example, while the former nineteen-year depreciation period for an apartment building allowed a larger deduction from your income tax each year than the current 27½-year depreciation period allows, the present depreciation rules still provide an enormous advantage.

Because accountants keep up with the modifications in tax laws from year to year, an accountant is going to be your best source for information about exactly how those tax savings can be maximized through your real estate holdings.

WHY EXPERIENCE COUNTS

I mentioned that the accountant with whom you would consult about buying, owning, and selling real estate must be one who is experienced in real estate. Accountants who don't deal frequently with transactions similar to the one you are making may not have the information you need on hand and have to learn the information you require—at your expense! When professionals have to do research before they can perform services for you, you may end up paying them to do research instead of paying them to share their expertise. What you get in this circumstance is a higher bill and less expertise.

Another value of using accountants (and attorneys) who deal in real estate on a regular basis is that they may lead you to other people who will help you. Often they have clients who are looking for real estate investments, and many such clients call on their accountants and attorneys to point them toward potential investment partners.

HOW DO YOU SELECT THE RIGHT ACCOUNTANT?

When you're starting out, don't go to a large national accounting firm. The fees they charge may be higher than those for similar services from a smaller firm, and as a beginner in real estate, you would probably be given to the firm's low man on the totem pole instead of a more experienced senior member of the staff. Your ideal accountant, then, is either on his own or with a small to medium-sized firm.

Talk to the accountant who has been preparing your income tax returns. See if he has clients who are serious investors in real estate, and what work he has been doing for these clients in terms of tax preparation and real estate investment planning.

If you've been doing your own tax returns and therefore don't have an accountant, talk to your friends, relatives, and acquaintances to find somebody who is a serious investor in real estate. When you locate this person, ask him who his accountant is. If the accountant is with a large national firm or if he commands top fees, then ask the investor for a referral to a smaller firm. If he doesn't know of one, you may ask his accountant for a referral.

The way to narrow down your choices is to start with the accountant who sounds the best to you and meet him face to face. Does he have the expertise to work for you? Does he seem right personally? Compatibility is important because, as you'll discover, accountants often become their clients' psychiatrists and confessors. At the very least, you need an accountant with whom you feel comfortable enough to be totally candid.

In order to find the right accountant—or to find out if the accountant who's been doing your tax returns is the right accountant for your new career in real estate—you have to describe the types of real estate deals you are considering and ask: "What kind of experience do you have in transactions of this nature?" If the accountant says, "I've had a lot of experience, I've been representing clients with similar interests to yours for ten years, and I haven't had any changes on any audits," then you have received a satisfactory answer. What makes it satisfactory is his ten years of experience, not that he hasn't had any changes in his audits.

Why is this so?

Real estate accounting is much more subjective than other types of accounting. There are many times when it is impossible to make a black or white choice. As a result, many situations come up in the course of a real estate transaction with a five-year history that a conservative accountant will interpret one way and an aggressive accountant will interpret another. Depending on the interpretation, there will be a very different tax result for the owner(s) of the property.

An aggressive accountant tends to interpret the gray area of deductions by taking advantage of them in a single calendar year; an accountant with a more conservative approach tends to use deductions over a period of years. The net effect of these sometimes vastly different approaches is that if you write something off quickly today, it may save you on your taxes today, but it doesn't save on your taxes five, seven, or ten years from now.

Here's how the difference in interpretation can affect you. The rules specify that certain items involved in owning and operating a property should be capitalized and other items should be expensed. Capital improvements are defined as work paid for to add value to the property; expenses are defined as operating costs.

Let's say that you want to add character and potential value to the ten-unit apartment building you've just bought by cleaning up the landscaping, painting the exterior, and improving the maintenance of the hallways and the other public areas. You also decide that in four of the ten apartments you are going to change over the old tenants to new tenants, and that you're going to install new carpets and draperies in the new tenants' apartments and raise the rents. One accountant may decide that the costs for accomplishing these changes should be depreciated over time as capital improvements; another accountant may think they should be deducted immediately as current expenditures; still another may view them as a mix of each. How an expenditure is interpreted thus has important effects on your current cash flow.

An aggressive accountant tends to save today whatever is possible to save today; a conservative accountant tends to spread any expenditure in this gray area over the longest possible period because that would be the safer route. A conservative accountant may never have had his tax returns changed when they are audited because he's so conservative that he's never taken an aggressive stance on anything. The other extreme is an accountant who is so aggressive that he takes an aggressive stance on everything, and his returns are consistently adjusted when they are audited.

No accountant is going to tell you, "I am an aggressive accountant. I write off anything." But you may find an accountant who says, "I'm very conservative. Our audits are always no-change audits, because everything I do is by the book." The point is that you have to be aware of these differences and realize that they may have consequences for you. Use this information in interviewing accountants to find the one you're most comfortable with. And change your accountant if he turns out to practice in a way that makes you uncomfortable.

Don't expect an accountant to be a financial counselor who says, "Invest in this" or "Invest in that." He can keep track of your affairs and answer your questions and do tax planning. The more specific questions and information you have on hand, the more you will be able to benefit from your accountant's expertise—and the less expensive your bills will be.

CHAPTER 19

BRINGING IN THE PROFESSIONALS: WHY YOU NEED A LAWYER AND HOW TO CHOOSE THE RIGHT ONE

After common sense and preliminary research have told you that you're looking at a good and affordable deal, your next step is to have your offer with contingencies written up accurately and in a manner that protects you totally. In making certain that the deal that is written up is the deal you think is being written up, and in making certain that you are protecting yourself against any eventuality, a competent attorney with a background in real estate transactions usually is required.

The key to determining if and when you should enlist an attorney is simple: Do you understand every word contained in every document connected with the transaction? Do the words say exactly what you want them to say? If the answer to both of these questions is yes—great; you may not need an attorney *yet*. If there's any doubt in your mind, you definitely need one now.

If you are bringing in investors as partners, you also need a lawyer to make sure your partnership agreement says exactly what you want it to say, and that you are protecting yourself in it against any eventuality in the future of the partnership.

DO YOU WANT A DOCUMENT MAKER OR A SELF-PROCLAIMED ALTER EGO?

The first thing you have to know about lawyers is that they generally come in two types. One type says, "Tell me what you want and I'll document it," and the other type takes the position of acting as an entrepreneur on behalf of his client and using a "literary license" on the transaction himself—whether it is requested or not. Since attorneys can handle your transactions in either of these ways or by combining both approaches, it's very important for you to be clear about what you want from an attorney.

An attorney of the first type will tell you if the deal is documented in the proper way, and he'll tell you what pitfalls lie ahead from the standpoint of contractual obligations. But he probably will not discourage you from making the deal even if he just saw somebody else make a deal for a similar property on better terms. He won't impose his business judgments on you, just his legal skills.

At the other extreme is an attorney who feels that nobody can do anything better than he can, so he'll tell you that whatever you're doing, you're doing it all wrong. "Why are you buying in Greenwich Village? You should be buying in St. Louis!"

I've been involved in real estate long enough and I have a strong enough personal point of view and personality that I'm willing to hear what people have to say, make myself the judge, and totally disregard anyone who tries to move me around arbitrarily. So I listen to the comments made by this kind of an attorney and then tell him, "Thank you. I'll plot the course, you do the legalese."

But a novice in real estate may very well want an attorney who acts as an evaluator because he needs help. In this case, he must beware of becoming totally discouraged if his attorney says something that makes the transaction look stupid. So if you find yourself gravitating toward a lawyer who will put his "business stamp" on your deals, make sure that while you give yourself the full benefit of his services, you do so without surrendering all your power to him.

You have to realize that an attorney (or an accountant, for that matter), expert though he may be, is still just a person with his own ideas. He is not a wizard; he may know even less than you do about the deal you're working on. Many good deals have been ruined because the client placed too much authority in the hands of other professionals.

The main precept to remember is that no matter what an attorney (or an accountant) tells you, think it through—and then test it. If what you hear discourages you, and yet you still have positive feelings and are therefore confused, go back and present the information to the rest of your Free Board of Directors once again. Start approaching people and say, for example, "Well, you know the attorney told me a lot of bad things are happening on the West Side. Uncle Fred, what do you think of that? Do you agree?" Take notes on what the attorney and the accountant say so that you are sure that you're presenting the information they've given you accurately. Was the attorney giving you legal advice, or was he just giving his own personal business opinion? It's unwise to make the attorney or anyone your authority figure. Listen carefully to their ideas and make sure you fully understand them. Armed with your integrity and your intuition, you and you alone are the final judge.

If your attorney's advice proves to be sound, and you think you can get an agreement from the other party to make the changes the attorney suggests, then by all means put his advice into action. But don't let the attorney get carried away in trying to carve out a better and better deal or you may end up with nothing. *If you're unsure about his negotiating style or his skill, don't let him show off his cleverness at your expense.* Keep checking your written notes: remind yourself of the figures and conditions that you felt constituted a good deal.

As you look for an attorney, keep in mind that you want to find one who represents you the way you want to be represented, both in style and substance. You want a person with whom you are proud to be associated. If you hire an attorney who calls everybody an obscene name, his behavior is going to reflect on you with the seller, the broker—anybody he deals with on your behalf.

MY RULES OF THUMB FOR WHEN AND HOW TO USE AN ATTORNEY

As a novice, you will find that the way to get the most out of your attorney is to:

1. come from the truth and tell the attorney that this is your maiden voyage in real estate;
2. describe the deal to her;
3. let her know if you simply want her to write down the components of the deal or if you want her to negotiate the deal for you.

This last point is very important. If you don't need an attorney to negotiate the deal for you, and if your attorney is charging you an hourly fee, then telling her you will negotiate for yourself will save you a substantial expense. If you are negotiating for yourself, then your attorney's job is to act as the legal facilitator in creating and reviewing the necessary documentation for the deal, and you have to make this clear.

While communicating about what services you want from an attorney should be easy, people often create their own difficulties with this task by regarding the attorney as being more successful and powerful than they are, and therefore they defer to them. Many people won't go to an attorney and say, "This is what I want you to do," even if that's exactly what they should be saying.

Many attorneys are aware of this problem, of course, and they may open their conversation by asking, "What do you want me to do? Do you see me as the negotiator? Do you want me to just write the agreement down? Do you want me to counsel you?" If a lawyer fails to put these questions to you, then you may ask: "How do you see your role? What can you do for me?"

YOU AND YOUR LAWYER AS A NEGOTIATING TEAM

If you're going to have an attorney negotiate for you, it's important for you to know that attorneys are often categorized as "deal makers" or "deal breakers." *You want a deal maker.* Unfortunately, you never know if he is a deal breaker until he is in the process of doing it—and then it may look as if he is saving you, not hurting you. Here is where you take your lumps and learn for the next time.

This is not to say that you want to make every deal you look at —you only want to make a deal that the process of checking and double-checking proves is right to make. But you don't want an attorney breaking a deal that you want by negotiating points that aren't important to you just to show what a good attorney he is.

Before your attorney goes into a negotiation for you, make certain that he goes over the deal point by point with you and that he will be stating exactly what you want.

If you are using your lawyer as a negotiator, you may find that it's effective to have him negotiate certain issues and that you will negotiate other issues yourself.

One attorney I know advises his clients who are first-timers in real estate not to tell anyone that they sought the advice of an attorney. He advises his clients to deal with the other party and just use him as a resource. He tells them that they can always bring him in at the last minute if they need him as a final means of negotiation.

He observes that sometimes if you admit to a relatively unsophisticated person that you have consulted an attorney, he may feel the need to get an attorney for himself and he may adopt a defensive posture. At that point, the attorneys sometimes get so involved in their own interplay that they overpower the buyer and the seller and ruin the deal.

DEALING WITH YOUR ATTORNEY'S ADVICE

Let's assume that you do bring in the attorney after a firm deal has already been struck.

If you, as the buyer, instruct your attorney to read the agreement and tell you if he sees anything inappropriate, then the attorney will give you professional advice based on what you've written up. As a smart buyer, I suggest that you add: "Do you see anything you think I should do that I'm not doing? Do you have any experience in transactions like this that you'd like to share with me?" Then you'll be getting the benefit of any advice the lawyer may have that's relevant to your deal—and his advice may help you to improve the deal considerably.

Remember, however, that after you hear what the choices are, and your attorney gives you his advice, you have to do what may be the hardest part of dealing with a lawyer: you have to decide what you want. As important as your attorney might be in the transaction, you and you alone are totally responsible for what is happening, even in your first real estate transaction.

Many times, your attorney will make good suggestions for restructuring a deal that is already agreed upon. Let's say that you're buying a furnished apartment house. You've already written up the deal and you bring it to your lawyer, who comments, "You know, if you could get some of the purchase price allocated to the furniture, the tax law lets you write off furniture faster than real property, so there's a tax benefit." A change like this may not cost the seller any money, because it's all purchase price to him. So as a potential buyer you can present this to the seller and say, "I'm sorry I didn't know this before. But this is more favorable to me, and it really doesn't cost you anything."

Agreeing on the Cost

It should be relatively easy to determine in advance the ball-park cost of an attorney's services for a particular transaction.

Describe to the attorney the kind of a deal you're going to make and ask him what his fee will be. Since your first deal is going to be a simple one, he should be able to give you a quick and reliable answer.

As you deal in more complex matters where the purchase price is much larger and more money is changing hands in all directions, it becomes more appropriate to work out a fee arrangement with your attorney in written form.

Once you decide on an attorney, it's crucial that you ascertain at the initial meeting what his rates are and what he's going to be doing for you. Then ask him to estimate what the entire procedure will cost you and, if his answer is satisfactory, make it clear to him that you are allotting that amount from the budget to cover his services; if he sees that his fee is going to rise above that figure he should inform you before you incur any more expenses. Have him put all of this in a letter to you so that you have a record of your agreement.

Remember that when you call an attorney on the phone to ask him a three-minute question he's going to bill you for more than three minutes because it's going to take him time to stop what he was doing when you called and to pick it up again and reconstruct where he was. Therefore, it might be more economical—and probably more informative, too—for you to schedule one fifteen-minute meeting or phone conversation with him to discuss several matters than to make five three-minute phone calls.

HOW DO YOU SELECT THE RIGHT LAWYER?

Ask friends, family members, business associates, and your real estate broker for referrals to find a lawyer who knows enough about real estate to be an appropriate choice for you. As a second step, go to the local bar association; most have specialty subgroups to which members belong on a voluntary basis. If a lawyer is paying to belong to the real property section of your area's bar association, he probably has more than a passing interest in real estate.

In narrowing down your field of choices you should find an attorney with a general practice and broad experience in real estate, rather than an attorney at a large law firm made up of specialists in all different areas.

If you work with a generalist lawyer you are building a relationship with one person who can perform many functions for you, from reviewing contracts and giving you advice regarding your buying and selling real estate to handling legal problems and even litigations. Not only is his service to you strengthened by your personal bond, but you may save money on your legal bills, since he alone is handling all your legal needs. In a firm of specialists, you may have to pay a bill for a counseling session with one lawyer, only to have to pay a separate bill for another counseling session with another of the firm's lawyers who specializes in another area. "Gang tackling," as this practice is called, is often more expensive for the client.

You are looking for someone you feel comfortable with, someone with whom you can communicate well, someone who doesn't sit across the table and regard you with a patronizing air. You are looking for a lawyer who sees himself as providing the exact service for you that you need a lawyer to provide, one who will act almost as your partner in the sense that whether or not he is going to negotiate for you, he is going to "live" the deal with you. His goal should be to see it completed successfully for all concerned.

Just as you don't want to go to a large national accounting firm, you don't want an attorney so prominent that your deal will seem insignificant to him—even if you can afford his fee. You need an attorney's best efforts, not his diluted attention.

I like to have an agreement from the lawyer that he will handle the affairs himself, not pass the matter on to a junior person in the firm—or even a senior person in the firm. You're building a relationship, and personal rapport is important. Every time a new attorney starts on your account, a new bill will follow for the time he's spent learning the facts—even when you've already paid to explain the facts to the first attorney!

One day can determine the outcome of a real estate transaction, so you should also have an agreement that your calls will be returned within the same day unless a major problem in the lawyer's life prevents him from doing so. I will use only an attorney who will make and keep this agreement.

On a fundamental level, you have to have faith in the skills and integrity of the attorney you hire. You have to say, "If I'm paying this person to represent me, I'd better well trust him. And if I don't trust him as a person or I don't trust in his expertise, I'm a fool for using him." You can protect yourself in your relationship with your attorney by constantly establishing the kind of objective standards I've talked about. When you ask your attorney in direct, specific terms what his role in this transaction will be, what the time schedule is, and how he envisions acting as your counselor, it prompts him to come up with a clear commitment. It also makes you start to think of other concrete ways he could help you.

HOW DO YOU USE THE ATTORNEY TO STRUCTURE A PARTNERSHIP?

Remember: only a fool enters into a partnership arrangement without a written partnership agreement.

As a matter of law, most jurisdictions require a written partnership agreement. If you want to take title to a property in the name of a partnership, and if you want to file a partnership tax return, you must have a name and you need some documentation. You want the document to define exactly what your role is, and what your partners' roles are.

When Joe buys his first property, he is going to bring in partners and use an attorney to help him draft a partnership agreement. The two basic choices available to him for this agreement are a limited partnership or a general partnership. With the counsel of his lawyer, he will decide on one or the other based on:

1. which type of partnership, according to the current tax laws, allows him the greatest flexibility in distributing the tax benefits to the investors;
2. whether he wants to have sole control of decision making or whether he wants the investors to share in the decision-making process;
3. which type of partnership provides the kind of exposure to risk that the investors agree to assume.

The real issues are: Who is in control? Whose deal is this? Who calls the shots? Who's primarily responsible? Who do you need to sign the documents? Where will they be when you need a document signed? Will making the investors into decision makers create a situation of too many cooks spoiling the broth?

Since you're going to win or lose on your efforts, my advice is to *keep the investors as investors and to keep control for yourself.* Have your role clearly documented as holder of the reins; have your investors' role clearly documented as that of investors.

People are often afraid to speak openly to their partners and say, "You know, I intend to do the following . . ." They are afraid that their partners won't like them, won't trust them, or won't agree to their conditions, and this fear keeps them from putting forth their intentions in writing. Ride through this fear if you find yourself experiencing it; the success of your deal is based on that documentation. The attorney's job is to draw up this documentation for you, to make certain that it is binding, and to see that it covers everything you want and need it to cover.

When forming a partnership, review a worst-case scenario with your attorney. The documentation you come up with has to prepare you for every "what if" that can be imagined. This has to be done with care, because you don't want to portray the "worst case" in such a way that it will scare investors out of the deal. But it does have to be done, and it has to be done accurately.

You should know that the most common problem that arises with a partnership is if the partnership becomes cash-shy. In these situations, there's always a dispute: Who's going to come up with the money? What do you do if he doesn't come up with the money? Spell out in the agreement what would happen if these problems arose.

As the entrepreneur, you must not assume that the person who promises to come up with the money will, in fact, come up with the money. Your contract has to plan what will occur if he doesn't. My lawyer friend keeps advising his clients, "Plan for an exit." Who gets to sell the property? Who gets what percentage of the money when the property is sold? State everything with complete clarity.

Sometimes there's a Pandora's box aspect to drawing up a partnership agreement with an attorney. Often, as the attorney and the client review all the "what if"s, the attorney comes up with a point the client either hadn't considered or had brushed aside. Because the attorney considers it his duty, he will say to the client emphatically, "This is something that you're absolutely taking a risk on." Very often I think that the attorney who maximizes the possibility of risk scares people off.

This is extremely unfortunate. It's like refusing to sign your will because you get scared by the thought of dying. *Remember: no deal is risk-free.* After your attorney has told you that something is a risk, you have to be able to ask him, "Do you think it's a good business risk to take?" If he's not the kind of person who's going to level with you about it—if he's only going to try to play it safe by saying things like "Do what you want, it's your decision, not mine"—then you're never going to make a deal. It comes back to what we noted earlier about active risk takers versus inactive risk takers.

In every transaction there's a point where you must take a risk. You have to be as prudent as you can and ask all the "what if"s and when you come to one that's probable as well as possible, you have to examine how you would deal with it if it did happen. Be aware that many attorneys have a tendency to overemphasize the risk involved. If you have a strong conviction that a deal is solid and that you have the resources within yourself to deal with a "what if" should it come to pass, then you are right to go ahead with the deal.

CO-OPS AND CONDOS: A SPECIAL GAME NEEDS A SPECIAL LAWYER

Although a generalist lawyer with real estate experience can handle most real estate transactions for you as well as most aspects of real estate ownership, there are certain situations in which only a specialist lawyer will be qualified to provide the service you need.

If you are interested in buying apartment houses for conversion to either cooperatives or condominiums, for example, you definitely need an attorney with vast experience in conversions in the specific locale in which the property is located.

A lawyer experienced in these conversions already has models of all the contracts you will need to complete such a transaction. For him, it's just a matter of going through the many steps of conversion that he's gone through before—steps that can consume time and your money if an attorney without conversion experience is retained.

If I were thinking about condominium conversion, I would discuss the possibility with a lawyer specializing in that field to find out if conversion was possible with a particular building I had in mind and what would be required if I could and did go through with it. The real question is, do you have something that's marketable once you've made the conversion? Be prepared to investigate and be the sole judge of that question. It is truly your decision.

CHAPTER 20

MYTHS VERSUS REALITIES: FORECLOSURES, PROBATES, "NO MONEY DOWN," AND AUCTIONS, OR ANGLES ARE SO HARD TO FIGURE

The four categories of real estate transactions that I'm going to describe in this chapter fall under the general classification of "playing an angle." These angles have been around for a long time, and today they enjoy a greater mystique than ever as ways of getting the most for your real estate investment dollar. Indeed, the mystique is so strong that many people play one or more of these angles without first investigating their realities.

The question I'm going to analyze is: Can you acquire a property more advantageously by playing the angles? In other words, in the broad picture, what's so good about these techniques?

I'm going to show you why you can often make better deals in the general marketplace without all the effort and struggle involved in trying to play an angle.

FORECLOSURES

When most people hear the word foreclosure, they think it means they have the opportunity to get something for nothing. They imagine that they're going to see a property that nobody else has looked at, a property that isn't known to the marketplace. They know that the opportunity has arisen because somebody else has defaulted on his payments, and they feel that that person's misery will be their good fortune.

The myth here is that foreclosures generally present deals that are as good or better than those presented in the normal marketplace. What makes it a myth is that it's based on two false assumptions: that the people whose property is being foreclosed didn't know that they had a gem and therefore didn't see the value in it, and that there was a substantial equity in the property that was being lost.

The truth is that a foreclosure takes a long time—often a minimum of three to four months—and since the people who own the property will have used that time in every way conceivable to get themselves out of their mess, chances are that if there was a substantial equity or value greater than the total indebtedness on the property, they would have made a deal with someone along the way to help them solve their problem. Most likely, someone who saw the value of the property would have either lent or given them the money, or someone would have bought them out or have bought a participation in the property to "cure" their mortgage.

Although it's certainly true that there are plums to be had in the foreclosure market, finding one is like looking for a needle in a haystack. You may know that somebody put the needle in the haystack, and you could search for a very long time to find it. What you will find if you search the foreclosure market is that most of the foreclosure properties are not plums; that's why the owners are losing them. They borrowed every cent they could against the property and then stopped making payments. Often they were months behind before the lender started the formal foreclosure process, and this situation creates large debts—back taxes, legal fees, and miscellaneous costs that eat up the property's equity— possibly totaling more than the property is worth!

The other assumption about foreclosures that people often make is that whoever they are going to be buying the foreclosure property from is going to be selling it at a bargain price. I want to make it very clear that nobody in the real estate game just rolls over and plays dead. Nobody says, "I don't have enough money to make the payments, so I'm going to lose my big equity." The probability is that when a property is foreclosed, there is little or no equity left, and the selling price will be about equal to market value.

The foreclosure process varies from state to state. In many states, the lender serves the property owner with a legal notice. The owner then has ninety days during which the lender can do nothing, regardless of whether or not the owner makes any payments. If the owner pays the lender what he owes within the legal period (including fees, penalties, and costs), they both act as if nothing happened: The default is deemed cured. A notice of sale has to be published a specified number of times in a legal newspaper and it must state the sale date. When the property goes to the sale, the sale has to be held in such a manner that any interested person can bid. The highest bidder gets the property.

The proceeds from the sale are distributed in a specific order of priority. The funds are applied toward the first mortgage, anything left over goes to the second mortgage, and anything beyond that goes to the third, and so on. Whatever is left after all secured loans are fully paid, including fees and costs, goes to the person who was foreclosed.

Now let's invent a scenario in which you as a potential buyer find a property currently in foreclosure.

The first step is to research the property in order to determine its value. We'll assume that the property is a house, and your research tells you that it would be a good buy at $100,000. In the public records—or through the help of a title insurance company —you discover that there are three mortgages (or trust deeds): a first for $70,000, a second for $10,000, and a third for $10,000, thus making a combined total of $90,000 in mortgages. Let's also say that the owner is currently six months behind in all his payments. It is eighty days after the notice of default, and still in the cure period. Assuming the average interest on the owner's mortgages is 10 percent, he owes about $4,500 in back payments. There are also penalties, fees, and miscellaneous costs of another $5,000, so that in all, $9,500 is owed on the property besides the $90,000 in mortgages.

There are basically three possible ways to acquire the property in this foreclosure situation.

1. You can buy out the person losing the property. This means approaching him and saying something to the effect of "You're going to lose the property anyhow. It may ruin your credit, and you'll have nothing. Why not sell it to me for $500? I'll make the back payments and you'll have a good credit rating and something in your pocket." (Or you can work out various other offers with him—such as paying him nothing up front and giving him some money later, when you sell the property.)
2. You can wait to see if the property goes to auction, and, if it does, you can be the highest bidder.
3. You can attempt to buy out the holder of the first, second, or third mortgage and continue the foreclosure on the note you've just bought.

But what have you bought with any of these three methods of playing the foreclosure angle?

If you use the technique of buying out the existing owner who is being foreclosed before the cure period is over, then you've acquired a $100,000 property by taking over $90,000 in debt and paying $10,000 in cash ($9,500 for the back interest and costs and $500 to the previous owner). So, at minimum, you've spent $100,-000 for a $100,000 property. (If you structure the deal differently, striking an agreement with the owner for him to turn over the property to you without your paying him anything up front but promising him cash at the time you sell the property, you will end up spending more than $100,000 for the $100,000 property, because you're probably going to have to offer him more than $500 out of your potential profit in order to induce him to accept a deal like this.)

If the property was beyond its cure period, you may also have to pay off with cash the mortgages that can no longer be cured because the lenders insist on cash now.

Using the second technique, being the highest bidder at the auction, the purchase price could be about the same, if the lenders insist on getting paid in full for their loans or they will take back the property themselves. If they are not firm about collecting the full amount and they are willing to take the highest bid, then you may get the property for less than $100,000. The point is that it's their prerogative, not yours. With this technique, your bid will have to be made in cash.

The third technique requires a great deal more effort and can be the most profitable. Using this technique, you would attempt to buy one of the mortgages from its holder, and continue the foreclosure yourself. Generally, these mortgage holders fall into two categories: those who insist on payment in full for their loans, and those who fear further economic and emotional risk in the property, and will therefore sell their mortgage for less than they are owed on their loan by the current property owner.

Several things might happen after you've bought one of these mortgages at a discount or at full value. If, for example, you buy a first, second, or third mortgage and continue through the foreclosure process, the existing owner may cure the mortgage and you will then simply be a lender according to the note's original terms. If you bought it at a discount, then the property's owner would still have to pay you the full amount, and you would therefore profit by the discount.

If the property owner doesn't cure the loans and the property goes to sale because you're foreclosing on it and no one bids, you end up with the property. The pitfalls are that if there are trust deeds with greater seniority than the one you just bought (let's say you bought the third mortgage, so the first and second are still ahead of you, totaling $80,000), then you must cure those in order to protect your position.

So, with this technique, if you are able to buy a mortgage at a discount, you have much more control. At a minimum, you have locked in a purchase price equal to the first mortgage ($70,000), the second ($10,000), and the price of the discounted third, plus back interest and costs. If you were able to buy the $10,000 third at a discount of 50 percent, then you would own the $100,000 property for the total of the $70,000 (first mortgage), $10,000 (second), $5,000 (discounted price for the third) plus back interest and costs of approximately $9,500—actually a little less because you would get a savings on interest and expenses attributable to the mortgage you bought at a discount. This gives you a total purchase price of slightly under $94,500 for a property you've appraised as a good value for $100,000.

By buying the mortgage at a discount, at minimum, you also lock in a profit if another party bidding for the property paid the total of the first, second, and the third mortgages. So, for example, if you were able to buy the $10,000 third mortgage for a 50 percent discount, and the highest bidder at the auction bought the property for $100,000, you would get paid the full value of your note ($10,000) even though you paid only 50 percent of that ($5,000).

The real key to foreclosures, then, is the same as the key to any other real estate transactions: the ability to see value. Making a profit on foreclosure properties boils down to finding foreclosure properties on which the total indebtedness is much less than the properties' true value. This is a sure thing only if you are willing to own the property. My experience is that the process of foreclosure itself eliminates most of these opportunities. Generally, people are so emotionally involved in their real estate that they don't let go without exploring every avenue of action, and, as I said before, the foreclosure process gives them time—months—to find the answer, to cure the problem.

Even after doing a great deal of work, you as the buyer can run into a surprise detour or a dead end. For example, the current owners may already be in the process of going bankrupt. Once you make a deal on the property, they can still go bankrupt, and the bankruptcy courts can stop the foreclosure, change it, or delay it.

Another aspect to consider is that when property owners know they are going to lose their property, they frequently try to salvage everything they can from it. Thus, in all likelihood, a foreclosed property may not be in good physical condition. Often, it will not be properly maintained. Sometimes, out of vindictiveness to the lender who is foreclosing, the former owners may intentionally damage the property.

Even if you can buy the property before it goes to auction as a foreclosure, the deal may not be as good a deal as you could make by going out in the general marketplace and finding a similar property.

It's also important to remember that all foreclosures have to be made a matter of public notice, so everybody who's looking in the foreclosure market can easily find leads. With so many people today writing books and giving seminars on foreclosures, a lot of potential buyers are trying to find a bargain; so in addition to the time constraint that is an inevitable part of foreclosure, there is also a lot of competition. And this competition means that you can do a lot of work and still not end up with the property.

Remember: you have the entire marketplace to choose from! And from that marketplace you can pick a property in your price range that you like, and you can negotiate a good price for that property. I can't repeat too often that in the general marketplace, because you're not playing an angle, many times you have the power to negotiate a deal that is much better than a foreclosure deal.

This doesn't mean that it's never wise to go to the foreclosure market—it just means you have to know that if you do, you're fishing in a small bay instead of an ocean, that you're dealing with far more restrictions in your process of fishing, and that there are a lot of sharks in the water.

PROBATES

The myth about probates is basically the same as the myth about foreclosures: that you're invariably going to get something for nothing.

What happens in a probate is that somebody dies and leaves a piece of property in his estate, and the estate decides to sell the property. The executor of the estate becomes the business manager for the property. She may expose it to real estate brokers; she may expose it in all the traditional manners of marketing a property. Sooner or later somebody makes an offer that is accepted. At that point, the court has to approve the sale.

The court generally approves the sale by announcing the bid the executor of the sale has approved, and then inviting other interested parties to bid a higher amount. In this way, the court is protecting the estate's interests and assuring itself that the highest possible price was obtained. In order to be fair to the original bidder who made the offer that was accepted by the executor, the court opens the bidding to other interested parties at an amount that must be higher than his bid. In California, the overbid must be 10 percent of the first $10,000 offered by the original bidder and 5 percent on every $10,000 over that. Thereafter, the court may set minimum increments for bidding. *Thus, the main problem with probates is that even if you negotiate a good price on a property, you can still lose the deal to a higher bidder.*

THE MYTH OF NO MONEY DOWN

One of today's most popular myths is that there are innumerable people who no longer want their properties and who are anxious to sell them to you with "no money down." *The truth is that even though people may not want their properties, it doesn't mean they will give up their equity if they are in a position to keep it.* Let's take the case of a seller who has tried to get his equity out of the property by selling it, and has had no success with traditional methods. Under the "no money down" theory, as his last resort that person finds somebody who says, "I'll buy your property, under one condition—if you finance the entire purchase price." The seller will take a note for his equity, and the buyer will then pay him off over time.

The general rule is that "no money down" deals are extremely unattractive to sellers, and thus rarely does this opportunity present itself on a good property: Owners of a good property feel they can make a better deal. Only a desperate seller will sell for "no money down."

An essential fact about real estate is that neither the buyer nor the seller makes a snap decision that cannot be altered. A seller who no longer wants his property and takes a "no money down" offer probably has gone through a lot of soul-searching to get himself to agree to it, and he's going to accept such an offer only if there's no better way for him to sell his property. This more than likely suggests that there may be something wrong with the property.

The trick to making money in real estate is to find the "best" property regardless of its down payment and create the down payment money; don't simply buy "any" property because its owner has little alternative but to sell with no money down. *Remember that in the regular marketplace by tying up a property with contingencies, you can get an option with "no money down" and nothing to lose.* Using *this* "no money down" principle, you have the entire pool of all properties on the marketplace to choose from. And you can make an offer and have it accepted before you spend one penny! Then raise the down payment.

AUCTIONS

Properties go to auction not only when they are in probate or in the last stage of foreclosure, but also when an owner decides that an auction is the best way to market his property.

The main myth about auctions is that as a buyer you're going to find a "steal"—a property that nobody else is going to know about and nobody else is going to see.

In fact, however, people often end up paying more for a property than they would have paid had they bought the property by the traditional method.

The primary reason is that once they're at the auction, people get infected with "auction fever." Say you go to an auction to buy an apartment building that you read about in the newspaper. You know the building's location and its rent roll. You've had the opportunity to examine it on inspection days, and you decided that it's worth $250,000. Often, even knowing this, people will get caught up in the intensified atmosphere of the auction and will buy the same building they've evaluated at $250,000 for $325,000 just because everybody else was bidding on it and the price rose so quickly that they were left without the time to reassess the situation.

In a straight auction that is not the result of probate or foreclosure, there are no standard rules. The seller and auctioneer decide how the auction will be conducted. Once the auctioneer points to you and says, "Sold!" there may be no alternative but to pay what you bid, no matter what you discover later.

In general, selling property in a real estate auction is quite similar to selling a property through normal channels, except the seller through his broker-auctioneer presents the property to all potential buyers at once. Usually the seller and the broker-auctioneer agree to a minimum price for which the property may be sold and below which there will be no deal.

Once the seller has made the decision to auction off his property, he generally pays the broker-auctioneer to advertise and expose it to the marketplace. By the day of the auction, the seller has already paid the auctioneer a substantial amount of money. So the seller and the broker-auctioneer—who works on a commission—want to make sure that, if someone ties up a property in the auction and doesn't go through with the purchase, he will still pay them a substantial amount of money. Even more preferable from their point of view is setting a rule saying that a person can't tie up a property without going through with the deal. If the buyer were given broad contingencies, the whole expensive procedure could prove to be a waste of time.

Worse, if the buyer has the prerogative not to go through with the deal, the seller and broker-auctioneer have, at least to some degree, spoiled the property because once potential buyers realize that the property went for *x* number of dollars, it's established in their minds that that's the most they should pay for it. So although some real estate auctions do have contingencies, most good real estate auctions do not.

Thus, as a buyer, you have to be aware that auction fever isn't the only problem with auctions. The other, equally significant problem is that, in most cases, you really can't evaluate the property as well as you would be able to were it in the open market. If it's a well-run auction, you have to come up with a substantial amount of money in cash and commit to the property at the auction. And since auctions rarely give you contingencies, they don't present you with the opportunity to tie up a property and then go out and prove or disprove the property's value. Also, you won't necessarily be able to bring your Free Board of Directors to the auction: even if you are able to do so, they are liable to catch auction fever, too.

So in an auction just about everything that normally protects you gets partially negated because you have to act instantly, and you are then committed to consummating the deal with very few, if any, ways to escape.

If you are irresistibly drawn to an auction, it's a good idea to write down the top price that you're willing to pay for the property being auctioned off beforehand. If you're tempted to keep bidding just to save face by staying in the race, just look at your piece of paper and stop there! Also be sure that you know in advance what the auction's cash requirements are (how much cash you would be required to put down as a deposit on the property) and whether or not you can have contingencies written into the purchase if your bid is accepted. Find out, too, if there are penalties for acting on these contingencies and not going ahead with the purchase.

Given the choice between traditional auctions, foreclosures, and probates, I would work on probates, because the process of buying probate properties comes closest to the traditional process of buying properties, and often probate properties are not widely exposed to the marketplace. Also, while foreclosure sales are forced as a result of insufficient financial resources or a lack of equity, probates result from deaths, something none of us can escape.

My major point is that while there are finds to be made with auctions, foreclosures, and probates, they rarely are as productive and financially rewarding as the traditional style of buying real estate.

WHY ANGLES ARE SO HARD TO FIGURE—AND TO PLAY

Angles are so hard to figure because everything with angles is based on trying to calculate hypotheticals on top of hypotheticals: "What if this happens? What if that happens? What if all of these happen?" It's the difference between a billiard player's making a bank shot, which is playing an angle, or having a straight shot at the ball right into the pocket. If you play it straight, the greater your probability of being successful.

An important part of the difference between playing the real estate game from one of the angles and playing it straight has to do with the whole principle of communicating from truth. *To me, playing the angles often amounts to trying to manipulate the other parties in a deal to do something that's in your favor but against their will.*

The angles present you with a narrower range of options under the illusion that you're going to get a bargain. The constraints of time and other circumstances (such as no contingencies) deny you the full range of checks and balances that would prevent you from making a mistake. Adding to the lack of protection in these "thrill-of-the-chase" situations is that once the adrenaline starts flowing in response to the intrinsic pressures, it becomes even easier to make poor decisions. If you're the kind of person who might enjoy watching the angles in action as a spectator sport, by all means do so. But *caveat emptor:* "Let the buyer beware."

CHAPTER 21

THE MYTH OF FIXING UP VERSUS THE REALITY OF UPGRADING

Another common belief on my list of real estate myths has to do with "fixer-uppers." *The myth is that the best real estate investment is to buy a property and fix it up.*

I think this belief finds its basis in the Protestant work ethic. Applied to a piece of property, this means you have to *do* something to the property to add value to it. *Though doing something to a property may, in fact, add value to it, you don't necessarily have to remodel it to add that value; all you have to do is add what I call "integrity" to the property.*

When I first started my career I bought an eleven-unit apartment building on Hobart Street in Los Angeles. It was originally part of a twenty-two-unit building which was later separated into two identical buildings, side by side. When I bought mine, the buildings were about thirty years old and dilapidated. I made mine fantastic. I spent a lot of money on new tile, new cabinets, new lighting fixtures, modern faucets, new hardware—I did just about everything I could to improve its appearance. The man who owned the building next door did nothing. I raised my rents; he didn't. But a year later, both were bringing in nearly the same rent, only I had spent far more money. My success at raising rents showed what the rents really could be. The owner next door figured, "Well, if Fogel, with an identical building that just happens to be nicer-looking than mine, is getting $300 a month rent, I should be able to get $290 for mine." So twelve months after I had spent a small fortune on my building, we were both getting almost the same income—and he hadn't spent anything.

The truth was that both buildings were already worth the higher rents—and neither of us knew it!

I'm not advocating leaving a building in disrepair and raising the rents because the market will bear it. Today I know that fixing up a building does not mean replacing items right and left but seeing to it that every item is in proper repair and 100 percent neat and clean. Many people prefer old cabinets, hardware, and fixtures to new ones—the key word is "perfect."

Upgrading real estate simply means adding integrity to a property. Adding integrity to a property is not a matter of spending a lot of money on the property to make it different, but making the property the best it can be as it is. It is making the property so clean and efficient that you, your tenant, and neighbors do not have to make excuses for it and instead take pride in it. Let me show you what I mean.

UPGRADING AN APARTMENT BUILDING BY ADDING INTEGRITY TO IT

Let's look at an apartment building that an owner has had for ten years. He's made plenty of money from it, and he's had the traditional attitude that he shouldn't spend money on a building when the expenditure is optional. If something doesn't need fixing, don't fix it; if a tenant doesn't demand to have something, don't give it to him. When the owner has this attitude, the first thing I would expect to see as I walked toward his property is overgrown landscaping. The second thing I would expect to see is that the building is partly clean and partly dirty. The owner's attitude so permeates the philosophy of management that the building superintendent believes that he's doing a good job by saving money in avoiding proper cosmetic maintenance. Since the property loses more of its attractive edge each day, the landlord compensates by getting slightly less on rentals than nicer-looking buildings get. Neither owner nor superintendent knows he could get more simply by adding integrity.

Let's say you're a prospective tenant looking at an apartment. As you walk through the apartment, you notice that the carpets and the draperies seem drab and unappealing. Over the years water has seeped in and cracked and ripped the plaster under the windows. The previous patch jobs show on the walls and on the ceiling where the roof has leaked. You notice that although the top of the stove is clean to the touch, no one's cleaned the inside in years.

This is a vacant apartment looking for a tenant; the apartment is 85 percent perfect. A perfectionist would want it to be 100 percent before he rents it, but most renters will rent it at 85 percent— especially in markets such as New York City's, where they're lucky to get apartments at all. Twenty years of experience have shown me that an absolutely perfect apartment always rents quickly in any marketplace for top rent, and the kind of person who rents it is a higher quality tenant who is willing to pay more for it. For the 85 percent integrity apartment to have 100 percent integrity, the plaster has to be done over so that there are no signs of water damage; the inside of the stove and the cabinets have to be immaculate; the carpets and draperies have to be cleaned or replaced.

A tenant who comes to an apartment that has 100 percent integrity will maintain it that way. When the 100 percent integrity standard is applied to the whole building, its hallways will always be clean—even back hallways that nobody ever uses—and the landscaping will be kept up, the elevator will be clean, and all repairs will be done properly. One of the most important facts to remember about adding integrity to a building is that just getting the right manager (or superintendent) for a building will add integrity to it. Doing this not only creates buildings that draw top rents, it also creates buildings that sell at premium prices.

Resident managers often have difficulty standing up to painters and maintenance people and demanding perfection. You have to stay on top of managers constantly in order to make sure that everything is done 100 percent correctly. If you own a building in the middle of the best blue-chip neighborhood and you hire a manager whose standards make it acceptable for that building to be filthy and full of cockroaches, you're going to end up with filthy tenants with cockroaches in their apartments. If you allow a wino to be hired as manager, the tenants will turn out to be winos. Conversely, if you put in a deacon of the church to manage the worst building in the worst neighborhood, all the tenants will turn out to be churchgoers. Like attracts like, and your building will reflect this principle.

I recently read an article about a man in Washington, D.C., who rented an apartment in a poor neighborhood that had been taken over by drug addicts and derelicts. He went there to live because it was the least expensive place he could find. After renting the apartment, he ultimately managed to buy the building. He organized the neighbors, who were primarily economically disadvantaged people, and enlisted his friends to act as workmen, helping him to improve his building. Eventually everybody in the neighborhood started helping one another. Now the neighborhood has been converted to a very up-and-coming area, and it has become an attractive part of the city almost overnight. It has become a safe area, thanks to community members policing their own streets. The man who initiated these changes was just taking a stand to create a place where he could live safely and cheaply. Because of his dedication, he ended up making the entire neighborhood a better place to live. This is what being a "fixer-upper" really means to me.

Thus far in my business career, I've cleaned up about 150 apartment buildings. And every time I made them nicer places to live, I got more rent and they went up in value. I did something for the community; the community did something for me. It wasn't a question of making a huge financial investment in these buildings to make them nicer; it was just adding integrity to them.

Part
Four

CHAPTER 22

CHOOSING YOUR FIRST INVESTMENT

Okay, the jig is up. The information gap has been closed. Now *you* know about real estate. You have an overview of the factors you have to consider in buying different types of property, a good idea about the factors to consider in financing a property, and an understanding of how to raise money, structure a deal with partners, and bring in the professionals who will support you. All that's left is for you to choose the property you're going to buy as your first investment and then to buy it. The purpose of this part of the book is to guide you through that process and to support you with practical, step-by-step suggestions for overcoming whatever barriers you may encounter along the way.

SEEING WHERE YOU ARE RIGHT NOW

In choosing your first investment property you will, of course, have to analyze your personal likes and dislikes as well as your financial resources. That means you have to ask yourself, "What do I want in a property, in general?" Then you have to set a goal and match your expectations to it, figuring out what it takes to get there. My guess is that if you ask yourself, "What should my first investment be?'' the answer will pop into your mind almost immediately, because on a gut level you already know. If you find you have much doubt about what kind of property is right for you, I suggest you get a piece of paper and a pencil and write down three choices of location. These three possibilities should all be within one or two hours from your home—the closer, the better. Then write down your expectation of the amount of money you can put into a deal, or the amount that you think you will be able to raise from investors. It is important to commit yourself to this amount in writing.

With these steps you begin to form your hypothesis about what kind of a deal is possible for you, both in location and in size of property. Soon you'll begin to focus on what's realistic by walking or driving through the three locations you've written down and asking what is available.

You'll discover that there is only a limited number of choices, because what you want as a first-time investor is a property that is:

1. simple to own and manage;
2. relatively close to where you live;
3. within your price range; and
4. likely to prove a good investment within the relatively brief time limits you will set for your first investment.

As you go through the locations and see what properties are available that meet these criteria, write them down and include all the financial facts you can get. Your next step will involve your Free Board of Directors.

For my personal Free Board of Directors, I have social friends who are successful businesspeople. If I'm talking about buying an old apartment building that may need to be torn down and replaced by new construction, and I have no real idea what it would cost, I'll call my friend who is a builder and ask him. When I'm buying a commercial property and want to know what rent a doughnut shop would pay for the corner store, I call my friends who are in leasing at the local real estate company. These members of my Board come and go in my life. For my more immediate and steady Board members, I use my partner, Howard, and our next-door neighbors in our office building, who are in a similar business. I tell them about my deals and ask their opinions and they do the same with me. We are Free Board members for each other.

When you ask people their opinions, acknowledge them for their support. If this acknowledgment really comes from your heart, they'll bend over backward to help you for years.

When you start thinking about your first real estate investment, your Board may be your spouse, or, if you're not married, perhaps someone you're dating. You'll need all the good business friends you can find as well as your brothers and sisters, father and mother, and one or two close friends—people who may be unsophisticated in real estate but may serve as a sounding board for you.

After committing to writing three possible real estate investments that meet the criteria of simplicity, proximity, price, and appropriate duration of investment, you will move on to the next step: talking about these possibilities with appropriate members of your Board. Always remember to check out what they say with your intuition and the duck test, and to take into consideration whether, generally speaking, they are positive or negative agreement machines. Using this process, you'll arrive at a decision about what type of property you want—a house or apartment building or office, commercial, or industrial property—the location, and the price. Now you're ready to find the property itself.

SHORT- AND LONG-TERM INVESTMENTS

Let's stop here to determine whether you'd like the investment to be short-term (say, three years or under), medium-term (three to five years), or long-term (over five years). Let's use Joe as an example. Joe is twenty-four years old, has never been married, and works as an engineer in the electronics industry. He has to think about whether his career might demand that he move from the area where he's now living. If it's pretty clear to him that in two or three years he'd like to change to a better job that might necessitate a move, then he'd better find a real estate investment that's a relatively short-term hold.

If, on the other hand, Joe were a schoolteacher, married, and had every expectation of working in the same neighborhood for the rest of his life, then he could look at an investment that he might do well holding for five or ten years.

Aside from considering his plans for the future, Joe should analyze his personal makeup. Is he a patient person who can look at everything as coming in due time, or does he need to do things quickly and get gratification from immediate results?

I know that my need for results changes, depending on what kind of an investment I'm making. For example, a day after I buy a new stock I start following the newspaper and calling the broker on the hour because I want to find out what's happened. I've learned that my long-term view of holding a stock is one week. Other people have a long-term view of the same stock that encompasses years. Yet although I act very quickly in real estate I can hold on to a property for years and be perfectly content to hold it. I can be patient because, in general, I am buying sardines for eating, so they are paying for themselves for as long as I own them. I know that time is making them appreciate and I'm confident that the longer I keep them, the better sardines they will be for trading. If there is an immediate buyer for a property, however, I will sell it to him if I can realize a substantial return on my investment very quickly. Thus, with real estate, I can be satisfied with long-term investments, short-term investments, and even ultrashort-term investments (overnight).

Joe has to be clear about his need for results, and he has to find a first real estate investment that matches his needs. If he wants to turn over money for himself within two years because he needs the result in order to continue his enthusiasm, then he should decide on a short-term investment plan.

An anecdote demonstrates the wisdom of this. A prospective buyer in the early 1960s asked a land salesman, "Should I buy in Hesperia or should I buy in the San Fernando Valley?" The first choice was being promoted on television and radio; the second was the place the salesman was representing. The answer the salesman gave the prospective buyer was, "Well, it depends. Do you want your children to think you were a genius in real estate or do you want your great-grandchildren to think you were a genius in real estate?"

How quickly do you want to make your money? If, for example, you want to make it in two years, you should be prepared to buy something and plan on selling it for a quick profit—although the profit will probably be smaller than if the property seasoned out for four or five years. Then repeat the process over and over.

HOW LONG DO YOU KEEP A PROPERTY?

The people who ask real estate syndication executives this question seldom consider that most of these executives have been in the business for less than five years; they assume that whatever plan a syndicator presents in his sales pitch is the way it is done when, in fact, everybody's transaction is different. Furthermore, they fail to realize that people who have been in the investment business for five years or less can't possibly have kept properties for as long as people who've been in the business for ten, fifteen, or twenty years.

My guess is that if someone analyzed all the real estate syndications that have ever been put together and found out how long the properties were held, there would be very little correlation between what the syndicators expected to happen and what actually happened in regard to the length of time the property was kept.

Although people who haven't invested in real estate before may expect to make their money quickly, it rarely happens this way.

I have probably bought over 250 pieces of property in my business career; we still own most of them. I discovered that the properties I owned turned out to be like fruit trees, orchards that are harvested. If I harvest the fruit properly, the fruit keeps coming year after year. I just continue owning the same pieces of property and, every few years, refinance them and then use the proceeds to buy more new property. This way I don't have to sell properties to get the money out of them. I think what I've experienced is typical for many people investing in real estate over a number of years.

This arrangement generally works out very well for investors, too. Our investors are people who have been with us for many years, people I've known since we started out. They were young professionals just beginning to make some extra money, and they believed that they should use money to make more money. Four or five years after we bought a property with the investors as our limited partners, when it seemed a good time to sell the property, we would ask them their thoughts on the investment. Typically, we'd find that they had made other money along the way and that in their own thinking they had put the money they had invested with us off to the side, more or less forgetting about it—though, of course, they didn't really forget about it. So when it came time to consider selling the property, they'd generally say, "Gee, it would be terrific to sell it," but on the other hand, "Why bother? I want to buy more. What else do you have to invest in?"

Not having a pressing need for the money, they just viewed the old investment as a component of their growing estate.

There is enormous satisfaction in the whole process of finding the property at the price and terms that make it a good deal and from watching the property do what you thought it would do. There's also great satisfaction in making the corrections on a property so that it will do what you thought it would do.

And if you have partners, they'll feel the same satisfaction that you feel; they'll feel terrific when they get their monthly or quarterly report showing that they're profiting. Furthermore, real estate investments generally go up in value all the time—and the investors know this, too. This is what makes real estate a good investment while you own it; it's not just a good investment the day you sell it. People take the psychological reward of the investment every day they have it.

How Do You Know If a Specific Property Is for You?

The main thing to bear in mind in choosing your first investment is that any piece of property, whether it is a house, an apartment building, or office, commercial, or industrial real estate, is a great investment under certain circumstances, and that any piece of property is a terrible investment under other circumstances.

If you buy a 100,000-square-foot building in a big city slum for $10,000 cash, all you have to do to make a 100 percent annual return is rent it for storage to someone who will pay $830 a month, which works out to less than one penny per square foot. You'll discover that you can always find someone who will pay that rent for that space in a highly populated area. So it would be a wonderful investment even if you wouldn't want to go near the property, because to rent it out for storage, you don't have to go near it.

On the other hand, if you buy the General Motors Building in New York City on Fifth Avenue and 59th Street (which is pretty much as blue-chip an office building as you can get) for $10 billion, you're not going to come out well with the investment in this lifetime. *Therefore, in order to choose a property you must decide what you want for yourself, and then go out and find it. It's not mystical. Choose what you want.* You will never be happy with a deal you don't like regardless of how well other people can justify to you why you should choose it.

If you are attracted to a property, then you start with the premise that it is a good possibility—meaning that it is the right type of property at the right price and the right location, that the figures make it a good deal, and that you can hold it for the length of time you want to hold it—then you see if you can disprove the premise. If you cannot disprove the premise that the property is a good possibility, then you know it's for you.

Occasionally I find myself in a dilemma over whether to buy a piece of property: I can't decide to go forward or retreat. To show you how I solve this, I'm going to tell you a story I heard about how monkeys are caught in Africa and India. A bunch of bananas is put in a big jar with a narrow opening. A monkey sees the bananas, puts his hand around the whole bunch, but his clenched fist *and* the bunch are too great a mass to get through the neck of the jar. The trappers approach the monkey and just carry him off with his hand still stuck in the jar; he still won't let go of the bananas. He doesn't realize that if he grabbed only one banana at a time, he could escape. As soon as I start feeling like a monkey clutching a bunch of jarred bananas, my personal strategy is to lower my offer on the property, get a better deal on it, or forget about it.

Why It's Easier to Succeed Than to Fail

Perhaps the simplest way of choosing your first investment is to get an overview of an area and then pick out a place where things look like they are going to happen. If you start making deals in an area where things are going to happen, you know you're bound to win. Basically, this is a very simple thing to do.

When wildcatters look for oil, they make a fortune only when the well they drill produces oil. Even if the area looks promising before, geologists never know if there really is sufficient oil under the earth's surface to warrant the drilling. It's very different with real estate. It's easy to find an area where things are happening or are going to happen. Just follow the trend.

The trends are easy to notice. Drive through the area and look for clues. Is there any construction? Are there many "For Rent" signs on stores in the neighborhood? Are houses and buildings well maintained or shabby? Are many renovations in progress? Do the retail stores seem to be aiming their marketing for affluent, upscale buyers? Are their shelves and racks well-stocked, suggesting high volume? Talk with the shopkeepers, businesspeople, residents, and real estate brokers. Tell them you are thinking of buying—ask them what they think of the future for the area. Call the local chamber of commerce and ask their opinion. The key is determining whether the area is healthy and growing, on a downhill trend, or just stagnating. If it is growing, your property will rise in value with it.

Although your first real estate investments should definitely be within one or two hours from where you live, in the future you may decide to expand your range of opportunities and buy properties in other parts of the country as well. If you decide to broaden your investment horizons this way, be aware that no matter how well you know your home marketplace, a new marketplace requires new research.

My own rule of thumb is to buy real estate only in locations where the population density is so great that somebody can't reproduce whatever building I buy one hundred times over within a few square miles. This means that I'm not going to buy any shopping centers or apartment houses where there is plenty of totally undeveloped land. But I *am* going to buy a shopping center or an apartment house where someone would have to buy another piece of land, tear down an existing building, and build a new one from the ground up in order to have a building like mine. In that situation, I know that I'm starting with the economic advantage, and my competition has to put up a lot of money to meet me.

The significant point is that whether the property is local or distant, you must do thorough research so that no matter what you buy, you're not going to overpay; at the worst, you'll pay fair market value. And the worst that can happen when you buy a property at fair market value is that you will sell it for about the same price you paid for it. It's not like the wildcatter who buys his oil lease and then spends his money drilling and comes up with a dry hole. When you're approaching your first investment and you find yourself being resistant to taking action, keep reminding yourself that it's really hard to lose money in real estate and it's very, very easy to make money.

How Much Time Should Looking and Finding Take?

The clearer you are about what you want—the clearer you are about your goals and expectations—the less time finding property will take. I have personally found that it can take almost no time. You can look at the newspaper, see an ad, and make an offer; you can make a telephone call or receive one, hear about a property for sale, and make an offer; you can walk into a real estate broker's office or have him walk into yours, hear about a deal, and make an offer.

Remember: it takes only a minute to make arrangements to buy any property. What may take a long time is getting yourself ready to come to that minute.

For a person who is slow and methodical, it may take six months to get ready for that minute. For a more impulsive type, it may take two weeks—or two days. The length of time it takes for the whole process is determined by how ready you are to make a move.

I can't overemphasize that you must back up your choice with solid research and debate to prove to yourself, once you've tied up the property, that the deal really is what you think it is.

One person will find a deal and discover that it's a reasonably good one. After doing all this solid work, he may still jeopardize the entire deal by worrying that his entire life rests on whether the deal turns out to be as wonderful as he thinks it will be! This person might put so much pressure on himself that he will never do anything; how can he make a deal if he feels that his survival depends on how that deal works out? The more one sees his life's survival tacked on to the job at hand, the harder it is to get himself to do the job, because there's too big a risk involved.

Another person in exactly the same set of circumstances, who takes the deal seriously but at the same time doesn't believe that her life depends on it and who sees that the deal is just a part of life, will make her decision relatively quickly, saying to herself, "What's the worst that can happen?" If she has done her homework, the worst that could possibly happen is that she loses her money, but the probability is that since what she is buying with the money is a piece of real estate, and since the deal is well thought out, if everything doesn't go magnificently, she'll own it for a year or two and sell it. If she takes the venture seriously but at the same time doesn't see her personal survival as dependent on it, she'll find that it's easy to make many deals while creating joy and aliveness in her life.

The briefest scenario you may find yourself in is that you could look at one building, get a good feeling about it, make an offer on it, put it into escrow with contingencies, and then do your homework during the escrow period. In this case, you would find out the specific facts you need about that location once you've made your offer, assuming you have proper contingencies in your offer. With this scenario, you could actually find your first investment the first day you are looking. Then you can use the contingency period to go through your proving process.

The opposite extreme of this is the Prince Charming syndrome that so many of us experience in the area of romance. We immediately find the person with whom we want to have a relationship, but rather than believe in our good fortune, we say, "My God, she came along on the first day! I just decided I was ready for a mate and I happened to meet this woman while I was waiting in line at McDonald's! She seemed very funny and bright, she looked pretty, she had all these wonderful attributes, but she can't be right. I haven't *looked* yet."

With the Prince Charming syndrome, you ignore what's in front of you because you assume you have to look harder to find the really right choice. With the Prince Charming syndrome in real estate, you can go on searching forever and never find a property.

HOW TO OVERCOME THE BARRIERS TO MAKING YOUR FIRST DEAL: KEEPING A DIARY

Because most of us resist taking action and assuming responsibility for doing something that could have powerful implications, I suggest that after you've completed the process of sorting out types of properties and locations in your marketplace and your goals and expectations for the amount of money you will create, you write a timetable for yourself for making your first real estate transaction.

I recommend keeping this information in a diary. It's been an invaluable tool for me, both professionally and personally. I write in mine every night, reviewing what I've done that day, discussing whatever problems I may be encountering, and laying out what I think and feel about them. I write down any business transactions I may be involved in or may be considering, along with any thoughts or feelings I have about them.

If you begin to keep a daily diary, I suggest that you keep a special section about real estate. Keeping a diary about any transaction you're interested in is a great way to raise yourself to the point of observation, which will start the process of seeing value.

When I started keeping a diary I had no particular reason for doing it except to find out how it felt. After keeping it for a year, I noticed that recording my goals and desires in writing seemed to crystallize my scattered thoughts. I saw that certain themes persisted for a while, and if they took the form of complaints, I realized that I had to do something to correct my attitude.

Make a special section to write down your real estate *goals* for one year. Be specific. Is it your goal to buy one property in that year? Two properties? Write down what price property (or properties) you want to buy in the coming year, and what kind: apartment houses, office, commercial, or industrial property, or private homes. How much of a down payment is it your goal to raise for each property?

Next, write down your six-month goals. What do you want to accomplish during the next six months toward achieving your one-year goals? Is your goal to become an expert on your local marketplace during that time? Is your goal to have made an offer on a property? Is your goal to buy a property within six months?

After that, write down how you plan to accomplish your goals. How will you go about finding the area you want to invest in? How many properties do you expect to see each week? How many hours a week do you plan to devote to seeing them? How do you plan to create the down payment? Who will be on your Free Board of Directors?

Next, write down your *expectations* for the next twelve months. This may seem the same as writing your goals but it isn't. This is a process that will help clarify if your goals are in line with your expectations. Do you expect to buy one property in that year? Two properties? How much of a down payment for each property do you expect that you can raise?

Write down your six-month expectations. What do you expect to accomplish during the next six months toward achieving your one-year goals?

Now write down what you expect to do in terms of fulfilling your plan. Is it your expectation that you'll follow your plan—that you'll keep the commitment of time that you've allotted per week toward building your real estate career? That you'll create the down payment in the way you've stated in your plan? That you'll create and use the Free Board of Directors made up of the people you've listed? Through this process you'll get to see whether you may be playing a game of noncommitment, and, if so, to change your decision about playing it.

If you find out that your expectations and your goals are different, write down the reasons for the differences. Can you align them? Is there some particular aspect of putting a transaction together to which you feel a resistance? Is there any aspect that seems like a barrier to you? If so, write it down, and then write down what you plan to do about overcoming this barrier.

I suggest that you keep a day-by-day record of what properties you looked at. Write down their square footage, the number and type of their units or offices, or any other relevant characteristics by which they can be defined; what price the sellers are asking; and what the suggested financing was. Next, describe your quick impressions of the properties, including what you feel they are worth.

If you do this for a hundred pieces of property over a period of six months, I suspect that you will pick up as much expertise at appraising as some professionals have. This means seeing a little more than fifteen properties a month, a goal that could be accomplished by your seeing approximately four properties per week. The mere fact that you've written down the facts and figures for each property, what condition it was in, what the financing was, and its price will start the process of your seeing value in your price range in your area.

The mere fact that you're writing down something means that you've made a commitment. You're engaged in the ongoing process of turning your fantasies into realities by making and following —and, if necessary, revising—your own personal plan.

Give yourself permission to change any aspect of your plan or the entire plan at any step along the way. By approaching the process in this manner, you are actually making movement in your life.

GETTING ALL THE ADVICE YOU NEED

If you find yourself dwelling on how much you don't know about real estate instead of how much you've just learned, remember that there is a way to get the best advice in the world for free: *All you have to do is to ask for it.*

Similarly, remember that there is a way to investigate every piece of information you are given about a property or location: *All you have to do is test it.*

A final suggestion on overcoming potential barriers to making your first deal: if you find yourself intimidated by the figures involved in real estate transactions, remember that you can always get a calculator to help you with the numbers, you can always get a member of your Free Board of Directors to help you with the calculator and with double-checking your calculations, and that, if necessary, you can get an accountant to triple-check.

Also remember that one of the things that makes real estate exciting and satisfying is the human element. It's extremely challenging to deal with people and create a situation in which everyone wins. You're not just dealing with numbers. *Real estate takes place on two levels at the same time: the level of numbers and the human level. The building is just the medium by which everything happens.*

CHAPTER 23

THE ART OF SELLING, OR SELLING THE SIZZLE AS WELL AS THE STEAK

Real estate isn't *sold,* it's *bought!* When a buyer sees something he likes, he buys it. As a seller, the trick is to make your property fit the buyer's "picture" of what he wants.

Thus, in order to sell, you first have to figure out what the buyer has in mind to buy. You do this by looking at the world from the level of observation. If you observe what people picture as good investments, you'll see that they want things that look as if they still have an element of bargain left in them; they want things they feel they can make money on. They often want things they feel they can improve, acquisitions to which they can apply their own artistic abilities. They want things they'll be proud to own and things they feel they're capable of handling. So as a seller of property, the question is: How do you make certain the property you're selling has these elements?

Maintaining a property with integrity is the best preparation for selling it at a good price. As we've noted, it isn't important for you to remodel the property; what is important is to let people know through your presentation how they can remodel it.

I know of a large house in Bel Air, California (on a block where no house sells for less than $3 million), that was on the market for a long time. It finally sold for about $2 million to a man who bought it as an investment, planning to resell it at a profit. There were three reasons why he was able to buy it so far below the market price for other houses on the block:

1. the seller had overpriced the house for a year, asking $4.5 million for it, and it had gotten a reputation as "not being seriously on the market";
2. it was filthy;
3. it was for sale during a down market.

The sellers had lived there for fifteen years and had originally paid only $300,000 for it. Despite the prestigious address, they had failed to maintain it and it was a mess. Potential buyers who walked into it said, "It's going to cost millions to fix this place up!" The new owners took this advice. They decided to improve the house by spending about $500,000 on it; then they planned to put it on the market for $4 million. They ended up spending $1 million on the improvements. Their final selling price was $3 million.

The truth is that no investor had to spend anywhere near $1 million on this house. Instead of spending money to remodel, the new investor-owners simply could have upgraded it by meticulously cleaning it both inside and out and making it 100 percent perfect the way it was—which would have cost them about $100,000. Once this was accomplished, they could have put it back on the market and spent some money to promote and market it.

What we do when we sell the sizzle as well as the steak is make sure that the properties we're selling don't look too overwhelming to take on. All cleaned up, the large house on one of the best and most beautiful blocks in town is not at all overwhelming; it almost shouts, "Bargain! Bargain! Come buy me and fix me up yourself!" It shows you where *you* could fix it up. By just adding integrity to the Bel Air house the new owners (or the old sellers) could have sold it for $3 million, which would have made them the $1 million profit they had hoped for, only with less time, money, and risk.

When we're selling the sizzle as well as the steak, we also show potential buyers where there's profit to be made in the property.

Let's say, for example, that you want to sell an apartment house.

In marketing it, you would show the potential buyer that the rents can be set higher. In the past you have raised the rents annually, and it's just about time for another increase.

HOW DO YOU DETERMINE WHEN TO SELL?

In general, you really don't have to sit and think about when to sell a property.

We usually sell for one of three reasons: either because something turns into a problem and we want to get away from it; because someone approaches us and says, "Can I buy this?"; or because we need to unlock capital for something else.

In the case of wanting to be free of a property, that desire is reason enough to sell it, and we start the ball rolling. In the case of someone's approaching us about a property, we figure out what we think the property is worth, add a little to the figure for good measure, and then say, "If you want to buy it on the following basis, it's yours." Generally, however, I find that the very act of figuring out what we want for it frequently starts a whole chain of events.

For example, somebody might contact us and say that he wants to buy a specific property we hadn't really thought about selling. We figure out what would be an attractive sale price. Then we say, "Okay, you can buy it for X amount of money." Next the potential buyer will ask us for facts and figures, so we're forced to commit to writing the income of the building, the expenses, and the financing. We have to prepare a fact sheet. In doing this, we start inspecting the property from a buyer's point of view. This quickly makes us review our strategy for the property and update our view of what the property is worth. Next, we send the setup (fact sheet) to the interested party.

Invariably, the simple fact of our new energy in this property creates four or five other people who are interested in it. As they apply their various methods of investigation to make sure they want to buy it, still more activity is created. Soon it is on the market and everyone knows about it.

The third circumstance that signals the time to sell is when the circumstances present a new opportunity and you find yourself saying, "Let's do this!" Say we have a piece of property that we're content to be holding and managing, but suddenly a much bigger, better deal comes to our attention. We start looking around and decide to sell a property we already own to finance the new deal.

So, in terms of when to sell, generally I let the momentum of the property and marketplace do the planning and it does a very fine job.

READING THE MARKET CONDITIONS AT THE TIME YOU SELL

No property stands alone. Every property on the earth stands on a specific block, in a specific neighborhood, in a specific village, town, or city. You can tell what the trend in your marketplace is by reading the newspapers, calling the local brokers, and finding out what prices other properties have sold for and what price current owners are asking for properties now on the market—activities that come naturally to you by now and that you enjoy.

Of course, the market for selling properties depends on many factors other than just real estate. It depends on interest rates, on whether or not it's an election year, the general feeling about the present and future economy, and even the season. If you have a house for sale in Palm Springs, California, it's common sense that in the summer, when it's 110°F. outside, you're not going to find many prospective buyers, and those you do find are going to see that there's no activity and expect to make a better deal as a result. But if you put the house up for sale at Christmastime when vacationers come to Palm Springs from all over to enjoy the weather, many people are going to say to themselves, "Gee, I'd like to live here. I wonder if there's a house I can buy." Consequently, there are not only a lot of lookers during this season, but the spirit of the buyers is very high.

On the other hand, if you want to sell your property at Christmastime in a colder or even a moderate climate that is not a resort, you may meet with some resistance. We all know that the majority of people generally tune out to purchases other than gifts during the holiday season, recovering from the holidays sometime in February, and then complain about business (or bills) until after tax season. If you can see these cycles, you can see other cycles, too.

When the economy is doing well, it's a better time to sell than when the forecast is doom and gloom.

But there's another factor that has to be taken into account, too: sometimes money has more value to you personally than at other times. *What often happens in real estate is that it doesn't make a difference if you sell your property at a better time or a worse time as long as you have a need for the money.*

Let's say, for example, that you're going to build your estate through real estate investment in the way that I'm suggesting, that you bought your first piece of property a year ago, and that right now the economic climate is bad. If you sell now you'll realize a profit from the property, but you don't think the profit will be as high as it would be if it were a better year. If you're selling your existing property to buy a second piece of property, then logic would suggest that you'd get a bargain because your new acquisition is being purchased when the economic climate is bad. In this case, it would make sense to sell the first piece of property if that's your only way of buying the second. This is why the time you sell the property may not be all that important as long as you're going to place the money you get from the transaction into a similar vehicle that you're purchasing at a good price. If you're selling to get out of real estate altogether, this logic won't apply and the bad timing may be very costly.

PRICING—DO YOU *REALLY* WANT TO SELL?

Pricing has to be viewed on two levels: what a property is worth and how to price it when you're truly ready to sell it.

Most people think that it's absolutely fine to sell if they can get a premium, that it's okay to sell if they can get a fair market value, and that it's ridiculous to sell if what they'll get for the property isn't what they think it's worth.

If your motive for selling is simply to make yourself feel good and to make a potential move to another investment that you haven't picked out yet, perhaps you'll price your property at your highest possible fantasy of what it's worth and let it sit on the market until you sell it.

The other side of the coin is if you have a serious need to sell.

For example, a couple with three kids discovers that the wife is pregnant again—with twins—and suddenly they need to buy a bigger house. The babies are coming in January, and it's already October; they want to sell their house immediately and buy a new one. Since the couple knows that there's a tremendous pressure to sell the house so they can buy a new one, they're not going to be unrealistic about the price they want; their motivation is to sell the house quickly.

The person in the first example really has not taken the stand that he wants to sell; he's taken the stand that he'll sell only if he gets a premium. Once he actually puts his property on the market, he goes through a unique process. That process usually starts with real estate brokers' telling him what he wants to hear—that he may be able to get the kind of money for his property that he's asking. At this stage, the seller has his fantasies intact. Then, if he's lucky, along comes a potential buyer who'll say, "I'm interested, but I'll give you less." The seller gets indignant and says, "No!" After three or four months of doing this and eliciting a few more of what the seller considers insulting offers, he starts to transform his thinking. Eventually he changes brokers, and then he changes his mind and finds out that he *was* asking too much. When he *really* gets ready to sell, which may be the next day, he gets realistic, lowers the price, and sells the property for what the market says it's worth.

Overpricing a property can be a very expensive way of finding out what price the property will bring, since it may mean that the property will stay on the market for an extended period of time. If you have need for the money that will be generated by the sale—either because the property is costing you money each month to own or because you have other needs for the funds—you'll feel more pressure the longer it's on the market. Then, too, when a property is on the market for a long time, potential buyers may suspect that something is wrong with it. They may also make very low offers with the idea that the owner is desperate because it hasn't sold yet. If there is a financial pressure on you, you may actually end up taking a lower price for the property than you would have had to take if you'd initially listed it at a more realistic price.

Given the fact that pricing is very important to the quickness of sale, how you approach a broker about selling the property is crucial. If you tell the broker that you're interested in what you believe is the highest price for the property and you seem unwilling to list it for less than that, the broker may well take the listing at the price you're insisting on although he's really saying to himself, "Well, okay, if that's what the seller wants, we'll try and we'll see what happens. He'll come around and drop his price." If, on the other hand, you go to ten different brokers and ask, "Look, what do you think it's going to take to sell my property in sixty days?" chances are that you'll get ten different opinions. Consequently, you will have a totally different attitude about pricing than you would have if you'd approached only one broker and told him the price that you want.

After you get input from ten brokers, you'll be dealing not from your fantasy, and not even from your own reading of the market, but from information provided by people who are actually selling properties, who are not emotionally involved, and who, therefore, know realistically what price you should ask if you want to turn over your property within the time you've indicated. You must remember, of course, that the lower the listing price, the greater the brokers' chances to earn a commission. So the seller still must test all the advice and information he receives and search for the best consensus of opinion in determining his price.

The selling price of a property is very much a function of how determined the seller is to sell. As the seller of a piece of real estate, you must decide on the least amount of money you're willing to take for the property, and if you're really ready to let go of it for that price.

It seems as if this should be easy, but we return to the fact that in our society there is a tremendous emotional investment in the buying and selling of real estate. People mull it over endlessly, putting much more pressure on themselves than they do with almost any other decision they make in their financial lives. That's just part of the psychology of real estate, and we all have to accept that whether we're buyer or seller, the other potential parties to our transaction are going to be going through that same process. Even today, after years of buying and selling property, I always have a little bit of buyer's or seller's remorse at the end of the transaction —merely from having acted.

NEGOTIATING AS THE SELLER

As a seller, I generally negotiate by stating the simple truth: I tell the potential buyer the price I want, and no matter what he counters, I tell him, "I can respect your argument, but that's really what I want."

Frequently, people are dissatisfied with this kind of an attitude because they want to go through a ritual before they buy: they *want* to negotiate; they see it as part of the game. Having completed hundreds of transactions, I've learned that the ritual is not entirely necessary, so I let the other person go through his own process, and I don't participate.

If you just state the truth and not waver from it in order to satisfy others' desires to negotiate, you just have to wait patiently and give potential buyers the time to work through all their rationalizations as to why they're going to take your deal or leave it. In effect, this is just making the ritual dance a simple one because you're not much of a dancer.

Of course, if you want to participate in a more elaborate dance, you can also play the game of negotiating as the seller. You have to pick your own style: the point is to know at what price you are truly willing to sell the property—if, indeed, it is important to you to sell the property. If you feel the buyer won't buy unless he gets something off the asking price, then it may be smart to ask a little extra to begin with so you can come down later.

If you list your property for more than what it's worth, you're really testing your own desire to sell. You're going to find out what you really want to do and at what price; it's a variation of putting the question of what the property is worth before your Free Board of Directors and seeing what the Board has to say. In this case, the Board is made up of the potential buyers you don't even know. In essence, they are advising you to sell the property at a particular price. You listen to the debate between the other people and yourself and eventually you choose.

WHAT DO YOU DO WHEN YOU REALLY WANT TO SELL AND THE MARKET IS "SOFT"?

There is always a buyer, even in a high supply/low demand market. All you have to do is set an absolutely realistic price. Setting a realistic price means setting a price that is in alignment with the market at that time.

At any moment a combination of market factors can create an unpropitious time to sell. In 1981 the economy was so bad that everybody was saying, "I'm not going to take on any additional responsibility because everything is collapsing and I don't want to be burdened by any more things to pay for." Unemployment was going up rapidly; newspapers announced that breadlines were starting again; the prime interest rate was high; many people were convinced that another Depression was coming. Although there was nothing wrong with real estate per se, the psychological mood was against buying.

In an economic climate like that, there is only one answer to the question "To sell or not to sell?" It is summed up in one word: *Wait.* If you must have a quick sale and you're in a bad economic climate, you might have to take a loss. If, instead, you remind yourself that on average real estate does go up and you know your property is quality property, then you might say to yourself, "If I wait through this period, then I should be able to make a profit on my property. Now is not the right time."

Real estate is a very nonliquid business. If a person must be able to get his money back on short notice, real estate isn't the investment to choose.

Having the financial stability to be able to wait often makes the difference between making a lot of money on a property, a little, or none at all.

That's another reason why I recommend buying properties that at least break even: if a property doesn't run with a negative cash flow, it doesn't create financial pressure and it therefore won't force you to sell it. It makes sense to own a property with a negative cash flow only if you have abundant financial resources or if you have very strong financial backing from your investors in the form of an agreed-on fund that will meet the negative cash flow so you can hold on to the property long enough for it to actualize its theoretical appreciation.

This doesn't mean you should *always* wait and *never* sell at an unpropitious time. If a property has problems or develops problems that you can't or don't want to deal with, if a neighborhood develops problems that you don't want to wait out, it's time to take your money and move.

If you're able to wait out the problems in a neighborhood, you'll find that property values do generally rise again, although it may take decades. This is what's happened in many of our country's inner cities, which experienced a decline in the sixties and early seventies and a revival in the eighties.

SHOULD YOU USE A BROKER TO SELL?

Eliminating the broker's commission can sometimes mean a substantial savings. But deciding whether or not to use one depends on the circumstances of the sale, as well as on whether you need a broker's expertise and on how comfortable you'd feel selling your property yourself.

A major reason to use a broker is to expose the property widely and aggressively to the marketplace. Clearly, the "for sale by owner" approach doesn't have the advantage of attracting potential buyers that a good broker has. Selling a property necessitates your receiving many phone calls and taking the time to show the property, which, depending on your particular life-style, may or may not be appropriate on an everyday basis. If you can't be completely available, then you're eliminating a big part of the marketplace; the broker has all day to receive phone calls, show properties, and be enthusiastic about doing it.

What's really important in considering this matter is to place yourself in the shoes of the other player, the potential buyer. Ask yourself how you would feel seeing a broker's sign in front of a house or a broker's ad in the newspaper as opposed to seeing a seller's sign in front of a house or a seller's ad listing his phone number. How would you feel talking directly to the seller? With a broker, there's a prearranged agreement that we're going to be nice to each other. It's easy to ask a broker, "What do you think the seller wants, and how much less do you think he'll be willing to take?" Asking the seller such questions can be awfully delicate.

There's another consideration in favor of using a broker: a potential buyer is probably looking at comparable properties, and as soon as he's interested in yours, he's going to want help with his research —someone to validate your property, to make sure that it's decently priced and that the terms are fair. The person he'll most likely turn to at this juncture is the broker who's been showing him other real estate. And since the broker knows that he has no possibility of making any money on your property because you're selling it directly yourself, he's going to give the potential buyer all the reasons why he should steer clear of it. If your property *was* listed with him, he would support a buyer's interest even if he had to reduce his commission to make the sale. (Most brokers are used to splitting their commissions in one way or another anyway, since the listing broker is not always the one who finds the buyer.)

My point is that whether or not you use a broker for your property, the potential buyer is going to be dealing with brokers, and you may be making your potential market much smaller by not dealing with one.

A trend is developing that will probably make having a broker handle a sale even more attractive. While traditionally brokers may represent both the buyer and the seller, in the future some brokers will represent only buyers and some will represent only sellers. In addition, the computerization of property listings will greatly facilitate the potential buyers' ability to compare properties and will greatly shorten the time it takes to buy or sell a property. As computerized lists of all the comparable properties being handled by brokers find their way into more brokers' offices, it may be increasingly difficult for owners to sell their own properties. And if brokers' commissions do go down as a result, it may not be worth the savings to try to sell without them.

DO YOU WANT TO BECOME A REAL ESTATE BROKER?

As you've been reading this and other chapters in the book, undoubtedly you've noticed that not only do brokers have a pivotal role in real estate, but that they are well paid for their time when a deal is consummated. Wondering if, in embarking on your career as a real estate entrepreneur, you should perhaps become a broker is an extremely reasonable question; it is also a question that can't be answered with a simple yes or no.[1]

THE PROS AND CONS OF BROKERAGE

The potential earning power of a real estate broker is only one of the profession's many attractions. In most high-paying fields a lot of training and experience are required before you can reach the top. *In the real estate business in general, and brokerage in particular, there is little hierarchy—and most of the experience comes through doing.*

One of the great things about the real estate business is that it's true horse-trading. You don't need a formal education for it; all you need is the desire to go out and do it. This applies both to being an entrepreneur in real estate and, in most respects, to being a real estate broker. You need a license to be a real estate broker; in most states, to get the license you have to take a course and pass a test. Generally, the whole process can be completed in a matter of weeks. The total investment for becoming a real estate salesperson is small. The basic equipment is easy to acquire: it consists primarily of a briefcase, a calculator, and a telephone.

I want to state clearly that you don't have to have a license to be a real estate investor or entrepreneur. To people who say, "I'll do a lot better if I have my broker's license," I respond, "The fact that one is licensed makes absolutely no difference to a career as an investor or an entrepreneur."

Choosing to become a real estate broker is a matter of personal preference and individual disposition. It's a very hard way to make an easy living. Working brokers must be willing to spend a lot of time and energy in order to receive a payoff. In fact, most brokers spend 99 percent of their time making 1 percent of that time pay off.

I get at least five calls every day from brokers with properties for sale. That's how the real estate business—and especially the broker-

---

[1]There is a technical distinction between a real estate broker and a salesperson who is licensed under the broker. Colloquially, salespeople are also referred to as brokers, and that's how I'm using the term.

age part of the business—works: everyone's working hard at putting his fishing line in the water, hoping a fish will bite.

What ultimately makes a real estate deal pay off for a broker is if he matches a seller with a buyer. It isn't mandatory to be a particularly good salesperson, because the figures speak for themselves and the buyers are either going to be interested or not. But you do have to be in the marketplace all the time to attract sellers of properties and buyers who want properties, and you also have to keep exposing the buyers to the sellers and the sellers to the buyers until a transaction occurs. This takes a personality that's comfortable making new business connections all the time. You can't hide; it's a constant search to see who is holding your reward and what you must do to receive it. The major qualifications for being a broker are getting over fear, being able to meet new people, make phone calls, hear no, or meet with total indifference, and just keep going.

One of the primary barriers to being in the real estate sales business—and there are many of them—is that it's a commission business, not a salaried position: you get paid not for the amount of your work, which may be enormous, but only for the sales you make. The reason that this is a barrier for so many people is that there's a mystique around the selling of property that makes it seem as if it's complicated and difficult to do. Many people have a hard time conceptualizing what the process really entails. They know it looks inviting, but they can't get a handle on it, and they're afraid that even if they hear opportunity knocking, they won't know how to open the door.

Even if you feel that you don't have the disposition to become a real estate broker, it's important to get a handle on what brokers do in the selling of properties. Being able to put yourself in a broker's shoes, even just for the amount of time it takes you to read this chapter, is essential to finding out how the real estate marketplace operates. It will help you both as a buyer and a seller.

CREATING TRANSACTIONS OUT OF THIN AIR

One of the most common misconceptions about being a real estate broker is that you have to depend on someone's coming to you with a property to sell or someone's coming to you with a desire to buy.

Actually, all you need are your wits and a telephone and you can create business—cold. How? By finding buildings that appeal to you in one way or another—their location, architecture, size, or personality—and tracking down their owners to see if they are interested in selling, and, if they're interested, working out the price and terms for which they would sell. Once you've worked all this out, you can complete the deals by continuing to approach property owners you don't know to see if they are interested in buying the properties. This process is called *cold canvassing.*

The way to find the owners and the potential buyers is to learn by doing. There are many ways to find who owns a specific property. Each area has published directories that can be bought or rented that list ownership of properties by their street address. This same information is available at the hall of records in the city or town where the properties you would like to sell are located.

To find potential buyers, you can start with the premise that anybody who already owns property is likely to be interested in owning more. Your list of property owners is also your list of potential buyers. To sell an apartment house, for example, you could start by going to anybody who already owns one. Once you know who is willing to sell, call the others to find out if they want to buy. I know from personal experience that in any major city you could easily gather the names and phone numbers of a thousand qualified buyers in a month. There's an even simpler method: just put an ad in the local newspaper saying, in essence, "I have this to sell for this price." Hundreds of people regularly read through the ads looking for opportunities like this.

The second major supplier of buyers is the network of real estate brokers. Traditionally, almost every real estate deal involves two brokers by the time it is completed. One broker finds the property (the seller), the other finds the buyer. When you make the whole network of real estate brokers aware of the deal that you've put together, you've already started to sell the property.

There's often a role reversal in the deals in which I participate. A broker brings a buyer to me for one of our buildings, and I'll ask him, "What do you have to sell?" In these transactions, real estate brokers are like charged particles spinning around, moving all the time, changing places: one moment they're buyers, the next they're sellers. They all have so much energy that they keep bouncing off each other. Every once in a while they're in exactly the right place at the right time. When that happens, they make money.

WHAT MAKES SOME BROKERS BETTER THAN OTHERS?

There are thousands of brokers in America. Some make hundreds of thousands of dollars; most make hardly anything. If it's so easy to find buyers and sellers—which it is—then the question is: what separates the successful from the unsuccessful? *Besides the willingness to spend the necessary time and energy, the most important quality for a real estate broker to have is the ability to see value.*

Everything we've discussed up till now about seeing value applies to brokerage as well. Like being a genius real estate investor or entrepreneur, being a genius broker means understanding and recognizing value.

Most of the calls I get from brokers about properties don't lead to finished transactions. I listen to the information they give me and put it through my mental computer. Most often, after I sift through the facts I find that there's no "bargain" quality to the property being offered. That's because most brokers don't know how to see value, and as a result they're calling me with the wrong deals. The right deal for me is one with which I know I can make money when I buy the property. *For a broker, seeing value is knowing what a property is worth to a particular buyer.* If a broker wants to make a sale to me, he must be able to see that I will buy a property only if I can get it at the lower end of its potential worth.

The better or lower the price for which a broker can list a property, the more probability there is that he'll make his commission by selling it to me or another real estate investor. To be effective in his relationship with buyers, a broker has to price the property at a figure for which he knows he can have a sure sale— a price at which someone he knows would certainly buy the property, a price at which an informed buyer would immediately see the value of the property.

HOW A LITTLE EXTRA WORK PAYS OFF

I recently bought a building from a broker at a very good price. The broker called me as part of his cold canvassing, and the price at which he offered the property was so good that I completed the deal right away. One of the reasons the price was so low was that the owner of the building lived out of state (the property was in Los Angeles, the owner was in the Deep South), so the owner didn't really know the market and hadn't even thought about selling. The broker approached him on the telephone, just as he approached me; he'd never even met him. The broker had just kept calling apartment house owners to see if they were interested in selling their buildings until he finally called this particular owner—in Alabama. This is a smart way for a broker to get listings, because out-of-town owners, especially those who have held on to their properties for several years or more, are often willing to sell at the low end of the market, since they don't see or feel the market changing on an everyday basis. They're going to make a large profit anyway, and frequently they're thrilled by a price that still makes the building a bargain for the buyer.

Even a broker who doesn't see value can sometimes be valuable to you. If he just keeps exposing properties to you indiscriminately, he can sometimes bring a good deal to you. It just depends on how much time you have to waste in politely considering all the properties that aren't for you. This means that if you decide to become a broker, even when you don't yet really know the market or the ropes of the business, you can still make deals—and money—while you're learning, if you're persistent.

By now you know that you can get to the same spot by traveling other roads and not being a broker. Only you can make the choice; it depends entirely on your own disposition and goals. I received my broker's license in 1964 when I was twenty-two, and since that time I've earned only one commission in the traditional role of a broker. It's just one of the many routes to making it in real estate.

CHAPTER 24

How to Recycle Your Working Capital: Refinancing and "Flipping"

As you begin to be an active participant in the real estate game, you'll want to learn about ways of recycling your working capital. *Refinancing* and *double-escrowing* ("flipping") are ways of generating cash either to reinvest or to spend; both are attractive subgames in the larger game of real estate.

Because refinancing is perhaps the most common method that property owners use to create money to buy additional properties, it's important to see clearly what it's all about.

Let's say you've owned a piece of property for three years and already have existing first and second mortgages. During those three years the property has appreciated at almost 10 percent per year, so now it's worth about one third more than you paid for it. If you wanted to refinance that property you would restructure the financing either by paying off the first and second mortgages and getting a new loan on the property in a greater amount than the old loans, or by leaving the existing financing in place and adding a new additional loan. Refinancing in either of these ways would create cash for you to keep or invest—and all of this can be accomplished without your having to sell the property.

Let's say that your property is worth $1 million today and has an existing first loan of $500,000 and an existing second loan of $100,-000, totaling $600,000. With a new first mortgage on the property for $700,000, you can pay off the existing $600,000 and have $100,000 change, which you can put in your pocket or invest in another piece of property.

Using the same set of circumstances, an alternative way to refinance the property would be to put a third mortgage on it so that you would have your existing first ($500,000), your existing second ($100,000), and a new third mortgage of $100,000. The combined total loans would still be $700,000, and you would still have the same $100,000 in your pocket.

TO REFINANCE OR NOT TO REFINANCE

Deciding whether or not you want to refinance a property involves three major questions: How badly do you need the money? What do you need the money for? Are you economically better off refinancing the property or getting the money from another source?

When you borrow additional money you have to pay interest on it. If you're borrowing an additional $100,000 and you're paying, say, 12 percent interest on it, the question becomes whether putting that $100,000 to work again in another property will create an investment that between the tax savings and the cash flow or the appreciation will bring you a total greater than the 12 percent you have to pay for the use of that money. If your new investment produces a return greater than this 12 percent, then creating the money through refinancing is a good choice.

Of course, refinancing is also a good choice if the money is needed for a life-or-death matter, since in that situation it doesn't make a difference what it costs; you just have to have the money.

My own advice to somebody who is considering refinancing is that he take a doomsday approach. Assume that "everything that can go wrong will go wrong." And don't stretch yourself so far that if things do go wrong you'll end up overextended. In other words, don't build a house of cards that falls apart because each card depends on another card to stay up.

My practice is to refinance a building only at the point at which that building's income is sufficient to cover the new interest cost of the refinancing. I've generally kept refinancing the same properties when they reach the point where they can handle the debt service of the new financing and still at least break even.

There are significant tax advantages to refinancing an income property in order to generate money instead of selling it. Since cash generated by the sale of a building is taxable, if the owner receives money from the proceeds of a sale he must pay tax. When a property is refinanced, the owner can often borrow most of the equity—which means he wouldn't be getting much more if he sold the property —and because he's borrowing the money instead of generating it from a sale, he doesn't have to pay any taxes on it now, since refinancing is not a taxable event.

Another advantage to refinancing is that the building that is being refinanced may end up having more tax shelter, since the debt service is increased. Your accountant should advise you on this. Before the refinancing, the income of the property after its expense was theoretically taxable because it was profit; now that the income is going to pay for the increased debt service, it may not be taxable —and the cash generated by the refinancing is available for reinvestment or for spending.

Here's a specific example of how refinancing works. Let's say that our friend Joe refinances an apartment building that has appreciated greatly during the time he's held it. He bought it five years ago for $200,000 with a down payment of $50,000; today it's worth $340,-000. Before he refinanced this building it had an annual cash return that averaged about 30 percent of the original investment, so each year he got back about 30 percent (30 percent of $50,000 = $15,000). As a result of Joe's borrowing an additional $125,000 on the building, its cash flow goes down almost to the break-even point. If he invests the money from the refinancing ($125,000) in buying a new building, he is getting appreciation on a substantially larger amount of real estate. He owns two buildings instead of one, and he never had to put up anything more than his original investment.

What about the tax consequences of this new investment portfolio? Not only is he depreciating the old building, he is also depreciating the new building. So the entire package comes out better on an appreciation basis, and, depending on his tax position, he may have additional tax benefits—and it possibly may be better on a cash-flow basis as well.

DOUBLE-ESCROWING

Double-escrowing may be defined as guaranteed "no-headache" ownership of property. It offers another guarantee, too: even before you own a building, you know exactly what you're going to make when you sell it. The reason it has these fabulous guarantees is that with double-escrowing you actually sell the property before you own it!

Double-escrowing is accomplished by finding a piece of property that you intend to buy, tying it up in escrow, and then selling the property before you have actually bought it yourself. For obvious reasons, double-escrowing is also called "flipping." Clearly, you can double-escrow or flip a property only if you can find someone to buy it immediately. How do you do it?

Because I've been in the real estate business a long time, I know what properties would interest certain buyers, so it's often just a matter of a phone call to sell a property. As a newcomer to the real estate business you can learn to make it happen. Once you know about double-escrowing and you are aware that you can create such a situation, the opportunity just may present itself. After you've tied up a property, and while you're figuring out where to get the money and whether or not to consummate the purchase, you may find that it's such a fabulous deal that you discover someone to buy it from you at a profit before you have even closed on it.

Let's say that you have tied up a property at a bargain price— $100,000—and you're in your tenth day of a sixty-day escrow. That morning, you meet somebody who wants to buy this property from you for $125,000. Now, your contract says you have sixty days in which to buy the property for $100,000, and fifty days are remaining. So you contract to sell the property to the new party for $125,000, and you make a fifty-day escrow so that both escrows close the same day.

Even though you don't own the property yet, you are still the seller in the second escrow. So you inform your escrow officer to take an instruction from you as the seller in the second escrow to use the money that flows to your benefit from the second escrow and apply it toward what you owe in the first escrow, and the profit from the second deal will go to you. By doing this, you really need no money to consummate either transaction, and the additional money from the transaction ($25,000) will come to you at the closing of escrow.

It's amazing how many of these transactions occur every day. Part of the reason they do is that your enthusiasm as a real estate investor encourages people to buy you out of your own transactions. What makes double-escrowing particularly likely is that since you are looking to make your money when you buy the property, and you're going to be buying at a price substantially below the highest market value, you know there are going to be buyers at that very moment who would be happy paying a higher price than you are paying for it—and they will still be paying fair market value.

If you make a double-escrow deal like the one I described above, you will have made $25,000, and the whole transaction could end up costing you somewhere in the neighborhood of $1,500 in fees. With this kind of return, it's little wonder that some real estate investors specialize in double-escrowing, and have built fortunes doing so.

Some states have special rules pertaining to these areas. Check with your attorney to see if any special laws exist in your area.

This process isn't quite as easy as it sounds; it takes experience, skill, and possibly even some luck. But it can be done. The trick is not to depend on it. Be prepared to follow through on your deal without flipping it, and if you find you can flip it—great.

CHAPTER 25

You Don't Have to Struggle to Achieve Your Goals

Contrary to popular opinion—and to your worst fears—every aspect of the real estate investment game—from the process of choosing properties to owning and managing them to selling them—can be handled with little if any struggling at all. I learned this lesson through my own experience, and I still have to work continually to keep myself from falling back into the trap of "efforting" and struggling. If I can impress this lesson on you right now, I know I'll be saving you from a lot of unnecessary hard knocks.

WHY SUFFER IF YOU CAN DO IT WITHOUT SUFFERING?

I used to believe that in order to find one deal that felt good, I had to look through a hundred properties first. I thought that if I found one right away, it couldn't be the right choice. I was a prime victim of the Prince Charming syndrome, and as long as I was so afflicted, I created a tremendous amount of effort for myself. I researched and researched every facet of every property until I just about disproved the worthiness of anything, because I believed that if I didn't strain myself mentally, physically, and emotionally, I would make a mistake.

Today I go through the whole process quickly, with practically no effort. The difference is in my belief about how long the process should take and how much effort it should involve; it's also in my trusting what experience has taught me: that clarity can come in an instant. It's one thing to work hard all day long for your day's wages; it's another thing to find a ten-dollar bill on the street. You don't have to struggle to earn that ten dollars, you just bend over and pick it up.

People often believe that the process of making any big decision should be difficult, and consequently that making a decision about real estate should be torturous. However, if we go back to the premise that the truth is just the truth, we can see the truth is that if a deal looks good, then you go ahead with it, and if it doesn't, you don't. Neither decision should be a life-or-death matter.

This is true in the area of property management, too. Certainly managing a property responsibly and raising its level of integrity takes work, but whether that work requires struggling depends on your point of view. *The point is that you don't have to earn your worthiness on a business level through suffering.* If you know that because of your own emotional constitution it would be a strain for you to own a particular property, you don't have to buy it; you can find another property. Choosing a property that's right for your personality is one of the best ways of eliminating struggling before it even begins.

MAKING INSTANT DECISIONS ABOUT PROPERTIES: GETTING THE MARKET TO COME TO YOU

Today my style of acquiring property is simply to let it be known that I'm in the market to buy real estate. I do this through the contacts I've made over the years with various people in real estate who know I'm a buyer, and also through putting ads in the newspapers describing the kinds of properties I would like to purchase.

Having seen hundreds of deals over the years, and continually raising myself to the level of observation in the marketplaces I deal in, I now find that I know automatically whether I think I'm hearing about a good, workable deal or not. If I feel I am, I make an offer on the property; if the seller is interested, he either accepts my offer or he starts negotiating. I generally don't even leave my office to look at the building before I tie up the transaction with contingencies.

Once you are at the level of observation in the marketplace you are going to work in, you can make just as quick and effortless a decision about the potential viability of a deal. You should be clear that what is required to make an immediate and sound decision about a property is homework, not struggling. And the more experience you have in the field, the less homework is needed.

In addition to looking for properties out in the marketplace, you can even as a beginner place newspaper ads to generate potential deals coming to you. For example, once you know the average GRM and average CPU for apartment buildings in the location in which you want to buy, you can advertise for exactly the type of apartment building deal you're looking for by specifying the neighborhood, the price, the size of the building, and the GRM. Once you know the cost per square foot of office, commercial, or industrial space in the location you've chosen, you can place similarly specific ads for these types of property. Then, when the deals start coming to you, you can use the homework you've done in learning about the marketplace to make a quick evaluation. You can know if you're interested in making an offer on a property in a matter of minutes.

You don't have to wait until you have twenty years in real estate behind you to eliminate the struggling approach to real estate transactions. Remember: just putting in an offer with proper contingencies protects you in case the deal looks good but the property itself doesn't pan out as expected. You have plenty of time to check things out.

STRESS-FREE PROPERTY MANAGEMENT

Let's take an example of property management and see how to handle it without creating stress. Say you're having a dispute with a tenant involving a repair, and as a result the tenant is holding back his rent. What obscures clarity in a situation like this and what creates a lot of struggling on the part of both landlord and tenant is that the situation becomes a matter of the self-righteousness of one battling the self-righteousness of the other.

The landlord is likely to get stuck in his view that it would be un-American for him to spend money on maintaining or fixing up his real estate when it isn't justified. Landlords are so programmed to think this way that their thinking frequently clouds over their own sense of responsibility in a situation, preventing them from seeing when a repair is actually justified. If you as a landlord have a tenant who is paying his rent and isn't asking you for anything, you don't offer to repaint his apartment or put in new carpets or drapes; if he doesn't ask you for anything, you simply don't do anything.

But if a tenant suddenly comes along and says, "I've been your tenant here for x years, I've always done this and that and I've been an incredibly good tenant," and then adds, "and you know, I'm getting sick and tired of looking at that crack in the ceiling, I want you to fix it," you may very well start struggling to hold on to your idea that it would be wasteful to do this, too. You might become self-righteous and tell the tenant, "I don't want to do it." Then he would get even more self-righteous and say, "Look, I deserve it, and I'm not going to pay my rent if I don't get it," provoking you to respond, "I don't have to fix it and you shouldn't tell me what to do. So if you don't pay the rent, I'm going to call my attorney and throw you out." The tenant, by now overwhelmed with self-righteousness, will retort with, "Oh sure, go ahead and try! I'll get my son-in-law, the attorney, and he'll beat up your attorney." At this point, you're deadlocked, and both parties are living with a great deal of stress over a matter that doesn't really merit the attention you're giving it.

The stress in this situation all comes from the fact that the landlord failed to take an honest look at the circumstances when they first arose. Instead, he looked only at his point of view. If he had gone in and inspected the tenant's apartment and put himself in the tenant's place, the landlord probably would have said, "Well, it's ridiculous for me not to fix this ceiling, because if I don't fix it for you, I'll only have to fix it for the next tenant."

Most of the effort and struggle involved in dealing with tenant problems comes from the owner of the property going through his own personal process of determining whether it's appropriate or inappropriate for him to solve the dispute by giving in to the tenant's requests. In general, the struggle is initiated by the owner's not wanting to do what is honorable. Instead of making the choice that would have integrity, he makes the choice to be cheap.

ANALYZING WHERE THE STRUGGLING COMES FROM

In talking about the decision-making process involved in buying and managing real estate, I want to differentiate between struggling on the one hand, and time on the other. *Be clear that just because a task may take time does not mean you have to struggle to perform it.*

Nothing in life requires struggling if you're totally clear about it. When you have to struggle in making a decision, it's because you're not sure if it's the right decision. If you're sure it is the right decision, you don't think twice about it. If you have all the facts in hand and you believe you have to struggle anyway, you're probably obscuring the very facts that you already have that would tell you what decision to make.

The truth is that people hold on to their struggling because they assume that they cannot come to a good, clear decision if they don't do a lot of messy, hard work. As long as they retain this attitude, they'll never accept their answer unless it has a history of messy, hard work behind it. But you can view the decision-making process merely as a search for clarity; viewing the process purely as a search is certainly much easier than viewing it as a struggle in which you're convinced that the answer cannot be easily found.

This applies to the actuality of "doing" as well as to reaching clarity. The process of "doing" is really simple. But most of us don't acknowledge that the results of "doing" are valuable unless a lot of drudgery and discomfort were involved. The struggling comes in only when you say, "I don't want to be doing this." In other words, the struggling comes from resistance—*not from doing the work itself.*

But just knowing how to eliminate the frustrating situations isn't enough—one has to work at not being frustrated. Only recently I had to learn all over again that as much as I know the lessons, I have to constantly remind myself of them.

Several months ago, my partner Howard and I bought an apartment house in North Hollywood. We bought the building at a terrific bargain. It was one of those buildings that look like an overwhelming mess; in this case it was a mess primarily because many of the tenants were irresponsible roughnecks, even though the building wasn't in a roughneck area. We bought the building with our eyes open. Our plan was to change the manager and do a thorough cleaning of both the building and its occupants.

I had gone through the process of turning a building like this around many times by doing the work myself. Over the last ten years, however, I've gotten used to having our staff handle all the interactions with tenants, since I no longer enjoy doing it. So when I bought the building, I bought it with the idea that I would simply let our property management people handle it.

Despite my having decided this, and despite our having gone into the building with our eyes wide open and having set aside enough money to handle the problems of cleaning it up—and despite my twenty years of experience in cleaning up many buildings like this one—I still made the mistake of getting aggravated about this building.

My tendency to do this was played upon by circumstances. A week after we bought the building our regular supervisor became very ill and we were shorthanded, so I decided to play more of a hands-on role than I'd planned. Every day I hassled the people in my office to get the job done immediately. As you can imagine, this made problems for everyone. They were annoyed by my nagging, but that didn't stop me. Asking about the building became the focal point of my day. I would begin by posing questions to people and always end up by pressuring them to do the job I wanted done. With a hundred buildings to think about, I kept making myself and everyone around me miserable about this one. Every time I wandered into my partner's office to give him a blow-by-blow description of the situation (which is basically my way of getting support and nurturing from him), he would say, "Why are you getting yourself upset over this? It's no big deal. We knew all this was going to come up. Everything is fine."

My point is that my partner, who never got involved in the day-to-day operations of the building, could see clearly what I was overlooking: essentially everything was going according to plan. Consequently, he wasn't bothered in the slightest. He was perfectly accepting of the whole thing, while I kept making myself miserable over it.

A week into my aggravation, he helped me see my own frustration, and suddenly I could see what he saw: that my aggravation was coming from being shorthanded on our staff and being concerned about the supervisor in the hospital, not from problems with the building in North Hollywood. All the feelings of struggling vanished. I had forgotten that none of us owns higher consciousness: we have to work every moment to have it.

When we accept the fact that reaching our goals takes a certain amount of effort and we don't resist the effort, then there is no struggling. If we believe strongly enough that struggling is necessary, we are unlikely to know what the process really entails and what the goal is. If we believe that the process of deciding about properties is merely a search for clarity, then there is no resistance to the process—or to reaching clarity. If we believe that the process of running a property efficiently and bringing it up to the level of 100 percent integrity is just doing what has to be done to accomplish this, then there is no resistance to the process—or to accomplishing our objectives in managing the property.

Do We Deserve It?

A final issue that comes up in regard to removing stress from the activities involved in being a real estate entrepreneur is perhaps best expressed in the question "Do I deserve success?"

The best way to eliminate all the unnecessary stress that you can so easily create for yourself and others is simply to keep in mind that to deserve the rewards of real estate investment, all you really must do is put in the time, energy, and commitment that it takes to accomplish your goals.

CHAPTER 26

IF I APPLIED ALL THE INFORMATION I KNEW, I'D NEVER HAVE BOUGHT ANYTHING, AND OTHER UNCLASSIFIABLE WISDOM

No matter how risk-free a piece of real estate looks, there are still risks and pitfalls. I know about the potential for properties to behave in unexpected ways, and yet I make deals anyway. In a sense, I have to ignore some of what I know in order to buy properties and be a functioning real estate entrepreneur. As a beginning entrepreneur in real estate, you must grasp this essential point.

Of the hundred and fifty apartment houses that I've owned, for example, I doubt that many have maintained their expenses in complete accordance with the budgets we've made for them. This isn't because the budgets were skimpy; they were always very conservative. The reason expenses don't stay within the budgets projected for them is that it's not the nature of expenses to do so. Even so, when I look at the apartment houses I've owned, I observe that despite their deviations from the budgets we've projected for them, every one has turned out profitably.

The tendency of actual results to deviate from projections can happen with any type of real estate, even with the best piece of commercial property rented out by a first-class tenant with a triple-net lease. Let's say, for example, that you buy a building and rent it to the "Bank of U.S.A.," which signs a total triple-net lease making them responsible for all expenses connected with the building. Even this might not work out exactly the way you picture it. Someone at "Bank of U.S.A." might one day have a problem with an element of the building and write you a letter saying, "It's the landlord's problem." If the person doesn't believe you when you cordially tell her that according to the terms of the lease it is her problem, you would then hire an attorney to respond to the letter. The attorney might charge you $500 to review the problem and write a letter to the person at "Bank of U.S.A." Then the person at "Bank of U.S.A." would say, "You're right. Thank you." But you still would have added an out-of-pocket expense you weren't expecting for the attorney's fees.

This is a conservative example of why real estate deals generally tend to deviate from even the most careful projections. When I go into any investment, there is a part of me that still worries about the "what if"s affecting the projections. At the same time, another part of me says, "In the real world, I've got to take a chance, and I've done my homework." So I complete the deal even though I know that it won't be picture-book perfect.

YOU CAN'T HIT A HOME RUN UNLESS YOU GO UP TO BAT

No matter how flawless something may look, it still has the potential to go wrong. But if we allow the *potential* for things to go wrong to become a barrier for our proceeding, we will never get anywhere. What we have to do instead is to come to a peace within ourselves, to know that by putting into practice the principles I've described in this book, we have a responsible way of evaluating deals.

We also have to believe that nine out of ten is a large majority, and since we're almost never going to get agreement from ten out of ten people, nine out of ten is enough to make a decision. There is always a margin of error that we can't anticipate, and we must recognize that an area of risk exists, but we can't let that stop us.

Each of us has to negotiate within ourselves and determine, "At what point am I willing to take the risk and at what point am I not willing to take it?" At a certain point, each of us has to be ready to act.

Remember that life is participating, and that you cannot participate in life without taking some sort of a gamble. Even not doing something is a gamble.

Since I do choose to participate, I don't let the secret fears I have stop me from proceeding. If I did, I never would have bought anything. At the same time, I know that if my fears had been manifested as a reality, they could have been devastating. The reason I don't let my fears stop me is that I feel I've done a significant amount of research and I therefore know that the deal I'm considering has a high probability of working out. Knowing that the probability is still a possibility is just a fact of life, and it doesn't cause me to perceive life—or the real estate deal—as less perfect.

The more home runs a baseball player hits, the more he is worth, but if a baseball player put so much pressure on himself that he felt he had to be certain of hitting a home run, or at least of getting on base, every time he came to bat, then eventually he'd have to stop playing baseball. Or maybe, because of the pressure from the fear that he couldn't do what he felt he had to do, he would never have gotten himself into baseball in the beginning. If you put this kind of pressure on yourself, the possibility of striking out may well keep you from ever taking the chance of playing the game.

If you decide you can't drive a car, you can't. If you decide you can, you can—even if you may have a great deal of fear about driving when you begin, and think, Maybe I'm not going to be able to do this. I certainly felt this way when I first learned to drive, and I felt it again on my thirty-sixth birthday when I bought myself a Rolls-Royce convertible as a present. The day I went to pick up the car at the showroom, I was terrified of driving it. I thought to myself, "Well, I've been able to drive other cars, but *this* is a Rolls-Royce. How can I drive a car like this?" Now I don't worry about it at all. The only thing that made driving the car seem terrifying was the pressure I put on myself, pressure that made me see myself as unworthy to drive a car that I considered such a symbol of worthiness.

The point of all this is to urge you to have the confidence to act even when you see potential risks, as long as your intuition that a deal is good is supported by the facts.

PEOPLE WILL HELP YOUR SUCCESS

I used to play cards with the boys on the block when I was a teenager and I learned a lesson about success that life has taught me over and over again: it's easy to succeed if you live your life so that people like you, because then they want you to succeed and they will help you, even when things go wrong.

The card game we played was called Red Dog or In-Between. A big winner would win two or three dollars a hand, and a big loser would lose about two or three dollars a hand. I always used to bet high, and sometimes I'd lose twenty or twenty-five hands, so I'd owe a total of $50 or $75 in IOUs. You might think that all the other boys in the game would have been rubbing their hands in glee, saying, "Look at how this guy's losing all his money. Look at all the money we're going to make." But they didn't say that. I was a nice kid, and I always played the game with a sense of fun; there was a sense of outrageous pleasure in my tendency to keep betting all my winnings, and all the other boys enjoyed it. I treated the other boys not as adversaries but as friends with whom I was playing a game. And because they liked me, and they all felt so damned sorry for me that I was losing more than I could afford, with every new hand, they were hoping I'd win! If I didn't, they usually would continue playing until I did, even though I was perfectly prepared to save up from my part-time job and pay them back. From this experience, I learned that if you are a good person and you do things in an honorable, forthright manner, the world wants you to succeed; the world will even help you to solve problems.

That's why if you tell the truth to your investors, even if something about the investment doesn't go according to plan, their response is probably going to be, "It's okay."

This truth is complemented by another one: the business world is so uncomfortable about having a messy situation that all those who are affected by it want nothing more than to clean up the mess and go on with life. If you have the tenacity to stay with the situation and work it out, the world will tend to give you the support you need.

If you give people the opportunity to help you succeed, you get back their support for your success. People will even support you in taking risks that they themselves wouldn't take if they believe the risks are worth taking and that you can deal with them. Remember, however, that people are also supporting you when they give you all the reasons you shouldn't take a risk!

Nobody is going to say anything to you on the negative side that probably hasn't occurred to you already, but hearing somebody else say it is very important. It makes you check out the negative point of view instead of merely hearing it in your own head, where it's sometimes easy to disregard. When other people become the devil's advocate, they make you find the facts, if only to have the satisfaction of proving them wrong. And if you find out they're right, you have to be a big enough person to be successful by changing your mind.

CHAPTER 27

ARE YOU WILLING TO BE SUCCESSFUL?

I stated in the introduction that we all have the power within us to succeed in real estate or, for that matter, to succeed in almost any other venture that other human beings have ever succeeded in. In helping you to determine whether you are willing to be successful in real estate, I want to return to the issue of personal power. It's important to see that I'm speaking quite literally when I say that the power to succeed is within you, and that whether or not you use this power to succeed is your personal choice.

Here's a list of questions to ask yourself to see if you're ready to be successful in real estate.

1. Do I have the time and the interest to be a success in real estate?

If the answer is yes, then continue to ask yourself the following questions about real estate. If the answer is no, and there is another venture in which you think you can and want to succeed, then ask yourself the following questions about that venture.

2. Am I willing to face rejection, to ask people for their help and hear no?

3. Am I willing to accept the person who says no and continue to

have a positive relationship with that person even if he doesn't want to help me, or am I going to cross him off my list?

4. If the person I'm willing to ask for help says no, am I willing to find somebody else?

5. Am I willing to take the risks involved in real estate as well as the benefits?

6. If the deal doesn't pan out, am I willing to say I did my best, that whoever went along with me was responsible for his actions, I am responsible for mine, and it just didn't work out? Am I willing to end up looking stupid?

7. Am I willing to ask people for their help and hear yes?

8. Am I willing to accept responsibility for the deal whether it seems to be working out or not, and see it through to completion, even if it takes years?

9. Do I feel worthy of success in my new venture?

THE SECRET OF SUCCESS

There is only one thing you must do in order to be successful: *be willing to take a stand.* State that you will NOT do anything other than be successful. Taking this stand shows a commitment of your will to succeed, a commitment of your will to surmount whatever obstacles seem to be in your path.

Anything that threatens to deter you from your goals must be overcome.

The only thing that stands in the way of success for any of us is ourselves —and to succeed, we have to see and accept this. We have to accept the fact that we are the only judges of our own success, and that we are the only judges of the possibility or impossibility of achieving the success we seek.

The way to reinforce the fact that we can all achieve success is to aim our sights at a goal that's in alignment with our expectations. It isn't necessary to put together a deal on the Empire State Building for your first transaction. What's important is to have a plan and to have the tenacity and commitment to follow through—and to realize that the ability to find the answers you will need along the way already lies within you. You simply have to keep asking the questions in the ways I've taught you and the answers will appear.

There's no reason you cannot achieve the financial success in real estate that others have found. To see this brings an incredible understanding; to see this means you're ready for success in anything!

INDEX